MODERN SALES
MANAGEMENT

Alan West

**MACMILLAN
EDUCATION**

First published 1987

Published by
MACMILLAN EDUCATION LTD
Houndmills, Basingstoke, Hampshire RG21 2XS
and London
Companies and representatives
throughout the world

Printed in Hong Kong

British Library Cataloguing in Publication Data
West, Alan
Modern sales management.
1. Sales management
I. Title
658.8′1   HF5438.4
ISBN 0–333–42145–0 (hardcover)
ISBN 0–333–42146–9 (paperback)

Contents

List of Illustrations

The links between the discussion topics and case studies in *Modern Sales Management*

	Sales Rep's Role	Recruitment	Training	Appraisal	Discipline	Sales Organisation	Sales Mkting	Sales Information	Sales Process	Motivation	Buyers	Forecasting
Wizard	×		×	×	×					×		
Arctic	×		×							×		
Candidate		×	×			×						
QR		×	×					×				
Aeroflex	×	×	×	×				×	×		×	
Quick	×											
Snack			×		×			×	×		×	
Further Exercises	×		×						×		×	×
Uppers				×		×	×	×		×	×	
Maxim	×	×		×		×	×	×		×	×	
Channel				×	×	×				×		
Burrow's				×	×	×	×	×		×		
HandyMan		×	×	×		×	×	×		×	×	×
Pilgrim		×		×		×		×		×		
WXY	×		×			×	×	×		×		×
Breaker	×	×			×	×	×					
Brights'			×			×	×	×		×		
Circus		×				×	×	×		×		
Plasty						×						
TSC											×	×
Zeller										×	×	×
Sommer						×				×	×	

To R.

Preface

After many years in the international sales and marketing environment one thing is clear in all the companies with which I have had contact: how isolated the members of the salesforce are within the organisation and how little time senior management spend ensuring that sales representatives are fully effective.

Two personal incidents underline this. One in Belgium consisted of listening to a salesman for over two hours listing from his comprehensive memory the shortcomings of the company during the past 12 years, including the failure of the managing director to ever visit the territory in that period although Belgium was a very important market to the company. The second incident revealed the total confusion expressed by the members of a consumer goods salesforce during a test market in the west of England. They did not know what they were supposed to be doing, where they were supposed to be going, and expressed themselves pithily on the subject.

Despite all this there are clearly those for whom selling is an obvious choice as a career. Sales representatives generally enjoy their job because they tend to be the real entrepreneurs: practical people who prefer action to discussing action at meetings, who must enjoy going to meet and bargain with others although they are by no means certain that they will achieve anything definite. They are people who can cope well with being relatively isolated as they often prefer a job without a high degree of supervision. Furthermore,

selling is one of the few jobs in large organisations which satisfies the
needs of the individual who wants to see immediate results for which
he or she will take the personal credit.

Much of the literature in the area of sales management con-
tinues to treat the salesforce in isolation to the main objectives of
the organisation and this book strives to rectify many of these
shortcomings. It also provides over twenty case studies which
further define the company/salesforce interaction. They have all
been used for teaching purposes, but can also be read as examples
of the problems that management needs to overcome to create a
truly integrated and effective salesforce.

ALAN WEST

Perceptions of Selling 1

Any book on the role of the company salesman and how he or she should be recruited, targeted, evaluated and paid, cannot avoid consideration of attitudes to selling both within the company and outside it as well. This is because however broad-minded and objective any individual may try to be, all of us tend to react to others because of preconceptions about ourselves; the way we think we should react; and how we feel the individual will be happy to be treated. The clergyman invited to tea will not be regaled with the slightly *risqué* story of what you did on holiday, or conversely you are unlikely to discuss the plight of the hungry in the Third World with your football-playing cousin who will be the recipient of the funny story. In other words, the salesman will have prejudices about the company, the company about the salesman, and the buyer, or the public, about both.

1.1 The Salesman in Society

The salesman must earn a living through his or her persuasiveness: a quality that is regarded with a great deal of suspicion by many cultures especially when it is being used by a relatively unknown party. Some of Shakespeare's most infamous scoundrels – Cassius in *Julius Caesar* and and Iago in *Othello* for example – were past masters at the art of persuasion. But this quality has also been the

1

subject of satirical stereotyping in portrayals of the salesman. Historically, the sales representative has always been the object of barbed humour. Geoffrey Chaucer, writing the *Canterbury Tales* in fourteenth-century England, describes the 'honey-tongue' of the Pardoner, a rogue of the first order, who promised celestial salvation to the purchasers of his ecclesiastical relics.

> **He had a cross of metal set with stones**
> **And, in a glass, a rubble of pig's bones.**
> **And with these relics, any time he found**
> **Some poor up-country parson to astound,**
> **On one short day, in money down, he drew**
> **More than the parson in a month or two,**
> **And by his flatteries and prevarication**
> **Made monkeys of the priest and congregation.**

When one introduces the words pedlar or hawker into conversation or descriptive writing it is generally in a derogatory sense. Mass manufactured signs exist stating 'No hawkers or circulars'. More modern playwrights such as Eugene O'Neill and Tennessee Williams also paint a less than favourable picture of the salesman in society. In *Foundation* the science fiction writer Isaac Asimov portrays selling as an important component of achieving power over other peoples.

Romantic fiction, a reasonably accurate reflection of male social status very rarely, if at all, portrays the salesman in the leading role. Doctors, lawyers and even politicians are portrayed with often monotonous regularity but the poor sales representative is left at the starting gate in the race for female affection.

Studies investigating the amount of trust members of the public place in various professions show a more or less standard form across all Western cultures. Priests and doctors tend to be highly regarded together with teachers. Lower down the scale come lawyers and accountants. At the bottom the politicians vie with the salesmen. It is interesting that the combination of the low status of politicians with the salesman was clearly identified in the case of the attempted denigration of President Richard Nixon. He was labelled 'Tricky Dicky' and this comment on his personality was underlined by the phrase 'Would you buy a used car from this man?' One may reflect that though no one bought a car, enough of the American electorate voted for him to make him President of the United States.

In common with the low social status comes the sales representatives' role as a butt for humour. Catalogues of jokes exist, many commencing with the car breaking down near a lonely farmhouse. Hollywood in its puritanical period not only forbade the use of such words as 'sex', and 'madame' but stated that the expression 'travelling salesman' should not be used in any context with 'farmer's daughter'.

Together with jokes about racial minorities, jokes on salesman also build up and maintain the image of the sales representative as being of very low status. One interesting exercise is to ask a class of students to describe a salesman. The answer is generally rapid and highly detailed. He is perceived as wearing a 'sharp' suit invariably with a waistcoat. The shirt will tend to be white though stripes will also be common. A fairly wide, ornate, silk tie with some complicated design is obligatory together with the smart, black, leather briefcase topped with a combination lock. Highly polished black shoes will complete the ensemble. Hair will tend to be slightly long though always carefully brushed. The firm chin will be surmounted by white teeth shown in a warm, insincere smile.

Home life is also perceived in fairly great detail. Living in either a semi-detached or a small detached house on a new estate, the sales representative who is almost always considered in these discussions as male will have an obligatory blonde wife and two children. The living-room will be open plan with a large video/television/hi-fi system. The kitchen will contain fitted cupboards faced with real wood. The salesman's family will take their annual holiday in Spain, will not read a 'serious' newspaper, will tend to have right-wing political beliefs and college education at the best. This last is generally truer of Western European salesforces, in the author's experience, than of the United States where perceptions of selling are rather different and where the job is seen as requiring a higher level of education.

The sales representative's car will receive considerable attention and contain a complicated car stereo/radio. This car, one of a very selective few, will again be identifiable as a 'salesman's type' and will generally be supplied by the company. The characteristics of the company car are described in several books and are worth repeating to underline preconceptions of the sales role:[1]

1. They always travel faster in all gears.
2. They accelerate phenomenally fast.
3. They need cleaning less often.
4. Battery, water and oil levels never need checking.
5. Suspension is especially strengthened to carry concrete slabs.
6. Unusual engine noises are always drowned by increasing the volume of the radio.
7. Floor is shaped like an ashtray.
8. No security is needed.
9. Warning lights only provide useful additional interior lighting.

The personal qualities that are seen as accompanying the company car, three piece suit and new house are tenacity, aggressiveness selfishness and mendacity. When a similar exercise is carried out with lecturers' or doctors' public, personal and private lives, no stereotype emerges. It is probable that if such an exercise had been carried out in the 1950s or 1960s a similar pattern would have been apparent with different descriptions of hair, clothing, car and house accounting for changing fashions but nevertheless revealing the same underlying theme of low and undesirable status.

1.2 Buyers and Sellers

The impact of these prejudices on selling can be extremely important, for they inevitably affect the reaction of the buyer towards the salesman and the products that he is trying to sell. Buyers will receive information about products from a variety of sources – exhibitions, trade literature, direct mail, and television forming a considerable element.[2] The importance of each source will vary with the nature of the firm and the industry in which it is involved. For the majority of small industrial firms it still appears that the main source of information about a product will come via the salesman.[3] In the case of the printing industry the main source of information is given as follows:

	Small companies (%)	Large (%)
Technical press	28	60
Salesman	47	19

Exhibitions	8	12
Direct mail	19	9

Part of this difference is that in the small firm the salesman will be likely to be seeing two out of the three people involved in the buying decision, in the large firm where six or more individuals may be involved he is still only in contact with two or three.[4]

The identification of the individuals who make the buying decision is crucial for the sales representative in the proper preparation for a sales call (see Chapter 3). The majority of authors suggest that there may be up to five differing influences on the buying process; influences that may be represented by one or more people:

1. The initiator: the individual who becomes aware of the new product.
2. The influencer: the individual who, while not taking the buying decision, has a major impact on the decision making process.
3. The decider.
4. The buyer.
5. The user.[5]

Obviously these roles may either be independent; or combined in one or more people. There are a number of interlocking factors that will influence the decision to buy which will affect the attitudes to the sales representative of the people with whom he is dealing.

Buying structures vary with the company. Some have buyers others do not. One illustration of the various roles that can exist is the case of an industrial company purchasing industrial chemicals, where a number of individuals at differing levels and operating according to different criteria have an impact on the buying decision. Their importance, the factors they will consider relevant, and the degree of detailed knowledge that they have on the subject are summarised below.

Employee	Buying criteria	Knowledge of subject	Buying status
1. Managing director	Profit/ efficiency	Limited	Makes final decision

Employee	Buying criteria	Knowledge of subject	Buying status
2. Production director	Efficiency	Some but not extensive	May make decision but always influences
3. Plant manager	Ease of operation	Likely to be extensive	Recommends not decides
4. Plant foreman	Effect on workers negative	Limited	Likely strong influence
5. Research manager	Safety/theory	Extensive	Important if product tested, otherwise small

Each individual's contribution to the final decision will vary from company to company and also over time. Thus informal links within one company may mean that the plant foreman has the ear of the managing director, which in an otherwise identical organisation may not be the case. The type of product in question also will affect the nature of the buying decisions made at each level. For example, the purchase of industrial lubricant may be dealt with at a much lower organisational level than new machinery, even if the costs involved are similar. Within these boundaries the decision makers dealing with purchasing will also be affected by a wide range of non-objective criteria in coming to a conclusion about a specific project. The buyer in consequence can be operating at varying levels within the firm so that a representative picture of the average purchasing decision maker and how he will respond to the salesman is difficult to arrive at.

A classic description is:

The typical buyer is a man past middle life; spare, wrinkled, intelligent, cold, passive, non-committal, with eyes like a codfish; polite in contact, but at the same time unresponsive; cool, calm

and as damnably composed as a concrete post, or a plaster of paris cat; a human petrification with a heart of feldspar, and without charm, or the friendly germ.[6]

Owing to the diverse nature of the commercial sectors in which buyers operate this biased description has as much credibility as the jaundiced view of the archetypal salesman.

There is, however, little research on the exact attitudes of the buyer towards the salesman though in many instances there is a degree of common interest between the two professions, with national accounts sales representatives, for example, often being recruited for buying positions: the poacher turned gamekeeper concept. Available information on the industrial market indicates that there are a large number of decisions which are taken on non-objective grounds which tends to suggest that the large body of research on how individuals reach decisions to purchase a particular product will also hold true for the purchasing manager.[7] The only major difference is that the buyer may not only be as cautious as a member of the public, he may also veer towards excessive caution.[8]

The research suggests that for a substantial number of firms, personal contact with the salesman is the most important source of information in reaching a decision, with 'objective' sources of information such as direct mail being less important.[9] This cannot be ignored in any evaluation of the role of the salesman and the interaction with buyers is next considered in detail in what is essentially a general discussion of various social factors affecting relationships between the salesman and the customer – whether the purchaser is buying for a company or for himself or herself.

A number of important influences have been identified as clouding objective assessment of any particular problem.

Cultural characteristics

Culture has been and will remain one of the most important determinants of buyer behaviour. Gross differences are fairly easy to discern – the salesman attempting to sell English encyclopaedias in the suburbs of Tokyo would obviously be facing an uphill task when compared with someone similarly occupied in the suburbs of London. Yet even here certain religious sects might conceivably forbid the purchase of encyclopaedias as being against their particular faith. The salesman would have to be aware of the impact of such a subculture within the broader cultural grouping of his territory. Thus the salesman of English encyclopaedias in certain London suburbs with large non-English speaking minorities may be facing as difficult a task as his colleague in Tokyo! Cultural characteristics will therefore often be very significant in determining the sales representative and buyer interaction.

More important for the majority of companies involved in the international sales environment are the differing norms of acceptable social behaviour. There are numerous well known cultural variations in human behaviour ignorance of which lead to misunderstandings. Examples are: not offering Muslims alcohol as it can cause offence if they belong to a non-alcohol drinking sect; not offering items with the left hand in certain Eastern and African cultures and so on. Often forgotten in this catalogue are the normal methods of social intercourse. The first universal problem is that humour does not travel, even relatively short distances. The author, when lecturing to a group of West European students – not generally regarded as the most serious members of the community – attempted to introduce humour into a lecture on marketing in Africa, to liven up the day's proceedings which had till then consisted of exercises in international accounting. As a reward for these efforts accusations of racial prejudice were made in the post course briefing session by 15 per cent of the audience, unnecessary levity from another 10 per cent, while the remainder greatly enjoyed it.

Other factors are no less important. Japanese businessmen tend to be polite, circumspect, traditional in dress and manner. They also take decisions in groups, sit silent when they have not got something to say thereby acquiring the reputation for 'inscrutability'. When the American culture with its emphasis on individual achievement, personal drive, passion for informality at almost all stages of the business process, and with a sometimes overdeveloped taste for speech, meets the Japanese culture in sales negotiations, problems and tensions can arise if each nationality remains impervious to the other's ideas about acceptable behaviour. In many cultures the question of personal trust is all important as the legal system is cumbersome and unwieldy, and this again can cause conflict when two different cultures meet.

Social class/status

Every society tends to organise itself like the chickens in the hen coop by creating a pecking order with some individuals at the top and some at the bottom. Such a system separates humanity into social and economic groups each with its own behaviour patterns which are distinct from the others. People of high social class in certain cultures will not accept ideas from individuals of a lower level. This is particularly true in a country like India with a rigid caste structure. For example, the use of women in a salesforce in that subcontinent would be a disaster unless they were selling specifically to women. This can be clearly seen in the family planning field – clinics run by women find that men are almost always unwilling to attend and male staff have to be recruited to deal with them in order to persuade them to use a method of contraception.

The individual's life style is also relevant especially if he should be closely identified with a particular group, or heavily influenced by his family. These will have effects on his buying behaviour.

Another aspect of the social class equation concerns the status of the sales representative which is important in a number of ways. It affects the contacts that he will have with buyers and it also influences his position in his own organisation. The majority of companies appear to place the sales representatives above clerks and secretaries but below junior management in the organisational hierarchy when their job grade is determined, with area sales managers being placed on the same level. As authority in any large organisation is largely determined by status, the salesforce tends not to be consulted about organisational changes in the firm. The reverse of this, the salesforce attempting to raise issues at management level, often faces the same problems.

Motivation

A number of authors define some of the motivational factors that influence the purchase decision. The most quoted of them considers that there is a hierarchy of needs divided into:

1. Physical – (a) Physiological – hunger, thirst. (b) Safety.
2. Social – Group needs.
3. Personal – Development of self-esteem.[10]

Further subdivisions of the buying process are possible. Thus not only is there a division between individuals in relation to the role that they perform within the group, the personality of the individual himself can have differing effects at varying stages of the purchase decision. If these problems are sufficiently overcome by some benefit to the buyer, the sale will occur, if not, not.

The company buyer who is operating in the normal social environment will be influenced by the variety of factors described above, the most important of which can be memorised as the 4 'P's:

1. **Profit** – Is it going to make him personally, or the organisation, more money?
2. **Protection** – Is it going to be a safe decision which will not involve me in risk?
3. **Prestige** – Is it going to increase my social status or standing within the organisation?
4. **Popularity** – Will it be well received?

The product, if it is going to be successful will have benefits which can be assessed in terms of one or more of these factors. One can draw up a graded scale of likely success from the total fulfilment of all these main criteria by which success should be practically guaranteed, to the other end of the spectrum with total failure on all counts.

1.3   The Role of Organisations and Buyer Behaviour

There is a body of research that indicates that the size of the organisation in whichever sector has an important effect on buyer behaviour, with larger companies developing a more systematic approach to product evaluation.[11]

The professional buyer it is held will be more concerned with researching and evaluating likely suppliers than has hitherto been the case, using vendor rating schemes and other similar techniques.

A number of authors have also developed buying models which attempt to explain the inter-relationships of various factors both internal and external to the buying centre. The main three proposed are:

1. The Wind model.[12]
2. The Sheth model.[13]
3. The Nielsen model.[14]

The main problem with these models in common with other attempts to classify consumer behaviour is that they do not provide a *predictable* measure of likely buyer response. The salesman cannot by considering these models arrive at any useful insight into the likely path of the decision process. A computer package *The Human Edge* also attempts to structure both the sales representative's personality and the nature of the buyer to determine what likely sales approach should be used to produce the most effective results. This in common with buyer behaviour models is highly subjective, demanding a considerable level of self-knowledge and also a highly developed psycho-analytical understanding of the buyer.

1.4 Company Expectations

One of the amusing views of how the company considers the salesman can be seen below in a modification of the widely quoted chart.[15]

Performance

Job quality	Excellent	Good	Average	Poor	V. Poor
Aggress-iveness	Leaps tall buildings	Needs run-up	Gets stuck on spires	Crashes on buildings	Needs lift
Timeliness	Faster than a flying bullet	Fast as a bullet	Not as fast	Misses bullets	Shoots himself
Initiative	Stronger than a locomotive	Stronger than a bull	Like a bull	Produces bull	Smells of it
Adaptability	Always walks on water	Walks on water in panic	Washes with water	Drinks water	Passes water
Communica-tion skills	Talks with God	Talks with angels	Talks with himself	Argues with himself	Loses it
Earning power	Owns bank	Owns bank in South America	Has bank account	Has overdraft	Loses wallet
Tenacity	Teeth like sabre-tooth tiger	Ageing sabre-tooth tiger	Has tiger kit	Chased by kittens	Caught

When companies are asked what are the important qualities they look for in their salesforce they tend to have a fairly simple answer – that the individual should be able to achieve sales volume.

Closer inspection of the roles that sales representatives fulfil within the organisation tend to show that many other tasks are expected of them and that some of them are not given due recognition as being of importance to the company. Any list of such activities tends to be fairly lengthy:

1. Sales volumes/target achievement.
2. The discovery and development of new accounts.
3. The introduction and monitoring of new products.
4. Credit control – ensuring that new customers are credit-worthy or in many instances chasing and receiving payment.
5. Merchandising and controlling demonstrations of products.
6. Providing information on competitive products.
7. Maintaining accurate records, not only of sales, but also calls, mileage, time spent telephoning, and expenses.
8. Solving distribution problems.
9. Dealing with product complaints.
10. Public relations – when the company has had adverse press comment for example.
11. Manning exhibitions.
12. Organising test market activities.

Some of these demands made by the firm of its salesforce will always be in conflict with others. Time given to exhibitions will inevitably cut into time that can be spent in front of customers. The introduction of new products will be a time-consuming exercise – the sales representative will have limited time in front of the buyer – should that time be spent supporting new products or promoting the bread and butter lines that provide the current income for the company and the bulk of the salesman's own earnings on commissions?

Many of the demands made upon the salesforce also conflict with their perceived role within the company. Credit control, solving distribution problems, acting as a public relations representative all require different skills – an individual who achieves high volume sales may not have ability in these areas, rather like the marketing manager excellent in most respects who is unable to produce his own brochure material. It is one of the more interesting anomalies in companies that whereas the marketing manager will be allowed to use the services of an advertising agency to supplement his skills in the production of the brochure, similar leeway is rarely offered to the salesforce.

1.5   Expectations of the Salesforce and the Case Study

The conflicts that the various perceptions of selling raise are therefore more complex that they would appear on the surface and it is this issue that the case studies accompanying the chapter address.

The motivations that lead an individual into the field of sales and sales management are complex but there are a number of common traits shared by salesmen whether the person is able to objectively define them or not.

First, the salesman as the Arctic Case Study which follows will show tends to be an individualist. The nature of the job is very much one of personal freedom with long periods away from supervision, running the sales territory in a personal way.

Secondly, there will often be a strong desire for personal achievement. The sales representative is so clearly isolated from working closely with others by contrast to finance, distribution and marketing personnel at Head Office, that personal rather than group achievement (or survival) is more important. How this drive for achievement manifests itself will vary, the most common being the search for higher and higher earnings as a measure of achievement.

Thirdly, these personal qualities will tend to produce antagonism towards authority in varying degrees. The view 'give me the tools, and don't interfere while I finish the job' is quite prevalent, and in consequence many salesforces will resent activities such as supervising merchandising, and demonstrations, and attending meetings as time-wasting.

Fourthly, long periods in a particular industry and area tend to produce a growing belief that their knowledge of the industry/ customer base is unsurpassed and they know what their customers want and whether they will buy it. As the salesforce is spending more time with the customers than with the company it is inevitable that to a certain extent they will start to identify with the customer rather than the company. Equally the daily reinforcement of company goals given to those working at Head Office may isolate them from the world outside and salesforces will frequently feel that they are out of touch with customers. Not surprisingly it is often the activities foisted on the salesforce by the centre aimed at goals which are more important to the Head Office that cause the type of conflict described in the Blyth Case Study.

Lastly, the isolation of the sales role tends to produce slight paranoia in the individual. The expectations of full information on any particular topic are rarely if ever achieved, and in consequence the sales representative tends to be additionally suspicious of change. It has always interested the author that in national distribution companies the salesmen covering the capital city (where the Head Office is situated) are far more relaxed than those in the provinces – the first have the opportunity to learn all the gossip, the others have not.

The main contact between management/Head Office and the salesforce is usually a monthly meeting at which the main issues are discussed. An interesting group exercise after reading the chapter is to assume the relevant roles outlined in the salesforce below and play out the individual comments provided. The group should attempt to continue the discussion beyond the basic issues provided – it is the one opportunity you the salesmen have to make your views known to the management and it is the one time that marketing management have an opportunity to put forward important new developments. We shall look in detail at one such meeting.

Arctic Frozen Foods Monthly Salesforce Meeting

Once a month, the area marketing manager of Arctic Frozen Foods met with salesmen in the north-east of England at a motel in Chester. A bright young spark is his early thirties, the area manager Brian Devine had spent most of his life in the south of England, having been posted north by his company nine months earlier. On this his sixth meeting with the group, he was introduced by Sam Vickers who had been a member of the Arctic area salesforce for some ten years. Devine had already spent some time with Sam Vickers touring around the shops in the area where he had met a number of members of the salesforce present at this meeting.

Background

These monthly meetings were essential to the company's selling strategy. They were regarded as an important source of motivating the sales force, supplying details about relevant company decisions – promotions, competitions and other incentives – and exchanging information about product lines. Since it was rare for marketing managers to spend time in the field with them, this meeting supplied one of the few opportunities for the salesforce to improve their employer's awareness of developments at the grass-roots and to clear up any problems by discussing them together. Devine had already received complaints about the role of direct mail, fringe benefits, and promotional material. There was general concern among the group about problems at the Arctic warehouse.

Brian Devine

Devine was generally dissatisfied with the performance of the salesforce as evidenced by his field visits. He felt that their achievements compared poorly with his experience of similar salesforces in the south. He appreciated that morale was low but he felt that the representatives were more concerned about their own personal working conditions than with selling frozen foods. Merchandising of the Arctic range was very poor, and compared with the south, a generally very limited range of Arctic products were in distribution. The job of area marketing manager was the next step on the ladder of promotion to board level, which he and all his colleagues recognised. His predecessor had warned him that the group was unreasonably sensitive about a number of issues, but he did not consider that this should stand in the way of improved performance.

The Salesforce

The members of the salesforce attending the meeting on the other hand were beginning to feel increasingly restive under Devine's leadership. They felt justly aggrieved because he had consistently promised to clear up a number of matters, some of which would crop up again today, and had failed to do so. Their territory was a very competitive one with two local manufacturers Igloo and Glacier causing more and more problems to the premium priced Arctic range.

Sam Vickers

Born in Manchester, with a decade of experience of the Arctic salesforce, Sam Vickers was the senior member of the group. He was regularly consulted by his colleagues on matters relating to pay and conditions of work because he was generally better informed than others about the rules. He felt that he was therefore expressing the concern of the group when he broached the subject of Mike McAlistair's new car. McAlistair himself was first amazed, then pleased and finally embarassed when he discovered that he had been given a Ford Sierra GL – all others at the meeting had the no trimmings Ford Sierra and wanted to know why McAlistair had been so favoured. Vickers had carefully checked the rules and revisions to them which made no mention of upgrading the cars to which the salesforce were entitled, he had also examined performance bonuses and found that McAlistair's work was well within the average category.

Devine, who was not in the least interested in cars, did not know of the discrepancy but appreciated how this would impinge on views about conditions of work and perceptions of the company's attitude towards them. He offered to refer the matter to personnel and lightly remarked that he still did not know what sort of car he would be allocated, or when. He had been in the north for nine months and was still having to use his old Granada 2.0 litre.

Martin Green

'Bad luck. Some of us don't have the option of using even an old Granada', Martin Green retorted. He had arrived late, towards the end of the discussion on McAlistair's Sierra GL. A conscientious worker, dedicated to selling, he felt that the company did not do enough to support the efforts of the sales staff. In his hand he clutched a sales leaflet.

'It would help', he continued, 'if instead of creating mischief by going against the rules and giving people cars different from what they're allowed, time was spent improving the sales literature'.

He held up the leaflet. 'This thing goes wittering on about "negative clawback". One store manager said to me yesterday that he never read them because they either went rabbiting on and on about irrelevant matter and that even when he read them he couldn't understand phrases like "negative clawback."'

Devine: 'Well it's good to see that you at least discuss the promotional literature. But you know during my recent trips in the field, I've seen leaflets and folders crumpled by backsides on seats, and mud-coated and derelict in the crevices of car boots.'

Green: 'Well I've just given you one reason why we can't find any other use for them. I think that you should be concentrating on more important things like getting the price of some of the lines down so that we can compete with Igloo and Glacier rather than worrying about leaflets.'

There was general agreement around the table at this point as all had suffered from the same problem.

Ron Tyler

Ron Tyler took up the lead provided by Green to discuss another issue of presentation, packaging. He was a very neat, fastidious man whose selling experience had committed him to the firm belief that appearances told a great deal. He reported that in his area the current efforts to promote the new, genuine, beefy Uncle Sam hamburger were not proving as successful as his brief from the company had led him to expect. He blamed this on the packaging which gave the product a cheap and nasty look. Many of his customers had pulled faces on seeing the pack and, as it was an edible product, they thought it likely that the housewife might be discouraged from trying it.

There was general agreement among the group that the packaging for the new brand of hamburger was a disaster and was affecting acceptance of the product which had been test marketed only in the south of the country.

Robin Moore

Building up and maintaining good relations with his customers received a great deal of Robin Moore's attention. He became very peeved if any action of his company caused ripples on the smooth surface that he so carefully built. A fast food-store had found paper clips in a consignment of fish fingers and had complained to the Arctic customer relations. The reply was curtly routine, implied that the fault was the customer's, and referred to the company's excellent record of quality control.

'I suppose it was my customer's fault for buying our fish fingers. But we could have been in a very difficult legal situation if someone had been harmed by swallowing those paper clips. The shop manager also showed me a copy of the letter he'd received when something similar happened some time ago with Igloo hamburgers. It was so apologetic, refunded his money and gave him a week's free supply, that now he wouldn't think of even trying our Uncle Sam's. I've got a copy of that Igloo letter here. Perhaps that's why they're getting all the business.'

Devine who had seen a copy of the letter sent to the store, as Moore had guessed he probably had, said nothing.

Ranjit Patel

Ranjit Patel had sat silent for most of the meeting and when he spoke it was with great effort because he found his situation embarrassing. During the two years that he had been a member of the Arctic salesforce he had made special efforts to direct his attention equally over his area. He had just discovered that another member of the salesforce had recently begun to call on a store that was on the edge of his territory but still within it, or so he had thought especially as no one else had given it any attention over the past two years. The store had been upgraded to a hypermarket. Patel shrugged apologetically.

'It's not that I mind particularly', he said, 'but it's just that as its now a hypermarket I hoped to get a lot of business for Arctic, the manager now knows me very well, and perhaps I might win a prize for myself.'

Mike Tracey

The Yorkshireman, Mike Tracey looked sympathetically at Ranjit Patel. 'I bet I know who it is that's been calling on that Asda hypermarket of yours Ranjit. It's that ruddy Jones. There's nothing that man loves more than prize-winning and he doesn't care too much what he does to win either. I bet even when he's not working he's entering for some other competition. I get sick of seeing his smug face grinning out at me every time I open the newsletter because he's won another blinking prize.' Tracey continued, 'I think it's about time a limit was placed on the number of prizes any one individual can win over a period. I know it's supposed to be an incentive but with Jones always winning it puts a positive stop on anyone else even trying. I know that's what it does to me.'

Mike McAlister

'Jones may be winning all the prizes but he's not getting all the sales leads like some others', Mike McAlister muttered. 'Over the past six months all I've had is 13 leads from area office, all useless. Ranjit's had 30 over the same time and he says he's got a lot of business as a result. Surely you ought to try and encourage us all equally, it's just not fair otherwise.'

To Patel, Tracey and McAlister, Devine replied by restating the company's policy of directing sales leads to the sales representative for the particular area. He was aware, even as he spoke the words, that his confirmation of support for the rules fell somewhat flat.

There was general concern among the group about recent changes, technical innovations mainly, at the Arctic warehouse. Incorrect coding had led to wrong product delivery, and failure to inform the computer of special offer prices for frozen peas had led to invoice errors. This in addition to the more routine distribution problems had created a certain amount of exasperation. Devine was able to inform the group that the warehouse reorganisation was more or less completed and things should soon be straight. Again he felt that his words were failing to reassure the salesforce. There was a general attitude of scepticism and 'We'll believe it when we see it'.

Towards the end of the meeting, Sam Vickers said how pleased some of the group had been to have Devine accompany them on their calls. Al Turner intervened at this point. He was a friendly man who felt the loneliness of his job more than he should have done. He was also proud about his area and felt that its importance as a selling area was greatly underestimated and underserved. He grumbled at Devine.

'Well you haven't visited me yet, as usual. Nobody ever wants to come round the rougher bits of country around Birkenhead. They always stick to the towns', he said morosely. 'You men from the south are just not interested in seeing the nasty parts of the country. Nine months and you've yet to come round to see me.'

*   *   *

One of the most important issues that the management and the salesforce have to face is how expectations can change over time and the conflicts that this can cause within the organisation. Such issues are outlined in the next case study.

Wizard Computers and Blyth

Wizard Computers the computer and office equipment specialists received during February 1984 a series of complaints
about the dismissal of the manager of a largish Wizard Computers work station in Slough, Mr Fred Blyth. Running an
expanding computer and office equipment organisation
throughout the country, Wizard Computers executives were
inured to redressing the usual routine grievances of the general public about product quality and technical back-up services. The case of Mr Fred Blyth was different: complaints
came from small businessmen in and around Slough and
Windsor who were among the group identified a year earlier
as key customers essential to the success of the Wizard
Computers sales strategy. They questioned the company's
management policy and criticised the dismissal of Mr Blyth
as irresponsible. Steps were taken to re-examine the grounds
for sacking Fred Blyth.

The background

Wizard Computers had grown out of a company that had
made a name for itself in supplying reliable and durable office
equipment at competitive prices. With the advent of new
technology its directors had decided that the company should
be re-organised, diversifying into personal computers. From
its earliest days, as electric typewriters had become more
sophisticated, Wizard had run a number of training work-
shops for secretarial staff to ensure that its customers got as
much as possible out of their office equipment. In entering
the personal computer market the company decided that it
would give greater emphasis to its training programme
backed up with customer consultancy services so that the
systems used integrated smoothly with the requirements of
the customer. To achieve this an extensive re-organisation
began during 1980. The Wizard office equipment retail outlets
in and around major cities were supplied with a computer
work-station displaying the company's range of personal
computers, demonstrating the available software and acting

as a service point for the new technology consultancy services for customers within the area. A new staff recruitment policy was introduced with the old-style managers of the Wizard office equipment era being replaced with younger graduate staff with a background in applying new technology in business.

The new company, Wizard Computers, did not, however, lose sight of its origins in office equipment which still accounted for the major element of profits. To make sure that the new technology experts currently being recruited were able to give due importance to the other areas of company interests, Wizard Computers had developed a sophisticated training programme. Courses initially inform recruits about Wizard Computers' origins, and the diversity and complexity of its operations which included some office equipment manufacturing in the Far East as well as retailing.

At the time that Fred Blyth joined Wizard Computers in the middle of 1980, training in the field included satisfactory completion of six months as an assistant manager before the trainee was assigned to managing his own store. Constant refresher courses were provided as well as support from area and regional managers promoted from among the most able store managers. They were constantly in touch with store managers – it being part of the area manager's duties to visit each store once a month.

Once a year an evaluation of the store manager's performance was undertaken by the area manager. Performance targets were measured against actual achievements, areas for improvement and further training identified.

Mr Fred Blyth

Fred Blyth was in his late twenties when he had applied for a post with Wizard Computers in 1980. After he had completed his degree course in computer technology he and his wife had set up a small shop specialising in selling home computers and software. According to the comments on his file, Blyth had considered joining a business expanding into computers for some time as he became increasingly convinced that small shops like his own would be unable to remain competitive as larger retail outlets entered the computer market.

His application arrived following the recruitment drive designed to implement the new staffing policy. His interview report recorded his excellent academic achievements, first hand experience in running a small business profitably against the odds, farsightedness, enthusiasm and a pleasing manner. His references were exceptional.

Blyth as an assistant manager

Blyth's initial training before he was assigned to work as an assistant manager for six months had progressed well. He had the ability to absorb quickly the dimensions of any problem and to initiate prompt action to deal with it.

During his six months as an assistant manager he was well-received by shop staff and the manager John Yardley. His knowledge of his subject, his ability to simplify and make technical details comprehensible, and his patience in getting to the root of user problems had stood him in good stead on several tricky occasions. In his final report Yardley had mentioned these together with Blyth's tendencies to spend too long chatting with customers about generalities and his lack of attention to stock-control especially in areas of company activity outside new technology. These he regarded as essentially the problems of the beginner which would be sorted out by further training and experience.

Blyth as a manager

His file revealed that Blyth was given charge of a Wizard Computers shop early in 1981 where he was visited by the area manager of some two years standing, Eric Small. On one of these visits a few months after Blyth was installed, he was surprised by the appearance of the shop. Although it was buzzing with people, especially around the computer station, the stationery and filing equipment shelves were half-empty. Discarded cardboard and plastic wrappings lay on the floor as if a hasty attempt had been made to conceal the more blatant gaps on the shelves. Notices of that month's special offers on bulk orders were not apparent.

Small demanded an explanation, Blyth did not offer any but pointed out that during his time at the shop, takings had gone up significantly. Customers, he said would ask for goods if they were not on the shelf. His staff knew and chatted with the customers like office managers who were regular bulk purchasers and drew their attention verbally to special offers. Blyth pointed out that the small hand-out notices about the promotion had all been distributed and they had already sold out of the stocks of the discounted envelopes and index cards and boxes of the Wizard own brand.

Small reported that he stressed that this was not the Wizard Computers style of selling and pointed to the importance of placing goods on the shelves to the system of stock control. When he received information from the Head Office that a stock control refresher course would shortly be available he insisted that Blyth should attend.

At the end of Blyth's first year, Small felt that some of the initial problems were beginning to sort themselves out, that Blyth recognised that there was a problem and was making a real effort to deal with it and that his performance was just about 'average'. Small was able to report substantial improvement over the next two years as under Blyth's management, and with his guidance, the branch's turnover and profitability improved. His successor as area manager was Bill Smith – a man with a good record as a supervisor who was greatly liked by those in his charge.

Smith admired Blyth's concern for people and his ability to use that to the benefit of the company. Various bonuses and financial rewards for high performance were achieved by Blyth during the further year that he worked under Smith.

The fall of Blyth

The new area manager, Roger Lees, was eager to get on. He was younger than Blyth, aggressive and anxious to find ways of increasing sales. His first report on Blyth was satisfactory but he soon discovered difficulties with Blyth's system of stock control. He noticed that Blyth organised his count of goods on the shelf fortnightly and not weekly as the rules laid down. He could not understand why this had been permitted by his predecessors or how Blyth's store could be profitable under such a poor system. He required that this should be corrected. Lees was also critical that various product lines were not moving as fast as they should have done when compared with other stores in similar areas. Sales of new types of product and in particular electronic typwriters could be improved substantially. He established new objectives which he regarded as being more in line with those of the company for Blyth in this area. As Lees believed Blyth to be out of touch with new developments in Wizard Computers' retailing he recommended that he be seconded to a larger store for a six-month period of retraining.

This helped Blyth to achieve an 'average' rating for the evaluation carried out by Lees before his departure to greener pastures.

Similar ups and downs were recorded under the next two area managers responsible for Blyth. They too were younger and also commended his good relations with his customers. The stricter monitoring of the shop's achievements with new products continued and showed little or no improvements. More rigorous supervision of Blyth was pursued in an attempt to improve his shop's sales of new products. Both area managers spent time in the shop, rearranging shelves to attract customers to little avail. One of the managers reported a change in Blyth's attitude: he was now indifferent and even hostile. He was becoming unco-operative, questioning company objectives, and alleging that the efforts of the area managers were actually harmful to the business.

The area manager sent this report to the regional manager. On going through the now substantial file recounting the problems and the attempts made to overcome them, he concluded that very little had been achieved and that it was in the best interests of both Blyth and Wizard Computers that his employment be terminated.

Conclusion

During the week following the sacking of Blyth letters expressing disbelief and amazement were received by the Wizard Computer's chairman, members of the board and at the regional offices.

One horrified small businessman recounted the story of his company's experience in new technology. He had come across Blyth at the Wizard computer work station in Slough a year after his company, on the advice of a consultant, had invested in a new technology system with a potential for expanding to 120 terminals. His company employed 35 people and the system did not work. Blyth had visited the office, pinpointed the key areas of need, supplied three Wizard personal computers with the appropriate software, organised the staff training and subsequently made useful suggestions about corrective action when problems arose.

Another manager explained that he had asked Blyth for help one morning when he discovered that the data base programme would not run. Blyth had come in after work and discovered that one manager had inadvertently placed a security lock on the data. With persistence he broke the security code thereby saving the firm a considerable amount of effort and money because customer files were involved.

Blyth, said the letters, was excellent at reassuring staff about new technology teaching them to regard it as an essential tool rather than a threat to their jobs. His replacement seemed totally unable to do this.

Recruitment 2

People are the most important component of any firm's ability to cope with the increasing demands of a complex business environment; high calibre staff will overcome difficulties and seize opportunities that their less able colleagues fail to discern. From that general statement the conclusion that the firm should recruit the most able individuals for any given task is inescapable. But in order to do this, the limitations of the job within the overall management structure will have to be carefully studied since it is pointless to recruit individuals who are too highly qualified or able for the job that the organisation wants to fill; they will become discontented and leave.

2.1 The Seven Point Recruitment Plan

One can identify seven pointers for a good recruitment and appraisal system. It will:

- recruit the right number of individuals to meet the sales and overall company objectives;
- reduce the rate of manpower turnover by selecting the right individual for the job;
- maximise the return to the company of the investment made in the employee;

- maximise the use of management time in productive rather than non-productive activity – for example ensuring that training will be a building, positive process, rather than a problem solving, negative one;
- enable the firm to maintain long-term stable relationships with its customers;
- minimise disciplinary problems and eliminate any of the possible legal problems that are always inherent in the recruitment and continuing employment of individuals;
- maintain a high level of responsibility of line management for those staff beneath them.

To achieve these diverse aims the firm is faced with a number of problems:

- defining the nature of the job and from that determining the number of individuals required to carry it out;
- determining the type of person required to fulfil the demands of the job;
- deciding on where the responsibility for the administration of recruitment and appraisal should lie;
- evaluating the procedures in relation to employment legislation.

2.2 The Job Description

The job description is a cornerstone to the successful control of manpower planning within an organisation. In general terms it will consider these issues:

- why does the job exist?
- what kind of job is it?
- what are the limits of authority to the job?
- what degree of impact has the job on the organisation, and how many people will the individual be in contact with?
- what level of support will the individual receive?

The job description should be used to:

- analyse the organisation;
- provide a benchmark for performance appraisal and disciplinary action where necessary, by forming the basis of a contract of employment;

- provide a guide for recruitment;
- define training and career development paths;
- often define the level of pay that the individual will receive.

For the job description to provide this breadth of requirements it must be *detailed*, *systematic*, and provide *objective* criteria for assessment.

To meet these criteria for the typical sales representative or sales manager, the job description would include the following type of information, here applied to a computer salesman.

1. Job title

Senior sales representative.

2. Job function

The holder will be responsible for the sales of the company's entire range of office equipment within an assigned territory, and the achievement of an agreed sales value target derived from current and new clients.

3. Reporting structure

Reporting directly to the regional manager (southern). No supervision of other employees involved. Day to day contact will be required with the technical installation staff, occasional contact with personnel, transport, financial and marketing departments on a functional basis. Position in organisation defined in accompanying organogram (see Figure 2.1).

4. Responsibility

(a) The senior sales representative is under the supervision of and accountable to the regional sales manager.
(b) The senior sales representative will carry out all instructions given to him or her by the regional sales manager relating to the conduct of his or her territory.
(c) It is the responsibility of the senior sales representative to be fully aware of and informed about all the products with which he is involved, the customers with whom he is dealing, the

FIGURE 2.1
Job description: company organogram

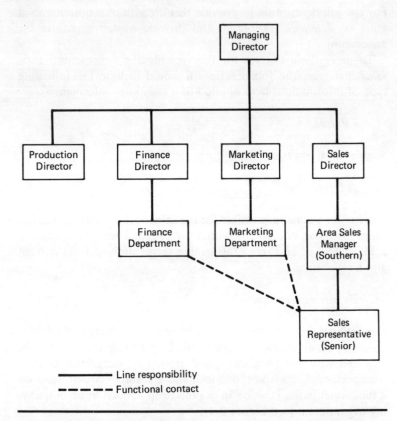

requirements of a professional sales approach, and the competitors that are faced in the market.

5.   *Degree of authority*

(a) The senior sales representative must adhere to the terms and conditions laid down in the company's current price list, unless authorised in writing to do otherwise by the sales director in conjunction with the regional manager.

(b) The senior sales representative is allowed to claim reasonable expenses for both entertaining and travelling. These limits are laid down annually by the company for all employees.

6. Products sold

The entire range of computer and accessory equipment developed by XYZ Ltd for the office equipment market.

7. Sales volume and value

The senior sales representative will be responsible for calling on 100–150 customers, representing an annual sales value of £1.5 million–£2.0 million.

8. Client type by outlet

(a) Institutions. All offices employing more than 100 personnel.
(b) Distributors. All distributors involved in the sale of office computer equipment with a turnover of more than £500 000 per annum.
(c) Consultancy firms. All consultancy firms involved in the development of office systems with a turnover of more than £1.0 million.

9. Client type by buying personnel

(a) Office managers, senior personnel involved in buying decisions on office equipment, organisation and method departmental staff.
(b) All personnel including management and sales staff.
(c) Senior consultants.

10. Nature of selling task

(a) Developing new accounts and new business will occupy 60 percent of selling time. The senior sales representative will be responsible for the definition of new accounts and determining the workload that each will require for profitable development.

(b) Maintaining contact and expanding current customer base will occupy 30 per cent of selling time. Current customers are ranked on the basis of turnover. It is expected that:

A grade customers will be visited once monthly;
B grade customers will be visited once every two months;
C grade customers will be visited once every four months;
D grade customers will visited annually.

(c) Liaising with distributors will occupy 10 per cent of selling time. Similar gradings applying to the current customers will apply to distributors.

(d) Routine travel within the territory will be necessary as defined by the customer requirements. Overnight accommodation when necessary will be allowed under company guidelines, in addition to other travel outside the territory to sales meetings, conventions and other venues that may be considered necessary by the sales director.

11. Promotional work required

(a) Arranging and administering demonstrations with clients either on site or using Head Office facilities.
(b) Assisting distributors where appropriate to train sales personnel or helping at exhibitions.
(c) Assisting where necessary with the development of new products – in agreement with the regional manager.

12. Administrative work required

(a) Sales documentation. This is to be sent immediately on completion of the agreement in the envelope provided.
(b) Weekly call records. These are to be completed on the forms provided and sent to the regional sales manager to arrive at the latest on the Wednesday following the end of the week under consideration.
(c) Competitive and personnel changes. Details of changes in competitive position and alterations in the buying personnel at any account should be completed in the account record which must be completed on a weekly basis, and despatched to arrive by the following Wednesday.

(d) Weekly expense forms to be despatched to arrive by the following Wednesday.
(e) Correspondence with Head Office departments on transport, marketing and finance departments. All letters will be answered within three days of receipt.

13. *Personal conduct*

(a) Car. The senior sales representative will ensure that the car remains in a correct state of repair as laid down in the Road Traffic Acts. He or she will report all accidents or prosecutions immediately to the regional manager.
(b) The senior sales representative will meet the company's policy on clothing and personal appearance.
(c) The senior sales representative will deal honestly with all customers and enquiries from the regional manager.
(d) The senior sales representative will report honestly on activities and the expenditure of company money.
(e) The senior sales representative will report any *serious* or incapacitating illness that may affect job performance as soon as possible to the regional manager.

*   *   *

This job description will meet the requirements initially laid down. It escapes the all too common pitfalls of job descriptions: that they are too vague. Statements such 'the sales representative will at all time use his best endeavours to further the interests of the company' are at best meaningless; at worst they can be a major demotivating factor. Clarity of job description particularly in the area of defining areas of responsibility and levels of expected performance will reduce the possibility of arbitrary action or assessment. Reference can be made to the English navy and the Articles of War which held the power of life and death at the time of the Napoleonic Wars. In addition to death for contempt, mutiny, sleeping on duty, cowardice, disobedience, and numerous other crimes, the Admiralty also included the catch all final Article: 'All other crimes committed by any person or persons in the fleet and not mentioned in this Act shall suffer death or a lesser punishment'. Many companies prefer to maintain vagueness in job descriptions for the same reason – to ensure that authority can be as easily maintained. They may, however, have to pay the price of diminished efficiency as a result.

2.3 Defining the Personnel Responsibility

In large organisations there will be varying degrees of delegation of authority for recruitment. Personnel departments will often be involved in all the preliminary stages of advertising for new applicants, often carrying out initial screening interviews to produce a short list. As it is essential that the responsible line management has the final decision as to the individuals chosen for a particular position, regional sales managers and sales directors will need to be involved at least at this stage. Indeed, it can be argued that the earliest involvement of sales management in recruitment will ensure that many of the pitfalls inherent in the exercise will be minimised; namely deciding on the type of person needed, the sort of advertisement most likely to attract them, and selecting the most suitable of the applicants for interview.

2.4 Selection

Once the job description has been drawn up, the type of individual best suited to the post must be decided. The requirements of each sales job will naturally differ from each other and also over time. There may also be geographic differences which would mean failure for any sales representative transferred to that area who might have been highly successful in another environment. Any approach that attempts to develop standardised recruitment methods will need to remember the problems that this local variation may cause.

Defining the basic requirements for a particular sales post will, however, supply a backbone on which the flesh of the individual applicant and the particular problems of the sales territory can be applied.

The most useful approach developed for a standard selection procedure is based on an application of the Seven Point Plan.[1]

This holds that the requirements for any job can be considered under a number of headings with elements that are essential and others that are desirable. Some companies will add a third column of factors that would disqualify an applicant.

Criteria	*Essential*	*Desirable*
1. Physical:		
eyesight		
general health		
hearing		
build		
age		
speech		
appearance		
sex		
2. Attainments:		
education		
career		
3. Intelligence		
4. Special skills		
5. Interests		
6. Disposition		
7. Personal		
circumstances		

This approach will produce a framework for comparing and evaluating all applicants. It can also allow the company to list the currently employed sales representatives, and their backgrounds to provide a profile of the likely successful sales representative for that particular industry or region.

Some companies evolve a points ranking system from such an analysis; 10 points for college education, 6 for 'A' levels, 4 for leaving with other qualifications, down to 2 for leaving school at 16 without any qualifications whatsoever.

Although valuable, analysing success and failure in this fashion can produce a too rigid system and a salesforce that lacks variety and the ability to cope with changing market conditions. Other companies use a more general approach to the application of the Seven Point Plan where there will be a number of key issues considered under each heading.

1. Physical

(a) Does the candidate need to meet certain physical standards – or are there physical problems that will create difficulties for the task in which he or she is involved?

(b) Does the candidate need to meet standards of appearance – does the male recruit need to be a clean-shaven with short hair?

2. Attainments

(a) What level and type of education should the candidate have achieved? Are there any special requirements in the school record? Will weaknesses in any subject such as English or mathematics be a problem?

(b) How well has his or her career progressed?

(c) How necessary is it that the sales representative should have received training in prior employment?

3. General intelligence

(a) What level of general intelligence is desirable for the job?

(b) What level does the candidate normally need to display?

4. Special skills

Has the candidate need for special skills to succeed in the job? There have been several attempts to define the special aptitudes necessary for the successful sales representative:

A high level of energy;
Abounding self-confidence;
Personally ambitious for status, money and prestige;
Hard working and competitive.[2]
Another approach demands that candidates for sales posts show two basic personality traits:
Empathy – the ability to understand other people's problems;
Ego drive – the personal urge to succeed.[3]

How these special skills can be best determined still remains an issue for debate. The value of aptitude tests have been put forward by some authors and denied by others.[4] One aspect of the problem that is often forgotten is that the sales representative is not (quite!) the typical rat in the maze. Many sales or potential sales representatives in the author's experience understand the issues at stake in aptitude tests with the result that they will do them well – whether or not they are in reality suited to the job at issue. Study of one of the several books of self-testing material available will bring any reader up to the required standard of aggressiveness and empathy within a short period.[5]

5. *Interests*

To what extent does the candidates' hobbies need to suit his or her likely employment?

It is possible to consider interests as falling into one of five categories:

(1) Those basically consisting of clerical work such as stamp collecting;
(2) Those of a practical construction type such as restoring old cars or building models;
(3) Those involving physical activity such as walking or sailing;
(4) Those involving close co-operation with people such as choral singing, or team sports and;
(5) Artistic pursuits such as writing or painting.

Team activities would appear to be a good indicator as to possible success at the sales task involving as they do the need to understand others' problems and requirements.

6. *Disposition*

What type of disposition does the candidate need? Should the individual be a good team manager for example? This will often be crucial for the successful selection of sales personnel, and many companies when recruiting numbers of sales representatives will run a selection board process by which a group of salesmen are asked to deal with a particular problem. This will show more clearly the candidate's acceptability to other people, his or her dependability and reaction within the group, giving important indications as to likely persuasive ability when dealing with buying committees. Specifically: does the individual help the group in acquiring information, listen attentively, summarise well, reduce tension, admit mistakes, or oppose views, withdraw from the group, fail to accept mistakes. How does the candidate cope on an individual basis; is he or she self-reliant? Able to put forward and maintain opinions without being opinionated? Issues such as all these will give valuable indications as to whether the candidate will be suitable.

7.   Circumstances

What are the ideal individual's personal circumstances?

(a) Has the candidate had a history of repeated house moves?
(b) Does it matter that the wife/husband is involved in another job that may preclude the individual from making as full a contribution as necessary to the job?
(c) Important for many sales jobs will be the degree of financial security: is the candidate under severe financial pressure which might make him or her take additional employment or encourage him or her to put in excessive expense claims?

Some firms adopt criteria which will lead to automatic disqualification of a potential employee. They can include:

1. Recent divorce or separation;
2. Inexplicable gaps in the employment record;
3. Excessive indebtedness.

Employment legislation makes the application of 'failure analysis' an extremely delicate procedure. The author has had experience of one company which firmly holds the view that *no* trade union members will be recruited. As this runs contrary to legislation, instructions to the recruiters of sales personnel are given verbally to ensure that no written record exists of such a regulation.

The firm has to consider whether there is a particular objective reason why a certain problem should mean automatic disqualification. For example management may feel that men over 40 or women under 25 are totally unsuitable for the job for that reason alone. Unless management can show from analysis of past records that failure is practically guaranteed because of this shortcoming, concentrating on this factor to the exclusion of others may mean that valuable potential recruits are missed.

Reaching likely applicants

First, the firm will consider the type of sales personnel that it wishes to recruit, whether it requires untrained personnel with a good educational background, or people with practical technical skills, believes in internal promotion, or recruits already established and trained sales personnel. This will determine which of the following possible sources of applicants is chosen as the most suitable:

1. Customers and competitors;
2. General advertisements;
3. Colleges and schools;
4. Employment agencies.

Most recruitment will rely on the advertisement, certainly within the United Kingdom, though in other countries the specialised employment agency is often an important source of recruits.

There are many books written on the design of a good advertisement and how to determine when and where it should be placed.[6] For the recruitment of sales personnel the following basic elements will need to be considered:

- the job description and requirements;
- the territory the job will cover;
- terms and conditions;
- contact procedure.

There will always be issues requiring careful attention. Should the company name be given for example? The exact nature of the job? More generally, the recruitment criteria will have to be examined to ensure that they are neither too broad – which will lead to a large number of unsuitable applicants – nor too narrow with few, if any appearing, wasting the often considerable expenditure on the advertisement. Adherents to the first school can be seen in the insurance company recruitment advertisements which offer large rewards while demanding few qualifications. The opposite is most amusingly put in an advertisement to ensure only a single applicant for the post of Prime Minister:

> *Wanted.*: **Prime Minister of Ruritania. Hours of work: 4 am to 11.59 pm. Candidates must be prepared to fight three rounds with the current heavy weight champion (regulation gloves to be worn). Candidates will die for their country, by painless means, on reaching the age of retirement (65). They will have to pass an examination in parliamentary procedure and will be liquidated should they fail to obtain 95% marks. They will also be liquidated if they fail to gain 75% votes on a popularity poll held under the Gallup Rules. They will finally be invited to try their eloquence on a Baptist Congress, the object being to induce those present to rock and roll. Those who fail will be liquidated.**[7]

Application forms

The use of standard application forms for those who apply has much to recommend it. It ensures that all candidates will provide information in a similar fashion and that no gaps will exist. Here again the application form should if possible be tailored to the job; using the application form designed for senior management may prove such an obstacle for many recruits that this initial hurdle is not passed.

Interviewing

Whether the personnel department is involved in the initial screening exercise or not, it is inevitable that sales management will at some stage be involved in the interviewing process.

Successful interviews like meetings, require planning. Sufficient time must be allowed to carry out the interviewing process. Far too often management see interviewing as a time-wasting exercise, which when one considers the implications of poor selection, is the height of stupidity. It is surely far better to spend an additional five hours selecting the right applicant rather than the 50 to 100 hours that may be involving in counselling, training, and perhaps eventually getting rid of the wrong candidate. Interviewers should remember the adage that it is difficult to make silk purses from sow's ears.

Secondly, the interview should be conducted away from the pressures of the office; it is tempting disaster to concentrate on recruitment when interrupted with telephone calls from important customers.

The role of the interviewer

The task of the interviewer is obviously to acquire as much knowledge as possible of the candidate's intellectual and social skills, level of experience, technical ability and motivation for the particular job in question, as well as general social attitudes, like the ability to work with others. These components need to be marshalled into some form of systematic pattern which will provide an overall level of acceptability or non-acceptability to the organisation. Each candidate will have strengths and weaknesses and every interview will demand a balancing act, an understanding of how the various components of the individual add to the overall picture of a successful or unsuccessful recruit. Because of the limited time available the interviewer is very much in the positon of the traveller walking by the sea-shore and picking up those things that are thrown up on the beach, and from them trying to determine the nature of life in that particular part of the ocean. Some of the things that this individual encounters will be red herrings and this will be no less true of the prospective interviewer.

The Seven Point Plan provides a useful departure station for the interview, enabling the interviewer to classify impressions and evidence as the meeting progresses. Certain key areas will provide valuable information as to how the individual has developed, and will also supply valuable pointers as to specific areas which should be probed in more detail:

1. *Early life.* Against what background has the candidate developed? What effect have these factors had? For example a broken home may produce insecurity, on the other hand it may result in a greater degree of self-reliance and the ability to cope. Continual changes in school in the same area may indicate other problems.
2. *Education.* The way the candidate has progressed at school and college will be very important in the overall assessment of the candidate's suitability. All other things being equal, the applicant

who did well at school both in academic and non-academic tasks and fitted in, will be equally successful in general terms in a job – the loner continually changing schools and achieving a mixed exam record may indicate problems. The type of exams passed will always give an indication of inclinations and dis- likes; were arts subjects stronger than sciences? What were the particular weaknesses? The type of sport played and at what level may also provide valuable pointers.

3. *Work record*. This for the older candidate will naturally provide a greater source of evidence as to the potential of the individual for the prospective job. Issues that need to be explored in detail include the reasons why previous employment was left: and how the individual responded to discipline, and the working environment. The claim that everyone around the candidate was to blame for leaving a job may be totally acceptable; if it is put forward more than once it becomes an issue that is suspect and requires closer investigation.

   The exact nature of the previous work often needs detailed 'excavation'. All of us will tend to claim to be slightly more important than we actually are, or to re-classify the jobs that we do, leading to such well known transmogrifications as waste disposal executive and rodent operative. One useful question is to find out who replaced the individual during the holidays or courses, as this will often give clear indication as to the value of the individual to the organisation.

4. *Interests*. The key issue in the evaluation of interests is whether they are coherent with the other aspects of the candidate's profile.

5. *Present circumstances*. It will be vital that the candidate can fit on a personal basis into the company and business environment that the job requires. The type of customer with whom the candidate will be required to negotiate should be carefully examined not for the sake of ensuring that they each have similar backgrounds, which is certainly not the issue – and can indeed be counter-productive, but in order to establish whether the individual will be comfortable in dealing with the customer.

Interviews should never be a one-way street: it is in the interests of the interviewer that the candidate should be totally clear as to the nature and responsibility of the job. Here the job description is a valuable document: it will clearly show in great detail what the job consists of. It is a useful personnel policy to send these out with the invitation to interview, as this will both reduce the interviewing load (candidates not interested in the job once they have received more details than were in the advertisement will cancel the interview), and allow candidates time to consider any issue that they want further clarification on.

Once all the questions have been answered and the interview is complete, an overall picture of the candidate will emerge against which the essential and desirable qualities required for the job can be judged. Balance and judgement will be essential: does the candidate's undoubted experience in national account negotiating make up for his lack of experience in the electrical industry? Will the tremendous selling skills offset an extremely prickly character?

Once these factors have been analysed the interviewer or interviewers (should a panel have been used in the final stages) will be in the position to decide on the suitable applicant subject to receiving references as to the business or academic performance and completing medical formalities.

2.5 Finalising the Appointment

It is essential that the hiring company checks the qualifications and the history of every applicant. How this is done will vary with the job, the candidate and industry.

Though it may be ideal for the interviewer to consider references before the appearance of the candidate, this is unlikely to be possible in the majority of cases, as individuals in employment are unwilling to divulge the fact that they are leaving until a firm offer of alternative employment is gained, a factor which has strengthened during the economic recession.

Personal contact whether by telephone or visit will tend to yield the best results for any reference, as line managers are normally extremely unwilling to commit anything on paper whereas they will be likely to be far more helpful over the telephone when they cannot be quoted. References by letter are much more likely to be guarded.

On the other hand, it is not uncommon for both candidates and employers to 'rig' references. The latter may put on rose-tinted spectacles to describe the skills of an employee whose departure is desirable; the former may name as referee a senior officer at their current place of work who regards them in a favourable light. Many large employers do issue instructions to staff about the correct procedures to be followed in the naming of referees in cases where employees are seeking alternative work. For fairly obvious reasons these may be disregarded and it is not always easy for an outsider to check that the referee named is indeed the individual authorised by the employer to write a reference for the person concerned. For example, in most sections of the UK Civil Service the responsibility of reference writing rests with the Establishments Officers. In practice many Establishments Officers trained in personnel management may wonder at the departure of civil servants from their sections without ever having been asked to supply a word for or against the skills of those leaving!

References can also be obtained via credit agencies which will also give information about how long individuals have been at their particular address; whether they have had credit problems, what is their level of debt and other issues.

Physical checks are also an important element in the pre-appointment period; are there any particular physical problems that will cause concern during employment?

Once the initial preliminaries are completed the candidate should be advised by letter of the contractual agreement between him or her and the company. This contract should include:

- an exact description of the job;
- the reporting structure;
- the probationary period (if any);
- length of notice on either side;
- salary, benefit and commission structure.

The candidate

Background

This exercise was in the first instance designed for two players: the job applicant, Jim Smith, and the personnel manager conducting the interview. However, it was subsequently pointed out that a group interview of the candidate could more effectively elicit the type of information essential to the company. Moreover trying out both techniques could well demonstrate the very different results that can be obtained by each method.

In either case, the representative of the employer organisation should if possible see only the curriculum vitae and references which formed the basis of the decision to interview Jim Smith. The latter will have access to the remaining information.

The company's position

During the year you are faced with the selection of an individual to fill the new post of sales information assistant in your busy office which deals with the sale of engineering products to the public and private sector. In the public sector it supplies some equipment to the armed services. The firm has a good reputation locally of being a steady employer.

The post had been created in an attempt to speed the flow of information between the office and the salesforce following complaints – which on investigation had proved well-grounded – that important information about products and competitors was not getting through to the salesforce. Part of the problem was that many of the senior staff at the sales office were frequently away travelling and important documents would remain unattended in in-trays. After detailed investigation, a consultant had recommended that the post of sales information assistant be created to look at and record all incoming information.

The job description

The job description of the post is as follows:

1. Main objectives

(a) To enable the company to respond promptly and accurately to requests for information about its products and operating environment.
(b) To help other staff keep abreast of developments which may affect their work.
(c) To support an information base for the work of the sales department as a whole.

2. Main tasks

(a) To monitor and catalogue all incoming documentation related to engineering companies, their customers, sales and products.
(b) To handle salesforce enquiries, in consultation with the relevant departments, about the company, its products, aims and objectives.
(c) To maintain a ready-reference system of information about the company, its markets, its competitors and developments in the market.
(d) To ensure that all documents are returned to a central bank.

3. Occasional tasks

(a) To handle routine press enquiries in the absence of the Press Officer.
(b) To collate information about the company and its markets for press briefing packages.

4. Main contacts

(a) All staff within the office.
(b) The salesforce.

5. *Responsibility*

(a) Sole responsibility for documentation in house.
(b) Sole responsibility for handling routine enquiries.

6. *Special expertise*

Ability to work without supervision; to set up and run an effective cataloguing system; to work quickly and accurately; to handle statistical information.

7. *Basic qualifications*

Experience of library/documentation classification systems; of handling technical information.

Copies of this job description were sent to all referees when a candidate's application was taken up. Candidates were required to name two referees: one being their current employer, another for character. In the accompanying letter the personnel manager pointed to a number of sensitive issues relating to the job: it was a new post; since the person appointed was dealing with in-coming documentation it was essential that he or she should not create a bottleneck – a conscientious, efficient worker was essential; it was inevitable that the incumbent would come across some confidential data and referees were asked to comment on the discretion of the applicant.

The appearance

One candidate who presents himself is Jim Smith.

Jim Smith's curriculum vitae

Name: Jim Smith
Address: 12 Farthing Close, Blackheath
Born: 1950, Malaysia
Educated:Eltham Comprehensive
          Charlton High School
          Bexleyheath College

Exams: 5 'O' levels.

Career history: 1969 to 1972 library clerk, Bromley Council. Reason for leaving: job lacked challenge.

1973 to 1976 warehouse despatch clerk, Splatford Machine Tools. Reason for leaving: firm went into liquidation.

1977 to 1982 administrative records assistant, Thames Barrier Project. Reason for leaving: rundown of project.

Interests: social clubs, cycling.

Jim Smith's referees

Both of Jim Smith's referees described him as a committed, hard-working and loyal individual. He had experience of library work and documentation systems and experience gained in his spare time, social club activities, gave him a good background in supplying information to enquiries. But this was in any case a facet of the record keeping tasks that he had undertaken at the Thames Barrier Project.

The reality

Here are some further details about Jim Smith which are not apparent from his curriculum vitae.

Born in Malaysia. His Malay father was in government service *but* not a British employee and Jim Smith is not a British citizen.

His early years were spent in an Islamic school in Kuala Lumpur having a curriculum with a high content of religious teaching from the Koran.

When the family broke up, his mother returned to England. He has a half-brother and half-sister. Currently his mother runs an adventure playground/activity centre in Manchester.

At present, Jim Smith lives in a 'shared' house which is in reality a revolutionary socialist worker's commune often raided by the police.

Jim has a violent dislike of authority in all shapes and forms.

He went to Eltham Comprehensive at the age of 11. Victimised by schoolteachers, he left because he says that he could not get on with the staff. In fact, he had laced the staff instant coffee with Eno's. The ensuing attempt to discipline the prankster had led to a row between the head teacher and Jim Smith's mother.

He next attended Charlton Park which coincided with the family moving house. Jim can argue that he moved school because of moving house, both in the case of Eltham Comprehensive and Charlton. He took 5 '0' levels at Charlton – Maths, English, Woodwork, Sociology and Geography. He obtained good passes in Sociology and Maths, and scraped by in the others. His career at Charlton terminated when he attempted to organise a solidarity group in support of the school dinner ladies who were on strike. He was asked to leave.

Jim Smith went on to Bexleyheath College on a book-keeping course. He can say that he had to leave because his mother had left home and he had to look after his brother and sister. However, he also had a series of rows over racism in the college particularly the victimisation of Asian teachers. He quit Bexleyheath in 1966.

He travelled for three years visiting Eastern Europe and the North of England. During that time he had also been sponsored by a constituency Labour party in the North of England to carry out studies on poverty in the working class.

While working for Bromley as a clerk doing standard administrative work cataloguing and filing for the housing department, he was also working on the implementation of equal rights legislation in the borough. He was now Branch Secretary of the National Union of Public Employees. He left because he claims that he found the work boring. However during his time at Bromley he had leaked information to the press and had an affair with the Chairman of the Housing Department's wife.

Subsequently he spent his time looking for the 'right' job. In reality, jobs with high union content were difficult to find in the area. His job handling sales ledger and bought ledger in a warehouse ended when Splatford Machine Tools went bankrupt. But the bankruptcy came as a direct result of a long and arduous strike called by a union of which Jim Smith was deputy convenor. He blamed incompetent management.

After the firm went into receivership, Jim Smith says he went on holiday to recuperate from trauma and became involved in community activity overseas: he was living in a commune in Hamburg for six months.

Employed as an administrative records clerk on Thames Barrier project, he was actually a direct nominee of the Greater London Council with a special responsibility for ensuring correct ethnic mix in the work-force. Since the entire project was funded by the GLC Jim Smith can easily evade this issue in any discussion. As the project wound down he had seen only very limited prospects for further involvement in politics of the work-force.

The reason that Jim Smith gives for wanting to change the type of employer for whom he has worked is that he is searching for greater work challenge. The reality is that he believes that unionisation should be developed as rapidly as possible among major organisations in the area to ensure that his political ambitions remain alive.

His stated interest in cycling, community-based activities, and sport has come about because his life revolves around a whole series of community/political clubs at which he is in great demand as a speaker. To get to them he cycles long distances, having visited Maidstone, Basingstoke, Luton and Oxford over weekends.

He reads and contributes to *Militant*. Does not read a daily paper. Thinks television has taken over from religion as the opium of the masses.

QR

One of four shortlisted candidates had to be chosen by John Dunn, sales director and Peter Bell one of the marketing managers of Quality Records (QR), the record and tapes division of Amalgamated Entertainment, the multinational group, to fill a new sales management post. These four were top of the list after applicants had undergone extensive intelligence and aptitude tests and interviews conducted by a consultant psychologist retained by the Head Office of A.E. to advise on all posts above a certain level. All four had been interviewed and John Dunn was compiling his report for the personnel director with his final recommendation and rationale.

Background

QR was one of the largest divisions of A.E. and had achieved sales in England alone in excess of £86 million in the last financial year. The parent company made films, computer software including games, television programmes and had a major publishing section.

QR manufactured and sold a wide range of records and tapes, mainly of popular music. They had developed a strong list of pop groups, ballad singers and with their American parent company were the leading label for Country and Western music in the world.

The 250 records and tapes currently in the range were sold by a salesforce of 50 to specialist record shops, department stores, and major retail chains which had steadily become more and more important in the record business.

The vacant post

The senior management of A.E. had decided that to improve cash flow within a very volatile industry, they should continue to expand the small classical record list throughout their world-wide subsidiary network. Though classical music provided far lower volumes, margins were substantially better than normal popular music. This was especially true of the new compact discs (CDs) which had started to appear in quantity. Peter Bell had been appointed as marketing manager to develop the product range and the next priority was to redefine the distribution system.

The directive had been issued by Head Office that a sales manager responsible for the development of the classical music division should be appointed as soon as possible.

Typically, the classical music specialist would spend most of his or her time negotiating at fairly senior level with major stores or store groups. He or she would also be responsible in the medium term for either training some of the current QR salesforce in the different demands of the classical music business or recruiting additional representatives to build up what had been proposed by the strategic plan of AE: a six to eight man salesforce directed purely to the classical record business.

Building up good relations with major accounts would be a special feature of the job. Initially it would also include arranging and conducting regional sales meetings, and attending others organised by representatives for distributors. These activities were considered as key elements in developing initial contacts with the salesforce.

Planning and reporting would be very important: A.E. Head Office had stressed their need to be kept in touch with the distributors and major customers.

Mr Dunn intended that the newcomer would report directly to him as did the other sales managers. He or she would need to develop a strategy designed to assist the new sales effort by deciding on which customers should be initially approached; training and motivating the salesforce and modifying the current sales information system to be more relevant to the requirements of the classical music business. Mr Dunn believed that this intensive thrust for new business could be relaxed after 18 months after which the sales manager could give attention to maintaining the key customers and organising the sales representatives.

Promotability was always an important issue for any A.E. management recruit; senior management were assessed on their ability to recruit and hold on to individuals who could progress through the company.

The job would require relocation to the QR Head Office at Welwyn Garden City, and perhaps a further relocation to south London if the classical music division grew as it was expected to. QR was a 'pressure' company: all employees had to clock in, offices were all open plan, and all decisions needed to be carefully documented for senior management review. The majority of sales managers with this level of expertise in the industry were in their mid-thirties and earned about £15 000 a year. Previous selling experience, some demonstrable administrative ability and further education were regarded as the most desirable qualifications, for the new post.

The candidates

Howard Field

Howard Field's application had been instigated by one of QR's largest distributors who spoke very highly about his ability as a sales manager. He knew a great deal about A.E. and its customers and had had experience calling on some of them, especially the major supermarket chains. Field had a pleasant appearance and an easy-going manner and although Mr Dunn on meeting him thought that he tended to be 'over-confident' he felt that he and the office staff could work with him without any difficulty.

The psychologist's report revealed that Field had not applied himself to hard work either at school or at university: he had changed his course at university and had had to resit his final year. He had worked for four years as a technical educational adviser in local government. Quitting because he estimated his job prospects to be poor, he went on to a small chainstore dealing in electrical appliances eventually becoming a manager of one of the stores. He found this became too routine and left initially to join the buying department of a nationwide department store chain. Here he had progressed to become second in command after the chief buyer but opted for redundancy during a shake-up. With the money so obtained he had set up a sheet music publishing business which had collapsed after 18 months. Although he was looking for work he did not regard the matter as urgent.

Field is the youngest of four children. His father had run his own business which had been something of a struggle. He is 38, married with two children. His interests include sport, representing Devon at pistol shooting in national championships, good food and wine. His knowledge of classical music was fairly extensive having been gained during his abortive venture in publishing sheet music.

Field's scores on the intelligence tests revealed him to be at the lower end of the scale required for managerial positions. He has excellent practical reasoning ability but was less good with abstract matters and figures. He approached problems well, thought before he acted, but the psychologist reported that his attitude to the tests was 'lackadaisical'. On reading, mathematical, and comprehension tests his rating was average. He scored well on resourcefulness and flexibility and was rated above average in judgement and comprehension. Overall the psychologist thought that he lacked self-discipline and the ability to apply himself constantly to the tasks in hand. Dunn thought that he would be likely to get on well with other people, and that his staid appearance might be very acceptable to the conservative classical record industry. Bell thought that he was lacking in 'drive' and might easily have to be pushed; Dunn did not agree.

Leonora Jackson

Leonora Jackson's application for the post of industry specialist with the QR of A.E. had been supported by a firm of head-hunters who spoke warmly of her ability. Mr Dunn had found her a lively companion and admired her personal motivation. She was exceptionally well informed about the company particularly about the product range and distribution problems. Of all the candidates she was the best turned-out, at 34, one of the two youngest of the four candidates. However, both Dunn and Bell were surprised that Jackson had not progressed further in her career. Bell thought that this was because Jackson was a woman and would therefore be naturally diffident and lack aggression. She was very eager for the job.

The report from the psychologist revealed that Jackson's school record was good. She had had to leave school at 16 because of parental pressures but had worked in the local library's music section while taking 'A' levels at the local college. While attending the local polytechnic on a business studies course she had worked in the evenings to supplement her grant, eventually leaving with a good degree.

For the first six years she had worked as a manager for a vending company before leaving to seek better paid work. She had then worked for a Birmingham based manufacturer of electrical components, in the sales support area, visiting distributors for training and advisory sessions. The firm eventually had gone bankrupt due to bad financial control.

Jackson's father died when she was young; she is divorced with two children. Her medical reports reveal that she had suffered from a string of illnesses in her late twenties as her marriage was running into difficulties. Current health was excellent.

Her hobbies revolve largely around the home; she is a keen DIY'er. Outside interests include the local operatic society.

On the various tests Jackson's rating was consistently above average with the exception of arithmetic. She performed well in organisational ability, resourcefulness, flexibility and creative ability, she appears to be both tactful and motivated but very tense. Neither Dunn nor Bell could decide whether this was her natural state or whether the interview had created it.

Andrew Flood

Andrew Flood had responded to one of the national newspaper advertisements for the post.

Both Dunn and Bell were impressed by Flood's encyclopaedic knowledge of the classical record business, his enthusiasm, and his ability to communicate. Bell, however, considered that the slight lisp and mildly eccentric clothing – he had arrived for the interview in a tweed jacket – might make him a creature of fun with the notoriously cynical salesforce.

The psychologist's report noted that the lisp disappeared when Flood became angry.

Andrew Flood's record at school and university was the best of the four candidates. He had left Cambridge with a good degree and had immediately joined the major music publishing company, Octave Press, which was based in Covent Garden. Starting in the despatch department he had worked for the last eight years in the prestige books department, producing and selling to the major chains the *Mastering Music* collection which had given him impressive contacts throughout the trade. Though he had been successful in this venture, Bell found out that the Octave Press did not carry out formal training for either management or salesforce, so that all his skills had been acquired 'on the job'. He has recently been unhappy with his progress in the firm and has been looking elsewhere.

Andrew Flood was 34, and unmarried. He had lived in the same flat in Hampstead (since leaving university) which he shared with a friend. His main hobby was music: he played the oboe for one of the leading amateur groups in the country and had gone on tour to Japan and the United States with them.

On the psychologist's report he scored highly on intelligence and analytical powers, though he appeared weaker in practical areas. He was extremely tactful, and appeared to be good at making decisions.

Hubert Hill

On his first meeting with Hubert Hill, Mr Dunn had been impressed by his ability as a salesman. He had a relaxed and convincing manner during the presentation he had made to Mr Dunn describing the differences of particular types of wine glass – he was currently employed by a glass manufacturer. He had also made a good impression on those Head Office staff who had met him, especially Dunn's secretary.

Hubert Hill's school and college career was bespattered with his passion for selling. With the money he had earned first from a newspaper round and then from a Saturday job he had bought items cheap in the market for resale to his school-mates. He had continued such activities while doing a business course at college where he earned the disapproval of the authorities by running a cut-price travel service; but since his work was average they left him alone.

After travelling around the world for two years after college he had worked for a while as a salesman for his father's company, which was a small printing works. When this was taken over by a larger concern he had gone to work for one of the major insurance companies. Finding that selling insurance was more difficult than he anticipated – because 'there were too few immediate benefits for the buyer', and he felt too constrained by 'rules', he had joined a sales promotion and training consultancy firm, for which he had worked for the last four years. In consequence he had had considerable experience of developing new salesforce teams, but now he wished to return to mainstream line management.

Hill, 35 came from a large family; his younger brother owned a record shop specialising in classical music near the cathedral of his home town Liverpool. He is unmarried and has no plans for 'settling down'. He spends his spare time windsurfing, racing cars, and hang gliding.

The psychologist found Hill has excellent practical and abstract reasoning abilities. He had performed well above average in the range of intelligence tests demonstrating resourcefulness, and flexibility. He appeared less competent in other areas; weak in organisational ability, tactfulness and motivation; and on tasks calling for immediate effort. Dunn thought that he would find it difficult to make decisions, but Bell thought that his background would make him well suited to the type of task involved.

Preparation for Selling 3

The art of sales preparation has three fairly distinct aspects: first which customers to see (prospecting); what to say to them when this has been achieved (discussion); and when to see them (organisation).

3.1 Prospecting

Prospecting can be simply described as the identification of suitable customers. How this will be achieved will naturally vary from industry to industry, the nature of the types of information available and the value of the potential sale.

The cost of prospecting should never be ignored especially as selling costs steadily rise. Take for example a typical salesman earning £12 000 per annum. On him the company will be annually spending in the region of £25 000 or more including the car, commission, insurance, expenses, proportion of salary of area sales manager, director, personnel department, and so on. His effective working year will be around 200 days, which means that the average salesman costs the company about £16 per hour. Should that individual then be required to spend time researching possible leads and using the telephone to establish contact after perhaps writing a letter, the expense can quite easily escalate to £25 per hour, for telephoning will have to be done during working hours even if the sales representative is researching the area during the evenings or weekends.

Investing in sales leads generated in this fashion should be compared with those that might be achieved through direct mail or exhibitions. A reasonable piece of direct mail will cost say 22 pence to despatch. Common levels of return in direct mail are of the order of 2 per cent in industrial markets, meaning that the cost of lead generation would be around £11 per customer.

An additional factor in the equation is the conversion rate, that is the number of enquiries that turn into orders. Direct mail or exhibitions also tend to be more efficient in this respect as the return of a coupon or enquiry at an exhibition does imply some form of interest in the product. In addition, they may score in reaching the relevant person within the organisation who can take a decision, a problem which is considered in greater detail below. Such identification is more difficult via the telephone, and two or more visits may be necessary to the organisation before the correct individual is identified.

As a result many firms are concentrating on providing the salesman with back-up in the area of lead generation to enable his or her time to be more effectively spent with the use of tele-sales system or direct mail. Obviously where labour costs are low different criteria will apply. Phillip Morris, the American tobacco firm for example, employ 300 salesmen in Venezuela, the majority of whom are used to prospect for new business. Similarly home improvement firms employ canvassers at low cost to identify customers on whom the more highly paid salesforce will call.

3.2 Discussion

Every sales representative can only achieve his objectives through conversation – often grandly called 'communication'. This skill is one independent of traditional classroom exercises – but one which is crucial for the exchange of ideas and for persuading others that one has a powerful case even though they may retain residual objections.

All of us have had experiences at school, university and in the business world of people who are expert at the art of monologues and who talk at great length about subjects that interest *them* whether it be horse racing or the office stationery bill. With such people genuine discussion is impossible and they make one feel that little if anything has been achieved in meeting them and that one does not really understand what the individual concerned really wanted. If such a person is very powerful and does not need the co-operation of others, he or she will continue to operate successfully, but once this position is lost the lack of ability to convince others will inevitably lead to disaster.

True discussion then is very much an exchange of both information and ideas, where an individual's status should be far less important to reach a conclusion. For the sales representative, who is essentially making a request of a more powerful individual in his own office that he should be listened to for a period of time, such a two-way process is essential.

The first task that the company and its sales staff need to face in the preparation for selling is to give due consideration to the techniques that build good conversation and how they can be improved. Let us examine some of them.

Simplicity

The language used is vital. In today's world groups acquire jargon using it as the badge of authority. It involves technical terms, specialised phrases, acronyms and abbreviations and other esoteric words that are used in day-to-day matters with colleagues and the office. Such words are often meaningless to outsiders. Anyone with a passing knowledge of the computer industry can appreciate how the bewilderment of the computer illiterate office manager faced with the sales representative enthusiastically mentioning bytes, networking, hard disk storage, and the like can change into antagonism towards both the salesman and the company that he represents, although the manager concerned may indeed be seriously wanting to examine the potential for new technology in his workplace.

Over-use of complicated words or phrases is a further problem in many product areas. Everyone is aware of house agent-ese the language of house buying, in which terms such as 'in popular area' or 'having great charm' require to be translated into 'near main road' and 'needs complete modernisation'. Though this may add a certain nervous excitement to the house purchasing process, it does little to help the uninitiated. The point is that sometimes these complicated phrases can rebound on the user causing suspicion and cynicism as demonstrated in the following illustrations of fairly common attitudes to a number of standard expressions:

Statement	*Means*
Seasonally adjusted analysis.	I have doctored the figures.
Lack of analysis may hide.	I have not doctored the figures.
There is no historical data.	I cannot find the file.
I represent a dynamic company.	We give good lunches.
I represent an industry leader.	We give good dinners.
The figures are straightforward.	They don't add up.
Your accountant will agree.	They do add up.

Similarly, the busy buying manager should not have to carry out complicated translations to understand exactly what a particular product or process can achieve. One office manager going around a computer exhibition became very peeved because no one could tell him how long printers would take to type out a page of A4 with varied spacing. Everyone quoted CPS – characters per second – at him. He was left with no option but to stand with a stop-watch to compare printers because his main concern was the rapid preparation of lengthy documents. Clarity in the descriptive use of language should also be accompanied by simplicity of structure – short sentences rather than long journeys through the language should be the rule as they will be universally understood.

Listening

Any individual with whom we wish to hold a discussion will have different ideas. If we wish the conversation to move forward to a conclusion we need to be able to accommodate these viewpoints especially if one is trying to achieve a sale. One of the problems of any profession which has a lot of contact with others is that many individuals cease to listen over a period of time. We are all aware of the doctor who facing the apparently same symptoms for the five or six hundredth time fails to recognise something much more serious because his preconceptions of what is wrong have already been formed. The salesman is often in the same position, with a mental conclusion that he has reached having been in fact invalidated by something that the customer had said earlier during the conversation. Each person will respond differently to the same proposal and by treating him or her as an individual the sales representative/doctor/clergyman/teacher/social worker will ensure that the best conclusion has been reached in any conversation.

Many of these views will not be conveyed verbally, the glazed look or the raised eyebrows may be very accurate indications of the success or otherwise of the sales discussion.

Asking

The quickest way of finding out the customer's views is to ask what they are. The direct question may easily produce the direct answer a *yes* or a *no* but this rarely is a full explanation of the buyer's views. What might easily be meant is 'Yes but not a present' or 'No but perhaps if it was in a different metal'. Open ended questions will provide more information which can lead to a more accurate conclusion; *what*, *how*, *who* are key opening words allowing the prospector to explain the problems that he faces. The use of hypothetical questions can also serve a valuable role in eliciting information. The various methods can be summarised as follows:

Question type	*Value*
(1) Open	Widen conversation and gain
'What is . . .?'	information.
(2) Probing	To acquire detailed
'Exactly how does . . .?'	information.
(3) Reflective	Problem solving.
'You seem to be	
saying . . .'	
(4) Closed	Confirming information.
'Do you dislike the colour?'	
(5) Leading	Trying to swing the argument
'I should think that . . .'	your way.
(6) Hypothetical	Introduces new ideas.
'What would happen	
if . . .?'	

Content

The consistency and logic of the argument are very important in maintaining the credibility of the sales representative. Gaps in argument or inconsistencies will generally lose any potential sale as the buyer will naturally assume that an individual making such a mistake will probably be wrong in other respects. The use of a standard approach for presentations can provide a valuable framework to ensure that the argument is consistent – it will also allow the company to concentrate on the elements that are most likely to be successful. Naturally, this system will also have the disadvantage that the salesman will tend to come to rely on the standard presentation instead of trying to structure the discussion in terms of what the buyer is most interested in.

Direction

Negotiations are not philosophy seminars exploring the meaning of life. They should have a clear objective around which the discussion can be built which should not be lost to view in a smog of generalities. While there should always be some flexibility, the salesman should not allow the discussion to wander too far from his structured agenda. Meetings without a clear-cut agenda and a lack of firm control from the chairman tend to be very unsatisfactory, because no firm conclusion is reached and all the participants will consider that their time has been wasted.

Straightforwardness

There will always be a large element of trust in any negotiation, and this will be a particularly important factor when one is seeking a long-term business or personal relationship. The admission that delivery cannot be guaranteed by the middle of the month may be excused, but the promise of delivery that never materialises will sour the relationship for a long period.

Objectivity

The introduction of subjective assessments into the conversation will make decision taking difficult. For example a heated

conversation on the merits or demerits of certain political parties
cannot be changed without great difficulty into a discussion on the
advantages and disadvantages of ball-bearings. An acceptance of
the other's point of view in the final analysis will be crucial for the
continuing maintenance of the buyer/seller relationship, the fact
that though the outcome of one discussion has not been fruitful
does not necessarily preclude future discussions.

Summary

One can conclude that the important factors in the development of
dialogue which hopefully will lead to a successful conclusion are:

1. The acceptance of the other individual as a partner in the
   conversation.
2. The willingness to listen.
3. The directness, simplicity and straightforwardness of the content of the discussion.

3.3   Preparatory Work

The skills of conversation must be supported by preparation in
other areas to make the dialogue more effective. Information
naturally takes time and money to collect and there will be a limit
to the amount which the salesman can collect or be expected to
collect. Both the company and the salesman will need to consider
investments of time and money to collate and spread information
in a number of areas.

The company

Knowledge of the company, how long it has been established in a
particular market, its past successes and failures is all important
information for the sales representatives. Often allied with this is
the company philosophy – what it is trying to achieve in the long
term, which is also important in establishing long-term relationships with end users. The company's financial systems and complaints procedures would be valuable additional information in
some negotiations.

The company's products

What products are available, how they are packed, how they are delivered, what promotional material is available, the advantages that the products have over the competition and, as important, how many disadvantages there are. Crucial to many negotiations is the degree of flexibility that the salesman has and can promise. It is very important that problems such as the level of discounting permitted and delivery times are clarified so that orders are not later cancelled due to misunderstandings.

Competitive products

Similar information on competitive products provides the sales-man with the knowledge necessary to compare and contrast, to determine strengths and weaknesses, and to deal with questions about these issues from the potential customer.

The market

Knowledge of who buys the products and where is important in deciding where effort would be most amply rewarded. Trends in the market place will indicate what the buyers will be increasingly looking for, such as changes in pack size or colour.

The individual salesman

Recognising the strengths and weaknesses of each salesman will be crucial for continuing sales success. The effects of personal appear-ance for example may be of importance for certain customers, less important for others. We all know that meeting new people is a tiring process, and one that is more exhausting when one is unwell. Negotiations should therefore be avoided if one is feeling unwell or particularly tired, as this can jeopardise the likelihood of success. Sufficient time should, for example be allowed to recover from travel before difficult discussions commence, as travel re-gardless of the existence or non-existence of jet lag, will always be stressful. Similarly, there are a number of studies relating illness to changes in personal circumstances. Death or divorce of spouse comes high on the list, but moving house is another event likely to cause illness, and any change in the nature of the job will also cause stress. The wise employer organisation will also take steps to make sure that it is informed of such circumstances when determining the work schedule for any of its employees.

Customer knowledge

This is naturally one of the key areas in which both the individual and the company need to acquire knowledge to determine the most likely customer problems and needs. The front-door salesman selling home improvements or life insurance is often provided with key factors to look for: books, records, furniture, car as indications of the status and likely buying intentions of the customer. One manual of a firm selling double glazing informs their salesforce that ownership of Des O'Connor records indicates a level of stupidity and that anything can be sold to the Max Bygraves fan!

On a less cynical level, knowledge of a firm's structure, its past record and other factors will all provide valuable pointers as to its potential as a customer.

(a) How large is the firm? Has it other subsidiaries in the area which are serviced from this centre or do they buy separately?

(b) Are they financially sound and a good credit risk? The company will tend not to rely on the salesman to comment on the credit-worthiness of his customers and employ an agency to carry out this work – however an impression of the firm's financial well being developed from a quick glance at the car park (are there a lot of new cars?); the outside of the building (neat, newly painted?); the reception area (tidy, with a competent receptionist?) will all help in determining the size of order that could possibly be achieved.

(c) Are they growing or contracting? A growing firm tends to be sure of itself and also prepared to experiment with new lines and techniques. The contracting organisation tends to be much more conservative in what it will accept as the employees do not want to accept the higher level of risk associated with innovation. The expanding firm will also be willing to carry a higher level of stock to meet further growth compared with the contracting firm reducing stocks to the barest minimum.

(d) What sort of business are they in, and who are their customers and competitors? Are they for example a sophisticated company with sophisticated end-users? The demands that this type of company will make will be very different from the down-to-earth company providing standard products, in areas such as price delivery, and quality of the items on offer. Every organisation will have problems and it is these the salesman should be endeavouring to become aware of. The fork-lift trucks may work all right but they have had continuous problems with the automatic palletising equipment. Whisky sells well compared with the other stores of the group because of the large Scottish community. Such facts would be valuable to any salesman approaching firms operating in this area.

(e) How long have they been established? New firms tend to be less conventional than those that have settled into a routine existence, and may be more open to new ideas, products and concepts than those that have been contentedly ploughing up and down the same furrow for many years.

Buyer knowledge

(a) The first important question that needs to be asked is whether the individual you are dealing with is in fact the right one. It is always easier to talk to people who have no authority at all, which will be a time wasting exercise for the salesman who needs to identify the individual in the organisation who has the Money, Authority, and Need. Where such an individual will be found is not always clear cut (though in a grocery chain there will be clearly designated buyers who take day-to-day decisions). If one takes the example of an industrial company buying components to manufacture machinery, buying decisions might be taken at three levels:

(1) The purchasing manager decides on various potential within his overall budget limit.
(2) Senior management determine the suppliers and the overall manufacture programme. The purchasing manager will then act as an administrator ensuring that the correct components are available at the correct time.
(3) The sales department with knowledge of its customers and competition provides a fairly detailed brief to the purchasing

manager. In this instance the purchasing manager would have considerable discretion on certain issues but very little on others.

Standard approaches like 'always speak to the man at the top' or 'speak to the man who pushes the paper' will not therefore necessarily yield predictable results. One needs to identify the person who in that particular firm has the final decision on the matter that one wishes to discuss.

Secondly, what motivates the buyer most effectively? Is prestige more important than profit, speed of delivery rather than credit terms? An understanding of the main criteria on which the buyer will be evaluating the proposed product or service will greatly help progress towards a successful conclusion.

Thirdly, the position that he or she occupies within the firm will be of considerable importance not only with respect to authority but also as regards influence over close colleagues who might have the authority to act in his or her absence.

Fourthly, special likes and dislikes will be relevant to determine whether a particular proposal will be of interest to him or her. Some individuals will agree readily to promotional material; others view it with scepticism and other aspects of the product would have to be emphasised.

Fifthly, career background and the level of skill that an individual brings to the position will often be important. It will, for instance determine whether the discussion can be on a highly technical level or whether the benefits of the product should best be stated in non-technical language.

Finally, the social background and life style of the individual can provide valuable points of contact with which to commence or terminate the discussion. Many commentaries on salesmanship concentrate on the personal aspects of the salesman/buyer relationship as being vital for the successful sale. Many individuals will react negatively to the fulsome enquiries of family, home and hobbies.

3.4   Time Organisation

The organisation of time is a problem for all of us and the sales representative with the added dimension of the distances that he has to travel often faces the problem in its severest form, as he has long journeys to make and will only have the attention of the buyer to whom he is talking for a limited period of time.

The first essential will be to maximise the opportunity that contact with the buyer allows. Naturally any individual in this situation will ensure that all literature is to hand and all information concerning the account, such as order levels and deliveries are to hand. More important and in the author's experiences of many salesforces most often forgotten, is the setting of objectives, the purpose and core of the visit. The physical noting down of the following points will greatly help both in the discussion itself and for the long-term development of the account:

WHERE AM I GOING?
WHAT CAN I DO THERE?
HOW SHALL I GET THERE?
HOW SHALL I MEASURE MY ACHIEVEMENT?

The setting of such objectives will enable the salesman to review in a hopefully objective fashion the progress or lack of it that is being made with the account.

The efficient use of time extends to how the sales representative organises his day. There will be a number of factors that the individual will have to assess:

1. when to deal with paperwork;
2. how long to spend at each call;
3. travelling time;
4. number of calls;
5. the order of calls;
6. the amount of time spent in the development of new business;
7. the amount of time spent in non-selling activities, merchandising and demonstrating;
8. social conversation with the buyers.

Bad organisation of the route to be covered, poor control over paperwork, and excessive chat can mean that two salesmen covering identical territories can show dramatic differences in the amount of time they are actually in front of the customer (Figure 3.1).

FIGURE 3.1
Concentration on essentials: two different allocations of time

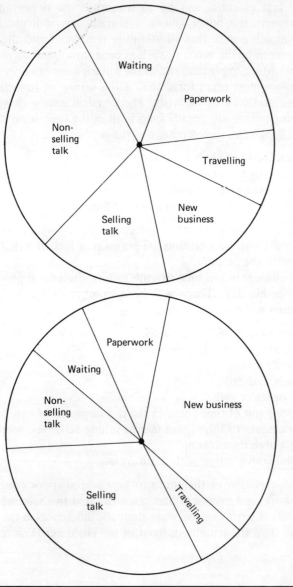

Industrial Cleaners/Aeroflex

Section I

Background

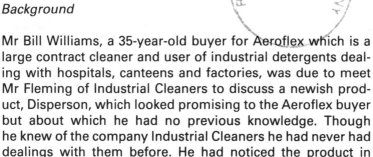

Mr Bill Williams, a 35-year-old buyer for Aeroflex which is a large contract cleaner and user of industrial detergents dealing with hospitals, canteens and factories, was due to meet Mr Fleming of Industrial Cleaners to discuss a newish product, Disperson, which looked promising to the Aeroflex buyer but about which he had no previous knowledge. Though he knew of the company Industrial Cleaners he had never had dealings with them before. He had noticed the product in *Cleaning News*, the main technical journal of the industry and had sent in a coupon for more information.

All sales representatives of companies calling on Aeroflex had to make their presentations to one of several buyers who were all chemical engineers with several years' experience. Each buyer had the responsibility for deciding whether or not a low cost trial should be mounted to evaluate any new proposal. Aeroflex were very aware of the need for performance guarantees on any cleaning system as they held several important hospital cleaning contracts. The final testing procedures were lengthy and expensive and the company was always trying to reduce the numbers of unsuccessful trials.

Each buyer was part of a profit centre and was evaluated on the costs of any trial and the improvement in performance and costs within their particular area. Recently the institutional division of which Williams was the buyer had been going through a period of reduced profits compared with the other divisions.

This division of Aeroflex purchased around £0.3 million of cleaning agents each year and Disperson could possibly account for 10 per cent of this figure if the product's claims were substantiated, and could significantly improve profitability. However, the testing procedure for this particular product would be especially prolonged as it would be used in conjunction with so many other chemicals. Currently Aeroflex

were using a silicate based dispersal agent which had worn
out their cleaning equipment with its abrasive action.

The interview

On entering Mr Williams's office, Mr Fleming introduced
himself by handing out his business card. He then proceeded
immediately to discuss the subject of his call:

Fleming: It's now about four years since we began work on
the problem of improving dispersal agents. A lot of time and
money has gone into this project and we've even gone so far
as to recruit university chemistry researchers to investigate
the surface thermodynamics . . . .

Williams: What aspect of surface thermodynamics?

Fleming: Well I'm sure you are too busy to want to go into the
technicalities of the product, which are all explained in the
information leaflet, so I will just describe the very special
efforts that went into producing Disperson. We think that our
efforts have produced extremely worthwhile results which
will greatly benefit our customers. Disperson is really rather
special. It can be added to almost any industrial detergent
and unlike many of the more primitive dispersal agents it
comes ready for use. No grinding or blending with water is
required so it's easy to use and it doesn't separate out or
evaporate either – so once you've added it, that's it.

Williams: Sounds fascinating but what do you mean by saying you can add it to 'almost all' industrial detergents. We
have to be specially careful about such catch-phrases. A lot of
our customers are hospitals and Aeroflex has to be absolutely
certain that any detergent used for hospital laundry isn't
going to give skin rashes to its clientele. At the same time we
can't possibly run the risk of any diminution of cleaning
power whatsoever because of risk of infectious diseases.
Have you tested the product in such an environment?

Fleming: Well, I can certainly reassure you on most of those
points. The only thing you can't add Disperson to is bleach, it
works well with every other cleaning agent although for

obvious reasons we don't suggest it be added to washing-up liquids though we are satisfied from the results of laboratory trials that even here it is harmless. Nor does it in any way reduce the cleaning power of the agents to which it can be added. We also think that we have stumbled on a revolution as far as allergic reaction is concerned. Disperson seems to reduce the abrasive feel, without affecting the cleaning power, of all industrial cleaners so it'll provide protection for both your employees and customers.

Williams: But what about the hospital environment?

Fleming: Well we have tested the product in a nuclear research laboratory and I would imagine that the standards required would be pretty similar.

Williams: We've recently spent a lot of money on new generation, highly efficient machines. They were very expensive but we're expecting long service from them – and obviously there are manufacturers' specifications that we have to observe about what we can and can't do and use.

Fleming: Close collaboration with the manufacturers of industrial cleaning apparatus was a major feature throughout the Disperson project. Together we carried out extensive tests to minimise any dust precipitate or abrasion which could harm cleaning equipment.

Williams: OK. Now tell me about costs especially when compared with other dispersal agents.

Fleming: We think that Disperson is likely to prove a very attractive source of savings on the quantity of cleaning materials you currently use because it spreads the active ingredient over a wider area thus lowering unit costs. Here, for example, is the results of experiments comparing the cleaning power and quantities of an industrial detergent containing Disperson with one containing a run of the mill dispersal agent. In every case a smaller quantity of the Disperson base detergent was needed to achieve the same results and in nearly three-quarters of the experiments Disperson was achieving the same results using two-thirds of the quantity of cleaner needed for use with the other dispersal agent. Experiments show that where purely routine cleaning is involved, say where hand-basins are washed daily, Disperson, using less cleaning agent, will clean more quickly. So there is also some saving to be achieved there.

A half-hour discussion ensued between the two men. Finally, Fleming rose and shook hands with Williams, thanking him for his time and saying that he could be contacted at Industrial Cleaners and would be happy to supply any other information.

Section II

Suppose that the Industrial Cleaners representative who went to see Mr Bill Williams at Aeroflex was Mr Morris because Mr Fleming was attending a trade fair.

The interview

Mr Morris entered Mr Williams's office, introduced himself and handed his card to the Aeroflex buyer.

Morris: I really am delighted to have the opportunity of meeting you in person Mr Williams. I was fascinated by the talk you gave the other evening, last week wasn't it, at the Industrial Society. You made some very valuable points about the pressures on service industries like Aeroflex to achieve a workable balance between responsibility to the general public and the need to run a profitable business.

Morris went on to mention the implications of Mr Williams's discussion as regards the dilemmas facing his own company.

Morris: I gave a lot of thought to what you said about Aeroflex's problem of meeting the very high standards required by hospitals of contract cleaners while keeping costs down in order to remain competitive. I think that I might have something that might be of interest to you as it will have an impact on this whole area. However hard we try, my company knows that the costs of industrial detergents keep going up and so we've developed dispersal agents which have helped to reduce the quantities of detergent needed but they've not been all that convenient. Crystals have had to be ground, or diluted with water in the right quantities, there have been difficulties with the solutions. If the crystals aren't kept dry they turn into blocks and that means that you have to be specially careful in storage. As a result, if cleaning staff are careless there's a high waste factor and higher energy costs because the resulting mixture of detergent and dispersal agent makes enormous demands on heat to work effectively.

Williams: Yes, indeed. You should see the lab's file on guidance for cleaning staff on dispersal agents but however much they try to cover all contingencies there's always a new one around the corner.

Morris: It was precisely to deal with these problems that we developed Disperson. It's a new kind of dispersal agent. It's a powder you can safely mix with anything except bleach and it doesn't crystallise, evaporate or change the nature of the solution. So straight away it reduces the level of supervision required. I believe you've also been investing in new machinery?

Williams: Yes, that's right, we have.

Morris: Well, you'll be delighted to know that as well as being good for staff, Disperson won't harm your machinery. It does not produce any of those dust particles or precipitates which not only can be lethal to machines but also increase your servicing costs. This dispersal agent really is a good mixer and requires little extra heat to activate the cleaners. One of Disperson's more interesting properties is that it seems to reduce the abrasive feel of powerful cleaners without reducing their cleaning impact despite the fact that you use less of the cleaning agent. This is why we think that it will certainly reduce your overall unit costs on industrial detergents as well as energy costs.

Williams: It certainly sounds very promising have you any definite figures for likely savings?

Morris: Well since Aeroflex currently uses one type of dispersal agent I thought you'd like to see how it compares with

Disperson. In all the tests a smaller amount of detergent mixed with Disperson was able to achieve the same cleaning impact as a mixture with a higher detergent level and one of the more popular dispersal agents currently in use. Generally speaking you can reduce the amount of cleaner by about a third if you use Disperson. When we tried to do this with any other dispersal agent cleanliness suffered. The tests also showed that where routine cleaning is involved Disperson can speed up the cleaning process. We reduced the length of the wash in several instances and found the clothes were just as clean but this did not happen with the other mixture of detergent and dispersal agent.

Williams: So it can be added to all cleaning agents with similar improvements in cost?

Morris: I think that that is clearly demonstrated in the tables that are in front of you.

Williams: And there will be no hygiene problems in any of the environments in which we operate?

Morris: Obviously Industrial Cleaners has a position to maintain in the industry and we would not be proposing any product that had not been fully tested.

At this point, a half-hour discussion ensued between the two men. Finally, Morris rose and shook hands with Williams, thanking him for his time and saying that he could be contacted at Industrial Cleaners and would be happy to supply any other information.

Achieving the Sale and Keeping the Customer

4

Chapter 3 discussed the techniques that must be mastered before a salesman is ready to call on a potential client. He or she must be well-informed, able to lead a discussion yet remain receptive to the needs of the potential client, and make the most of the limited time that is available to him or her. In this chapter we shall be concerned with using the preparation procedures and the information gathered through it to actually sell the product.

Four criteria, summarised in the mnemonic AIDA – everyone's favourite aunt – have been identified. They are as follows:

A = Attention
I = Interest
D = Demand
A = Action

The four are interdependent, devised to provide a bargaining technique allowing one step to proceed to the other thereby permitting the salesman to maintain direction throughout the discussion. The direction of the discussion is of paramount importance as it is designed to use the sales representative's time to maximum effect, ensuring that the highest possible percentage of the limited time that he or she is sitting in front of the buyer is being spent productively in attempting to gain an order for his or her employer.

4.1 Attention

Attention is the first vital ingredient. One very memorable training film begins with a comment on the length of time available to initiate interest from the average buyer in a particular discussion. This is the length of time that it takes for a match to burn down – if attention has not been developed by the time the match scorches the finger, the sales representative should consider the discussion to all intents over.

There are different ways of getting and keeping a buyer's attention but they all have one common thread. That is the relevance of the issues to the buyer. If they are relevant the discussion will continue if not, not. Relevance to a corner store will be profit margin and speed of turnover, to the delicatessen it may be image and product performance.

The emphasis is always on benefits. What does the fact that the washing machine has a cold wash feature mean to the average housewife? It means that she will save money by not heating the water – the feature has a benefit which can be easily understood. The advantage that this product has is therefore the sum of the feature and the benefit that it produces.

A product may have to fulfil not only rational considerations but more 'emotional' ones as well. Fabric conditioners are a good example of this. One objective benefit is that woollens washed with fabric conditioner tend not to become matted and flat. In addition to this is the fact that clothes will also smell 'fresh' when washed with fabric conditioner. The cleanliness of the washing can be objectively determined; but consumer research shows that the additional benefit of smelling 'clean' is a very important additional emotional benefit that buyers of fabric conditioners want.

Some buyers will concentrate on profit, others on prestige and still others on the various factors mentioned in Chapter 1. The same feature can on occasion be made to work on a number of different levels but will naturally need to be restated in a slightly altered fashion. This underlines the need for research to provide the information on which the salesman can tailor or individualise the presentation. People buy products for what they could get out of them, not what the firm has put into them, and it is essential that the salesman knows what the product can do, and understands what the customer wants.

4.2 Interest

The salesman is seeking to arouse the curiosity of the buyer once he or she has won the customer's attention. Essentially the seller is trying to establish a rapport with the buyer: attracting attention and inducing interest by making the subject under discussion relevant to the buyer's preoccupations.

Certain types of questions must be used to draw out and encourage the buyer to provide more information on: past and present situations, reasons for hesitancy, underlying objections, attitudes or bias, relationships with others in the firm and so on. Open questions will be most useful in this area. The WHO, WHAT, WHEN, and WHY techniques discussed in Chapter 3 are designed specifically to assist in this context. Specific questions requiring direct answers are most valuable as a means of analysing the effectiveness of a particular benefit, whether the buyer accepts a claim made about the product and is in agreement with the salesman's viewpoint. It is also important to use mechanisms such as a simple statement, for example, to encourage the buyer to make plain his or her own attitudes.

The buyer will be interested in his or her own specific problems and how the benefits of the product will overcome them. Generalisations and irrelevancies will lose the buyer's attention as he or she will not be interested in how other firms view the product and how it performs in other environments unless it is relevant to the one specifically facing the buyer's company.

4.3 Demand

Interest should lead naturally to demand: negotiation about the specific advantages and disadvantages of the product or service under discussion for that particular buyer.

The main obstacle to leading the sale discussion towards a conclusion, and action from the buyer to finalise the sale, will be one or more objections about some of the features of the product that do not match the benefits that the buyer wants. The ideal buyer will rely more on reason than emotion, be courteous and business like. Unfortunately objections will often come from buyers who are argumentative, ill-mannered, pompous, suspicious, or untruthful. Objections from such individuals will be difficult if not impossible to cope with as they are basically not interested in the job that they are doing – trying to provide the best service for the organisation that they represent. The only possible course of action in these circumstances is for the salesman to maintain his or her independence and to deal with each objection in an unemotional fashion.

Objections will always be a good indication of the underlying state of mind of the customer; whether he or she is seeking reassurance on minor matters but is basically accepting the proposition, whether he or she is prejudiced for some reason against the whole idea, or whether there is some genuine cause for concern. Often the true objection may not be voiced – the buyer may for example be over budget and not want to admit it, or he may misunderstand features of the product and not wish to appear ignorant by further questioning. The most common objection will naturally be one based on price. Such objections may be caused by a number of factors:

1. there is no money in the budget;
2. competitors have lower prices;
3. it appears to cost too much;
4. bargaining on price is a standard negotiating technique.

Should price become the sole method of judging product acceptability, the sales representative will be in a very difficult position. Such hurdles increasingly face the small firm trying to gain distribution in the hypermarket/supermarket sector, with competitive pricing becoming the only way to become established.

Wherever possible the emphasis should be shifted towards the quality of the product and the benefits that it provides. Concentration on quality in relation to the services that the buyer's organisation performs will produce more beneficial results than pure concentration on price. For example the buyer of components for industrial milling machinery could be asked whether the company he or she represents would cut service and quality to reduce price.

The objections raised will vary with the type of industry and customer. Studies of commodity markets such as oil suggests that price is the most important criterion contrasting strongly with hydraulic machinery where product and manufacturer reliability are rated more highly.[1, 2]

The sales representative can only cope with such objections and others by listening carefully to what is being said to ensure that there is no misunderstanding and answering positively rather than negatively. Objections can be very successfully used to restate the strength of a particular benefit – emphasising why it meets the client's specific requirements. They should, provided they are genuine queries be considered more of an opportunity than a threat to the individual sales representative.

Emotional reactions to any individual's comments in negotiation are almost guaranteed to lose both the sale and the future respect of the buyer. Answers to queries should be objectively stated, and rarely, if ever should the sales representative enter into an argument with the buyer. Contradicting the buyer also will often lead to disaster – few of us like to be shown up as either ignorant or stupid especially where our job is concerned, as individuals identify strongly with their role in the organisation and the position they occupy. To take an example, a buyer may happily accept that it was golfer A and not golfer B who won the recent international tournament, but is far less likely to accept that his knowledge of steel quality is inadequate should he be buying ball-bearings. Such problems become even more complicated when the buyer is not interested in the technical aspects of the job but spends as much of his waking life running the local golf club – obviously contradictions on the subject of golf would have considerable perils. Rules in the art of sales negotiation are like many others made to be broken. The author had experience of one very eccentric buyer who delighted in sales representatives who would engage in heated argument with him – those that did and stood up to him got the order; those that did not normally failed.

4.4 Action

The successful handling of the specific details defining need and demand should lead to the discussions coming to a conclusion. The successful conclusion for the sales representative will be that action is taken to place an order. The negotiation needs to be positively directed towards this end and the buyer asked to take the necessary action. This is the technique of closing, ensuring that the indecision and uncertainty at the end of the conversation is minimised.

Closing the sale should be attempted at the earliest opportunity, as this will successfully generate objections which can be overcome allowing a further opportunity to close. On the first occasion the sales representative attempts to finalise the order, buyers tend not to decide and it will require two or three attempts. The salesman that considers the negotiation as climbing a mountain, seeing the overcoming of objections as a step by step process until the peak of demanding an order is reached, will feel somewhat isolated and alone when the close fails, for what else can he or she do but go back down the mountain again! To take the hill-climbing analogy further the salesman who views the negotiation as a series of gentle slopes will not be nearly as despondent with the prospect of going down the reverse slope to begin the new ascent, as the effort is much less than that required by the intrepid mountaineer.

The standard literature on the sales process identify nine main methods by which the sale can be closed.[3]

1. *Request*. The straightforward request will either produce a 'Yes', 'No' or 'Perhaps'. Each of these will allow further probing and discussion, unless agreement is immediately reached.
2. *Sale or return*. Used in such industries as the recordings business, it obviously has high risks for the company concerned for two main reasons. First the cash flow of the supplier will be considerably lengthened. Second the buyer will never be very committed to a product in which there is no investment made by the firm, which may mean that it is stored under adverse conditions, or not properly used. The 'return' element nearly always produces disputes between the supplier and buying organisation unless the product is simple and the whole industry operates on that basis – newspapers for example.
3. *'Miss the boat'*. Commonly used by the home improvement salesman it exerts pressure by suggesting that should the buyer not take action now the price will go up; or the product will no longer be available in lime green. Occasionally, this method will work extremely well when a particular product is in short

supply, but in a competitive environment it is unlikely to succeed.

4. *Referral.* Should there be an example of a firm with which the buyer is closely connected successfully using the product, referral could be a very effective method of terminating the negotiation. The argument is that if firm A with problems very similar to firm B has found the product completely satisfactory the buyer B cannot go wrong. Naturally this approach will work better on some individuals than others.

5. *Pros and cons.* The listing of advantages and disadvantages may be a useful technique with buyers who are interested in detail, and how the product would fit into the organisation. A similar method is used by the double glazing salesman providing a fully detailed quote after a room by room inspection – the amount of work that that individual has put in tending to put the potential buyers under an obligation to purchase.

6. *Assumption.* The sales representative assumes that the order is finalised and begins to discuss the details that are involved with the order-delivery dates and credit terms.

7. *Alternative assumption.* In this, the sales representative also makes the assumption that the buyer is going to place the order and provides him with the alternatives that he or she can choose, attempting to limit the reply to placing an order for one item within the range. The classic joke question, 'Have you stopped beating your wife?' is similar in that replying 'Yes' or 'No' are both equally suspect.

8. *Reverse objection.* On receiving an objection the representative can turn it into a demand for an order; that if the company can meet the objection the buyer should be prepared to place the order. Thus if the buyer criticises the product for not being strong enough the sales representative while offering to have it reinforced would demand that the buyer must then place an order for it.

9. *'Why have I failed?'* The use of pity in the final moments can have a useful role to play. In animal society, submission to dominance is a very important survival technique and is maintained by a variety of gestures and movements. Providing buyers with an opportunity to show their dominance in the negotiation can lead to them telling the sales representative

exactly what they are looking for, or even ordering a product because they feel sorry for the representative and the role that he is being asked to play.

4.5 Keeping the Customer

Once a sale is completed, a new customer has been gained for the firm, or an existing customer is retained. In both cases it is important to keep the customer otherwise the company cannot expand, and will continually need to become re-established. It will forever be winning back customers that it has lost, and such an approach is extremely time consuming.

Of the three types of purchasing decision that occur: re-buy (the purchasing manager re-ordering identical products); modified rebuy (the purchasing manager buying broadly similar products from the same supplier); and new buy (new products from new suppliers) the first is the overwhelming majority.[4] Indeed, many purchasing managers are unlikely to go outside a favoured circle for their products.[5] This shows a similar pattern to many consumers that maintain a 'portfolio' of brands in a certain product field.[6] For example they may switch between Mars and Yorkie bars but will rarely buy Kit-Kat. To lose position in this favoured circle will therefore be potentially disastrous to the supplier company.

The continuing service element can be seen as consisting of two main areas: the provision of information, and the effective handling of complaints.

The provision of information to buyers is something that the majority of companies tend to ignore as not being of sufficient importance. However, when one considers the limited time that the sales representative has in front of the client, the more information that the buyer can be provided with before this meeting the more effective time utilisation will be. Leaflets describing promotional activities, new products, or invitations to exhibitions all build up the relationship between the company and the buyer. Even the mundane business card serves a useful function in this respect. Naturally a significant element of these items of direct mail will end up immediately in the wastepaper basket but the majority of buyers knowing that it is a company with whom they are dealing will at least read the material, and returns from such a system are always higher than the industry average of 1.5–2.0 per cent.

Complaints

How the company and the sales representative deals with complaints is also of considerable importance in the continuing business relationship. Mistakes will always occur, such as errors in invoicing, late (or early) delivery, problems with quality, slow selling stock, damage, or vandalism. Complaints when properly handled (provided of course that they do not recur with alarming frequency) can help to convince the buyer that the firm should be kept as a supplier. Should the handling of complaints be poor, the competitive world will ensure that someone else will get the business. Many of the arts of negotiation will again be useful in dealing with complaints. We are all aware of our annoyance when we make a legitimate complaint in a department store which is to all intents and purposes ignored. The salesman should therefore try to do as he would wish to be done by.

First, that the complaint should be listened to and accurately noted down. Second, that the receiver of the complaint should be both practical and at the same time sympathetic – not necessarily apologetic. Third, that something is *done* about the complaint and that the buyer is kept informed about the progress of the matter – too many complaints disappear into some forgotten limbo. Finally, the sales representative should ensure that the complaint has been satisfactorily dealt with by further discussion with the customer. This will have the benefit of underlining the salesman's professionalism, showing that he or she as well as the buyer are good businessmen. Providing such an approach to the handling of complaints is used the firm does not need to justify or explain itself, as there has been a problem which has been speedily resolved in a businesslike fashion.

Such procedures will decrease the buyer anxiety by confirming in his or her mind that the correct decision has been made to either continue, or commence purchasing from the supplier company.

Quick Snack Case Study

Bob Bland the managing director of Grand Catering Services Ltd was due to meet with the Quick Snack marketing manager, Ben Whittle, and James Deakin the Quick Snack national account salesman responsible for dealing with Grand Catering.

Whittle had requested the meeting after Bob Bland had written a letter to the Quick Snack national accounts manager about various contentious issues which had directly arisen from an understanding reached with the national accounts salesman.

Grand Catering Services Ltd

A company based in London, Grand Catering Services Ltd had grown substantially under Bob Bland who had formed the company some five years earlier in 1974 and who acted as both its managing director and buyer. He considered that the main reason for his company's acquiring a significant foothold in the very competitive atmosphere of fast food catering in the capital was because he had succeeded in tailoring its services to meet the special needs of each customer more rapidly than his competitors. By combining the jobs of managing director and buyer, Bland felt that he could cut through red tape concluding deals quickly and efficiently. He knew what his company wanted and now that he was in a position to offer substantial business to the manufacturers of catering food he felt that his negotiating position was much stronger. Initially a supplier of hot drinks vending machines for 100 or so snack-bars, Grand Catering now had 178 firms employing more than 50 people and six main line railway stations among its clients, ten conference and exhibition centres and had more recently added 106 schools and hospitals to the list following a rigorous campaign for more business. As a supplier of vending machines for small shops Grand Catering had achieved a dominant position.

Quick Snack

Quick Snack, an offshoot of a multinational confectionery company, manufactured and developed vending machines and supplied the food products for them. As one of the first vending machine companies it had managed to substantially improve the quality as well as the packaging of foods and drinks supplied and it still maintained a lead in this area. Its efforts had been largely responsible for changing negative consumer attitudes towards vending machines. For several years now the company had failed to further penetrate the market despite the evidence that the size of the market had grown. Competitors were more successful except in cases where customers were very concerned about the quality of the goods. Quick Snack also had very stringent guidelines which had to be met before it would agree to supply a vending machine to a particular site: the customer had to guarantee a minimum number of sales at each site. It also refused to set guidelines on price for its customers. There was a feeling among managers that greater flexibility was needed in order to increase the Quick Snack vending machine's market share. Time and again salesmen had pointed out that at some work-place sites the price of drinks were so high that employees preferred to buy drinks outside. This had the obvious effect of decreasing the number of drinks sold and put the future of the vending site into jeopardy.

Quick Snack and Grand Catering

For James Deakin the Quick Snack national accounts sales-man the acquisition of Grand Catering as a client was a personal triumph. He had watched the growth of Grand Catering which made it a potentially important customer as it was now involved in catering at sites which could meet the Quick Snack minimum sale requirements. When Grand Catering had acquired accounts at main line railway stations and conference halls Deakin had supplied Quick Snack vending machines to the company for the first time.

Bland had been impressed by the quality and reliability of the Quick Snack goods. He found Deakin very efficient and although Deakin did not know it, Bland had given Quick Snack the rail and conference hall business because Deakin had been able to supply the machines more quickly by side-stepping a great deal of routine in the new accounts procedures. By doing this Deakin had created some minor difficulties in the delivery dates promised to other new accounts but these were sorted out satisfactorily.

Deakin had called on Bland early in 1979 at the time when he was seeking to rationalise the company's dealings with vending machine manufacturers to improve Grand Catering's bargaining power by reducing the number of suppliers. Part of this process would involve the acquisition of orders to supply Grand Catering's newly acquired sites in schools, community centres and hospitals as well as the 100 or so snack-bars. An agreement was reached between Deakin and Bland whereby Quick Snack would supply the vending machines. The value of the sales generated through this deal would make Grand Catering Quick Snack's fourth largest customer, if approved.

Deakin placed the order and was surprised to find that given its magnitude and importance to Quick Snack, he heard no more. Bland as always was in a hurry and, aware of the value of the order, demanded that Deakin supply further details of discounts, delivery dates and the like. Pressed so far, Deakin contacted the Supplies Department and was told that various aspects of the deal were under review. It was at this point that the national accounts manager received Bland's letter which basically complained that Quick Snack was not giving his business the attention it deserved. He had heard nothing from Deakin despite strenuous attempts to get in touch with him. He demanded an explanation. It fell to Ben Whittle the Quick Snack marketing manager to try to smooth things over and keep the customer.

The Meeting

The meeting between Bob Bland, the managing director of Grand Catering, and the Quick Snack's representatives Ben Whittle, marketing manager, and James Deakin, national accounts salesman, began in a tense atmosphere.

Bob Bland again stated that he felt that Quick Snack was being dilatory and was not giving his order the attention it was worth. Given its value, it was currently worth half a million pounds and its value would increase as his company grew, provided that Grand Catering and Quick Snack could come to some agreement as soon as possible. Deakin in their discussion had not given him the impression that there were any significant obstacles in meeting the order which would lead to delay. Time was all important and cost money.

Deakin intervened to remind Bob Bland that when he had taken the order he had said that it would be subject to detailed scrutiny by the Quick Snack marketing department because it was both substantial and complex involving a number of different types of site. He had himself become anxious because of pressure from Bob Bland but on examining the details of the order he had realised that it would take time. Bland snorted in disgust in reply.

Ben Whittle felt that there was a basic lack of understanding about Quick Snack and its marketing policy and that there would be a better chance of sorting things out with Bland if he knew a little more about them. He described the economics of providing vending units as perceived by Quick Snack. In its view, there was a minimum number of items which have to be sold from a site before it became viable to put in a dispenser. In the case of some of the proposed sites in his order, schools, which were after all closed for most of a 24-hour day, and some snack-bars and take-away food shops, it was simply not viable to even consider putting in a Quick Snack dispenser.

Bland considered that this was humbug. Marketing was about selling one's goods not keeping them under lock and key as Quick Snack seemed intent on doing. Grand Catering Services had started from just such the base that Quick Snack was now denigrating. Drops of water make up the ocean.

Whittle, however, pursued his original line as well as pointing to some of the advantages that the Quick Snack policy had for its customers. His company did not charge for the vending machines or even levy a rental fee as some others did. The dispensers were supplied at a nominal charge of £400 when they cost about £900 to make. As they were in business to make money the remaining cost of the vending machine could only be recovered through the sales of drinks at the site: this was the reason behind the minimum sales requirement.

Bland could see that there was some sense to this approach but he was a businessman who had succeeded by adjusting his company's services to meet the requirements of his customers. He said so and added that Quick Snack would do well to display some flexibility of approach when failure to do so would be at the cost of a large order.

Mention of the flexibility provided an opening for Ben Whittle. He acknowledged that the Grand Catering account was very important and would become more so. He could not alter the economics on which Quick Snack vending policy was based but there were options available to benefit both parties. He then supplied the Grand Catering managing director with the details of a unique promotional package which he said his department would run for Grand Catering alone. A competition with a Caribbean holiday for two as the prize would be organised to boost sales at the vending machine sites. It would run over three months and when it came to an end the turnover in each outlet would be reviewed.

The proposal appealed to Bland. He appreciated that at the end of the competition he might have to find other makes of vending machines for some sites but then Grand Catering would reap the advantage to a promotional campaign which would benefit its customers alone, offering an attractive prize, and which cost them nothing. He gave his approval.

Further Exercises

The Quick Snack case study underlines some of the dilemmas encountered when one company is involved in selling to another. Obviously the objectives of the salesman's company will differ from those of the customer company. Each party is bargaining to achieve the best deal for his employer and it is normal for supplier and customer to find a workable solution satisfactory to both sides. Yet each has different parameters to meet and they alter according to the industry and product and the type of customer that the salesman is seeking. It is these that may cause the type of problem discussed in the Quick Snack case and the exercises given here provide a résumé of considerations that seller and buyer must take into account in order to close an order. They can be successfully played through in class exercises to demonstrate bargaining between buyer and seller.

Whisky, SaveAway, and Highland Fling

The Highland Fling national account salesman wants to persuade SaveAway, a national grocery retailing chain with supermarkets in city centres and hypermarkets on the outskirts of towns, to stock its new, cheap but classy brand of whisky. The total Scotch market is worth about £60 million but has been declining as the market has shifted in favour of wine and white spirits, vodka and gin.

The SaveAway buyer's position

The SaveAway buyer is over the age of 40, is married with two children and plays golf.

1. There are about 200 SaveAway stores nationally catering mainly for customers in socioeconomic groups B, C, and D many of whom read the tabloid newspapers and are TV audiences.
2. The total shelf space available is increasingly limited.
3. SaveAway already stocks five major brands: Teachers, Black & White, White Horse, Famous Grouse, and Bells.

4. SaveAway fixes its own retail prices. The current shelf price of £6.70 gives a percentage margin of 15 per cent on gross. SaveAway own label whisky at £6.30 gives 17 per cent gross. A cheap new whisky would have to sell at about the same price as SaveAway's own brand. Three of Highland Fling's competitors have already offered deals of 40 per cent Scotch at £5.20, £5.35 and £5.40.
5. The buyer has a remaining budget for Scotch of around £50 000.
6. SaveAway experience is that during the Christmas high whisky sales period it is mainly the well established brands that sell well. Litre bottles are bought by the chain at Christmas.
7. In the past SaveAway has had delivery problems with Highland Fling's sister company. The chain expected all products to be delivered to individual stores throughout the country.
8. SaveAway buys on 90 days credit with small suppliers but this can be negotiated downwards for special price deals.

The Highland Fling salesman's position

The sales representative is fairly new to the company, 27 and unmarried. He has been steadily falling behind on his sales targets and is currently highly unlikely to achieve any sales bonus.

1. The product is expensively packaged, 40 per cent alcohol by volume.
2. The company aim is to promote it as a premium blended Scotch superior to Bells and Johnny Walker.
3. The current advertising campaign is £40 000 spent in magazines such as *Autocar*.
4. The company also is sponsoring the new Invercaddy Pro-Am Golf Championship which will be televised north of the border.
5. The target retail price is £6.95, above the premium blended Scotch brands.
6. Trade price list is as follows:

10 case   £5.60 a bottle
50 case   £5.40

7. The sales representative has been given leeway to negotiate on price for 'substantial' orders down to a base of £5.20.
8. The salesman has available copies of the Highland Fling calendar.
9. The product is blended from lighter coloured products and is designed to meet the consumer demand for lighter products, which is underlined by the growth in the market for vodka and gin and the decline in the rum and cognac sectors.
10. Distribution throughout the country remains something of a problem. The company is using third party haulage firms to do their distribution except for the London area. This means that deliveries can take anything up to fifteen days and cannot be guaranteed for any particular time.
11. Credit terms for Highland Fling are normally 60 days, but for 'substantial orders' the sales representatives are allowed to negotiate extended credit.
12. The company does not have a litre bottle, nor does it provide product in gift packs over Christmas.
13. The target audience for Highland Fling is ABC1 socio-economic groups.

The Dallas Discount Store buyer's position

1. Dallas is a national chain of discount electrical stores with 80 outlets.
2. Their main turnover is in white goods – fridges, freezers, dishwashers and washing machines but they also maintain a substantial audio element.
3. Currently their sale of compact disc players is expanding by 15 per cent per annum in contrast to the sale of racked hi-fi systems which have declined by 5 per cent.
4. They sell two products Hitachi at £280 on which they make 40 per cent margin and the Philips unit at £300 on which they make 42 per cent.

5. Their main consumers are Cl-C2 socioeconomic group.
6. The buyer has the authority to spend up to £5000 on merchandise without approval of senior management.
7. The buyer is interested and knowledgeable on hi-fi systems as this used to be his managerial position before he became one of the buyers for the group.
8. The group are vitally concerned with both reliability of the products and the service arrangements if they go wrong as this has always been a problem with new suppliers.

The Mustang Laser position

1. The Mustang Laser compact disc player is new, British and the most sophisticated product on the market with features such as freeze frame, computer interaction facilities which the other models do not have.
2. Voted 'good value' in *Which* consumer magazine analysis of players except for problems of reliability.
3. Priced at £350 retail which gives the store 45 per cent margin.
4. Supported by advertising in consumer hi-fi magazines, with a budget of £35 000 in the last six months with more expenditure currently planned.
5. Service arrangements through Head Office; players returned within two weeks from date of receipt.
6. Currently stocked by one of Dallas's six main competitors.
7. Main market AB 'sophisticated' player user.
8. Sales representative is 21, without much experience of the compact disc market; he is currently ahead of quota and has earned good commission over the previous months.

Supporting the Salesman I: Training and Support Systems

5

The average well intentioned company will establish a cafeteria for its staff; own or share sports facilities; even provide an on-site dentist and crèche. In contrast, the look of blank surprise that normally greets the questioner when the company is asked how it supports and makes the job of its salesforce more effective is often symptomatic of how isolated the salesforce can become. A salesman costing the company £25 000 a year will during 40 years of employment imply a one million pound investment. This could be a conservative estimate: General Foods, for example, put the average cost of a salesman at £30 000 in 1984. The salesforce has a major contribution to make towards the achievement of the company's objectives, yet far too infrequently does the company strive to maximise the return on the considerable investment that they have made in the salesforce.

The company should accept that it has an important part to play in each area of the sales representative's job, from the first day that he begins work until he retires or leaves.

5.1 Training – Its Relevance

The literature on developing the skills necessary to effectively carry out any given task is immense, but all authors agree that the speed at which work related ability is acquired can be increased by

FIGURE 5.1
Effect of training on traditional 'learning' curve

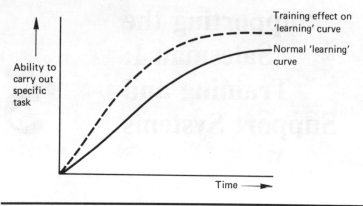

specific training. Animals of all shapes and forms when confronted with a new task gain new information fairly rapidly in the early stages, levelling off after a period of time.[1] The shape of this so-called learning curve can be altered by structuring the information in a more easily assimilable form. It is in the interests of the organisation to do this as a steeper learning curve will mean that an individual will become effective more rapidly (see Figure 5.1).

Naturally there are costs associated with this speeding up process which must be considered but for the majority of companies the nature of the return on the investment involved in the training process has probably not been given the attention it deserves. A study of 500 UK companies revealed that spending on training and retraining amounted to less than £4 a week, or 0.15 per cent of turnover. The average offered 2.1 days off-the-job training a year contrasted with larger German employers aiming at 40 hours off-the-job training per employee. Interestingly companies' training records improve as they become more successful. A study over five years showed an increase of 25 per cent in training activities among the high performance companies; 15 per cent among medium performers; while the low performing companies reduced them by 20 per cent.[2]

The figures are reflected in the training allocation for the salesforce. IBM for example has an exceptional record in that it will train its salesman for three or four months initially with additional refresher courses; far in excess of the average for the industrial salesman of 28, and retail salesman of 6 days training.

The nature of the information that the organisation will need to impart will inevitably vary, accounting for at least some of the difference in training between the industrial and consumer goods sectors, the degree of technical information in say the hydraulics industry making far greater demands than the consumer benefits of various brands of breakfast cereal.

Training will also need to extend into the development of effective selling techniques for the particular industry, the specific problems encountered, company practices on credit, delivery, and so on. In some contexts this is becoming increasingly important. For example, buyers in large retail stores are trained in negotiating techniques – the salesman that is not trained to counter them will be placed at a considerable disadvantage.

The maintenance of training at a fairly intense level is considered very important by a number of highly successful firms and would appear to be a major component in their success. This is underlined by the authors of *In Search of Excellence*.[3] In this study of 62 American companies that had been consistently successful over a 25 year period, the authors identified a number of factors leading to success. The conclusions of this study were that all successful companies had a unified policy in a number of areas:

1. They were more interested in action than reaction.
2. They attempted to understand their customers.
3. They delegated effectively allowing freedom of individual action while retaining coherent management goals.
4. Top management were always closely involved with change and innovation, and were not prepared to be diverted from the central goal of the company.

The authors stressed that the entire organisation lives by these criteria: in other words the training that the new entrant undergoes is crucial to consolidate the company philosophy. The criteria put forward in this thesis do not however tell the whole story as 15 of the identified companies have since run into difficulty – Hewlett Packard, Digital, Texas Instruments, Avon, Tupperware, Delta,

Levi Strauss, Fluor, Cheseborough Pond's, Disney, Revlon, Caterpillar, Eastman Kodak and P & G for a variety of reasons.[4,5] Too great an emphasis on training and company cohesion can therefore have its own perils, such as creating a degree of isolation between the company and the market which is difficult to overcome.

5.2   The Need for Information

The flow of information from the company to the salesforce need not of course depend on specific training sessions; information letters and regular meetings can do much to keep the salesman informed of the company's progress. This is particularly important when major changes are taking place within the organisation – clarity of information that is passed on to individuals in the field will do much to present a coherent face to the outside world via the customers the salesforce meets.

The aim and object of marketing information techniques should be to improve the effectiveness of the salesforce. Such considerations are quite frequently forgotten. Is it an effective use of sales representative time to man an exhibition stand? In the author's experience this question is rarely asked, and salesmen are used as additional support staff particularly when the exhibition runs over several days.

There are further opportunities for the company to improve the effectiveness of their investment in the salesforce through the preparation of information for the customers and the salesforce. The provision of professionally bound folders with information about the product clearly laid out and structured can greatly aid the presentation process. The home insurance market is now leading the way in visual presentations by providing salestaff with computers which, when linked to the home colour television set, will give graphic illustrations of the benefits of investing via their company. Other visual methods like film loops can add dramatically to the impact of the sales presentation.

Good catalogue material can be invaluable where the product range is complex or detailed specifications are involved to which the buyer will need to refer. It is interesting to compare the sophistication of holiday brochures with the standard of material prepared for the industrial market or retail buyers when both will generally always be ordering goods or services worth many times more than the average value of the family holiday costing around £1500. Catalogues can also supply additional direct mail material to existing clients to acquaint them with changes in price or product, or act as a structured way by which the sales representative can in addition to his sales folder, develop the sale.

Of crucial importance for the sales call is the simple visiting card: a ready reference for the buyer which is often a highly effective promotional aid.

Many companies go beyond the provision of catalogue and leaflet material and consider that the supply of promotional items can do much to sponsor goodwill from the buyer. Sometimes these ideas become an end in themselves; the Pirelli calendar becoming a status symbol rather than a means of promoting tyres is an obvious example. Emphasis on such promotional methods can cause major difficulties. Buyer turnover in many organisations may be of the order of 25 per cent per annum and informal arrangements developed with one individual will fall foul of another. Secondly many companies regard the offering or accepting of promotional gifts as an offence and in consequence the sales representative and the company that he represents can be black-listed if such a rule is broken. In consequence the buying of business will generally be a hazardous route. Innovative promotional items may, however, be very effective – the mysterious black box that turns colour slowly as the temperature changes for example will sit on the desk providing a continual reminder of the supplying company – until of course the next executive toy appears.

5.3 Direct Mail and Advertising

Further facets of the task of supporting the salesforce include the identification of possible clients and arranging appointments for further discussion. Direct mail, and the use of coupon return systems in technical magazines are two methods by which the individual with the buying responsibility within the organisation can be identified. Recently, the development of postcard-based information packs directed at specific markets, such as office equipment, education, and so on, has opened up new areas for direct response. Exhibitions can also be considered as a form of direct marketing as specific interest groups will attend, being particularly valuable for demonstrating expensive technical equipment to prospective purchasers. The advantages for the company using such systems are:

1. They can specifically direct their activity at one market type or geographical area, whereas prospecting by the salesforce will generally lead to more diffuse activity.
2. Direct marketing can reach individuals involved in the purchase decision who would not normally be seen by the sales representative, cutting through a number of subsidiary layers.
3. They can monitor the cost effectiveness of each individual item with great accuracy, which again is difficult when only the salesman is involved in prospecting for new accounts. The total cost for each operation will be self-evident, as will the number of appointments arranged and the number of new accounts gained.
4. Response to direct marketing techniques implies a level of interest in the product which will generally be higher than that shown by the individual that responds to the telephone call from the salesman.
5. Direct marketing will have similar effects in the long term to other types of advertising, building up the knowledge of the company within the industry.

Consumer advertising research tends to suggest that people need to receive a certain message a number of times before they respond and industrial buyers probably also only act if the message is sufficiently often repeated.[6] Information is also rapidly forgotten, with investigations of the consumer media showing that around 30 per cent of the message is forgotten every month.[7] It is unlikely therefore that the salesman can without difficulty maintain for each prospective account the necessary level of repetition, either by telephone or in person, to reach this response threshold. Over-concentration on an account in this fashion may indeed cause a level of antagonism in the buyer which is unlikely to be caused even by frequent direct mailings, the post being considered as more neutral than personal contact.

Within the retailing environment television or advertisement in consumer magazines will also have its positive effect on the retail buyer. First, he or she will be aware that the advertised product is likely to sell more effectively and thus the more profitable. Second, the buyer has been made aware of the main benefits of the product and thus a major hurdle of the sales presentation process can be overcome.

Advertising can therefore serve specific short-term company objectives by reducing the level of risk the buyer considers involved in the buying of new products. This attitude is well summarised in the famous McGraw-Hill advertisement:

I don't know who you are.
I don't know your company.
I don't know your company's products.
I don't know what your company stands for.
I don't know your company's customers.
I don't know your company's record.
Now, what is it that you wanted to sell me?

Media coverage need not, however, always be expensive. The simplicity and ease of receiving free space in numerous trade and consumer magazines should not be ignored for the expenditure of small amounts of effort. Most technical journals have great difficulty in filling their columns with relevant information, and seize on any contribution with heartfelt sighs of relief. Providing a black and white photograph and a simple account of the product, venture or process will stand a good chance of gaining free publicity leading hopefully to enquiries which can be passed on to the salesforce to follow-up.

5.4 Customer Follow-up

The company will have a major role in developing and maintaining customer records, crucial in the preparation of the sales call. The use of a database system can provide a range of information both for the company and for the salesman, allowing both to control the business environment in which they operate.

Management information systems often lose track of their prime

FIGURE 5.2
Information loop in management decisions

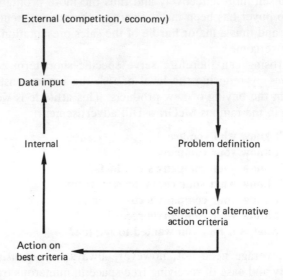

objectives which is to provide accurate, useful, and simply understood data. When the system becomes too complex the amount of data entering the system becomes large and subject to inaccuracy, and the output becomes obscure and difficult to comprehend or too time consuming.

The information provided should be seen as a means by which decisions can be taken and not an end in itself. Data will reveal problems: there will be a number of alternative solutions. The best possible route should be chosen to resolve this dilemma, and then the problem should be re-evaluated. A decision loop will therefore be formed (see Figure 5.2).

Most companies in the sales information area, establish a standard format for the way in which information about their customers in recorded. This data can be easily computerised either on a mainframe or a personal computer system using such packages as D-Base II or Delta. Main items included will be:

1. Customer address.
2. Type of business. Standard industry classification (SIC) codes will give a new sales representative an impression of the likely area of interest.
3. Area code.
4. Telephone number and extension if relevant.
5. Name and title of buyer and colleagues if possible.
6. Day of the week on which appointments are possible.
7. Delivery address (if different).
8. Credit terms and or financial status assessment.
9. Discount policy.
10. Company size – for retail stores this would be categorisation by size, for industrial customers an estimate of turnover.
11. Callage frequency. The number of times the sales representative visits an account will be determined partly by the amount of actual business achieved but also the potential of the account. Some accounts will need perhaps weekly visits, some monthly and so on, each being coded in a particular fashion.
12. Orders for previous years broken down by product either in volume or value.
13. Orders for the current year broken down by product volume or value.
14. Forecasted sales for the year (valuable for major accounts).

From such a system the organisation can produce a whole variety of reports some of which will be more valuable than others. The account record will provide Head Office with the ability to develop support procedures such as direct mail or to institute a telephone sales operation which can deal with small repeat orders or arrange appointments for the salesforce. Such methods can be highly effective in certain industries – the great majority of advertising space is sold via the telephone, and many books on sales techniques stress the value of developing effective telephone sales techniques.

The sales representative will have a succinct and clear picture of the account – its potential, the progress that the company has made over the previous years in particular products and the lack of success in others, and whether there are many problems with the account which would require an element of caution. For the major accounts progress against forecast will provide a useful yardstick as to the short-term problems or opportunities. Such a system can be used to minimise the loss of time in travelling between accounts. The combination of the day of the week that the buyer will see the sales representative together with the callage frequency and area code will supply a list of accounts that should be dealt with on a specific day reducing the time wasted in unnecessary travel. The advantages of such an approach can be shown diagrammatically when one compares two particular travel routes over the same territory (Figure 5.3).

The company can obviously extract figures such as progress against forecast for the current year in major accounts: comparison against last year by product group; total number of accounts by sector; percentage turnover by key accounts; turnover by region; profitability per account if the correct cost figures are included; effects on cash flow by reducing credit or changing discount levels; average sales per account, and many more. The criteria on which these should be judged is as stated previously whether the information can be and will be used to improve decision making.

Part of the information flow will obviously be the data that the salesman sends back from the field. A substantial part of the sales representative's documentation is not, however, integrated into the main management information system but stands alone, often producing a duplication of paperwork. Many companies insist on the completion of a daily sales record or DSR which lists the calls made, time spent at each call, distances travelled, orders achieved, and time spend in administration. This is often claimed to have a central role in the management of the salesforce, though in many companies the reality is very different. Consider the average area sales manager supervising eight sales representatives. Every week he or she will receive 40 daily sales records. Should the representative on average be calling on six customers a day approximately 30 items of information will be included per individual per day or 600 for the week. It is unlikely that this quantity of data will receive any analysis beyond a cursory inspection. The sales director supervising a 30 strong salesforce will be in an even worse position. This is particularly true when the field salesforce are required to supply other documentation such as expense sheets and competitive price listings. The effect on the salesforce of this excessive documentation is also often deleterious. The sales representative tends not to see the role as being administrative in nature, and will resent the

FIGURE 5.3
The importance of journey planning: route B is 10 per cent shorter than route A

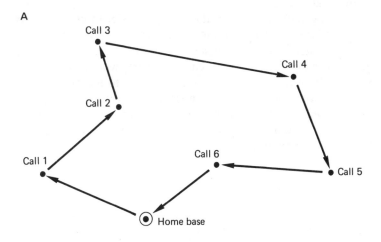

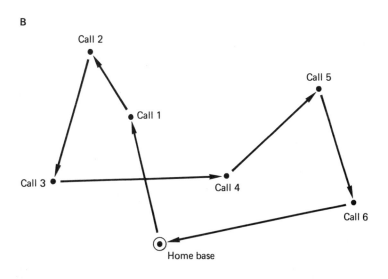

imposition of such tasks to a greater or less extent. In consequence some of the important, but not mandatory note-taking may be put on one side to complete the company's requirements, notes such as those on the setting of objectives, how the buyer might be convinced at the next call and so on.

All management are aware that it is far easier to create a new item of paperwork than to remove one, and that companies tend to evolve rather than appear in a complete shape one fine morning from a primeval swamp. As each industry will have its own problems there cannot be a universal solution to the problems of documentation. Each organisation should, however, evaluate the use each item is put to in the control of the salesforce. In the experience of the author daily sales records are rarely integrated into company planning.

Uppers Ltd

Mr Philip Merrydew the general manager of Uppers Ltd – a UK shoe manufacturer – was considering a report prepared by Gillian Wright, a company executive, which recommended that the recently installed management information system be expanded to improve the management of the salesforce, and to comprehensively provide information for the marketing, sales and finance departments. Gillian Wright argued that the improvements in efficiency would more than justify the expense since recent developments were forcing the company to re-examine the structure of the salesforce and an expanded management information system would supply a large element of the necessary groundwork. The new Uppers' computer system was already revolutionising the type of data analysis available to the company, particularly in the production area.

Background

A medium-sized shoe manufacturer with about 5 per cent of the market, Uppers' main competitor was the British Shoe Corporation which accounted for about a quarter of High Street sales in 1984. There were about five other UK firms of similar size to Uppers manufacturing shoes mainly for sale in the £2 billion a year retail market.

Originally the company had concentrated on the production of safety shoes, footwear for the services and boots for climbing and hiking. It had then expanded into manufacturing quality leather fashion shoes for men and women and into children's shoes as well. The numbers of retail outlets available to Uppers had grown and by 1975 it had around 2000 active accounts making 55 per cent of sales to independent retail shoe stores, 45 per cent to department store groups, and 5 per cent to mail order and retail chains.

Shoe production had risen for the first time in six years in 1983 but Uppers was by no means out of the sea of troubles of the past few years. Sales were still well below the pre-1975 levels. Competition from cheaper, imported shoes in conjunction with the recession had made it extremely difficult for the company to maintain customers in the north of the country. London, Manchester, and South Wales now accounted for 70 per cent of sales. Changes in value added tax which had given importers a seven month period of grace had led to a flood of imports to beat the deadline and a consequent over-stocking by retailers. The independent shoe shops share of Uppers' sales began to decline during the recession while sales to department store groups increased slowly but steadily. But the latter were also proving increasingly difficult to sell to as the stores themselves were coming under pressure from specialist retail chains.

Department and chain store buyers generally spent a lot of time researching the market before placing an order reading trade publications, consulting other buyers, looking at salesmen's samples, and attending many fashion and trade fairs. With the advent of the computer the role of the buyer was changing: with computerised sales slips they no longer needed to spend time in the stores to see what was and was not selling. They were therefore becoming less involved with selling in the store and more with purchasing and turn around of stock. The computer made it possible for buyers to determine sales and inventory in each price range by style, colour, and size, and the manner in which sales of each of the categories varied in the branch of each chain store. Trends could be accurately assessed, re-orders speeded up and the element of chance reduced. Nevertheless the industry depended on a large amount of forward ordering; a range of summer shoes would be presented during the winter to ascertain likely demand, with buyers firming up the orders later in the year.

The Uppers range was large, numbering hundreds of items as the company aimed to cater for practically all footwear requirements, a variety of tastes and income groups. The company manufactured some 30 types of shoe in a variety of materials as well as more seasonal footwear such as training shoes and winter boots. These all varied considerably in style, colour, size, and price. About 5 million pairs of shoes were produced each year.

The salesforce

The majority of the Uppers salesforce of 20 spent most of their time calling on their customers, though a significant proportion of time was spent in attending exhibitions which had long been thought of as providing valuable sales leads. The new sales director Alan Goodeve, recently arrived from a sophisticated motor company, had over the past 18 months steadily increased the amount of information that the salesforce had to provide Head Office. The list now included:

1. Daily expenses (broken down by customer type, mileage covered by call).
2. Callage reports (time spent with each customer, status of each customer whether prospective, new – under six months, established – currently ordering or old – not having ordered in the past year but having done so in the previous five).
3. Competitive analysis by store, reporting on price changes in the market.
4. Orders received broken down by product and pack.
5. Discounts and promotional offers taken up by each individual customer.
6. Source of new business report (exhibitions, advertising cold call etc.).

The installation of the computerised management information system was part of an exercise to improve the company's control over the salesforce. Previously, adjusting territory size and varying the amount of co-operation from the Head Office regarding the development of promotional material had been thought to have severe limitations as methods of control and had not been used to any great extent. By contrast the new management information system would enable the company to ascertain which salesmen's accounts obtained rapid delivery of reorders of fast selling goods. At the same time Head Office was also experimenting to see whether more control could be exercised over the salesforce if their income depended not only on taking orders, but also on co-operating with Head Office plans, in the development of new products or product ranges.

There were now only three salesmen covering the entire north of the country, and management wanted to be able to develop a planning system by which the effectiveness of increasing the number of sales representatives in that area could be tested and what level of increased sales could be expected. Management also wanted to ascertain what problems could be caused with the development of a national accounts sales team and how this could interact with the current geographically based salesforce.

A sales forecast had been used by management for both production planning and in evaluating the salesmen. In the fast moving industry in which they were operating, the forecasts had frequently been inaccurate and had had to be revised several times a season.

Similarly, until the arrival of the computer, management had had relatively little information with which to evaluate each salesman. Previously a report had been prepared four times a year, and another on a weekly basis. These reports based on the salesmen's own weekly accounts from their daily records showed sales for each salesman listed by account; sales for each salesman of individual items listed by group; and total sales per week for each salesman.

The sales information proposal

Gillian Wright suggested that a file be created for each salesman from which management could evaluate the salesman and decide what changes should be made. A summary sheet based on all the information would be prepared weekly for each salesman to allow management to appraise each one without becoming involved in excessive detail. The salesman would be provided with the information as well so that he could prepare more effectively for each sales call.

For each salesman the total information available would be:

1. Gross sales in current month compared with previous year.
2. Actual sales in the year compared with the forecast, providing an analysis of the variance.

3. Success rate by salesman by account type.
4. Highlight strengths and weaknesses in product lines.
5. Use industry figures to provide an estimate of area potential and compare territorial sales against this figure.
6. Investigate specific trading areas comparing the year's accounts with those of the previous year.
7. Provide a measure of the total number of accounts called on including prospects, new accounts, current accounts and old accounts.
8. Catalogue the number of times a product was sold in each account.
9. Add up the total number of accounts including those sending in orders on the catalogue ordering form.
10. Number of product lines sold to various accounts groups.
11. Measure the length of time that an account was kept on average.
12. Provide a measure of how many orders were cancelled compared with last year.
13. Compare expenses on a territory to territory basis.
14. Identify major areas of strength and weakness on a product by product basis territory by territory.
15. Identify major changes in pricing of competitive products on a region by region basis.
16. Profitability analysis on a store by store basis.
17. Measure the miles covered per salesman per effective call.
18. Discount and credit levels by account type.
19. Percentage of new business being generated from various areas of promotional activity.
20. Top ten selling lines.

The documentation that the sales representatives already provided could be keyed into the computer and would provide most of the necessary information, with the production information and costing system providing the remainder.

The company had for many years had a large data processing department during the time that accounting systems had been developed. Recently the work-load in this area had decreased and Gillian Wright was of the view that one of the programmers, paid around £10 500 a year would be available to carry out the exercise. Gillian Wright estimated that it would take 40 per cent of the programmer's time over the period of a year to complete the programming of the as yet unprogrammed portions of the proposal. She anticipated that the routine processing of the additional portions of the proposal would involve costs of £5000 in computer and operator charges.

In evaluating the proposal Mr Merrydew was concerned about its likely impact on the salesforce, whether management could make effective use of the information developed, and whether the system could adequately prepare the company for the challenges ahead of the shoe market. In particular he wondered if all the reports were necessary, whether they might not be too complicated for management who had responsibilities other than the salesforce; what the summary sheet for evaluating salesforce should contain, if some other type of reporting system would not be more useful to management, and whether it might not be simpler to buy in one of the standard reporting systems available in the market, costing around £3000 which though more basic than the sophisticated information system proposed would perhaps be more functional. Such a decision would have consequences in the data processing department. He was also worried that the proposal was perhaps trying to do too much while not addressing specific problems that sales, marketing and financial departments might have. He was also increasingly concerned about the amount of information that the salesforce were being asked to provide and felt that this might be having an adverse effect on overall performance.

Supporting the Salesman II: Motivation and Compensation

6

Any job will give rise to expectations: for the employer and the employee. The former will use various methods to motivate an employee in order to ensure that its expectations are met. The employee will also be keen to make sure that any system of motivation adequately accommodates his or her own expectations of the job in question. It is to the advantage of both employer and employee to see that these expectations do not diverge too drastically. There will be various control systems in operation to prevent this from happening – recruitment procedures, for example, endeavour to employ those whose job expectations will harmonise most readily with organisational expectations. Motivation schemes will also seek similar goals but they have a tendency for mainly administrative reasons to align themselves with group rather than individual expectations: what type of package will prove sufficiently attractive to act as an incentive for a particular group of workers with similar qualifications and experience. What can they reasonably and fairly expect from their employer? When the salesforce is considered, designing and controlling an appropriate motivational system for what is basically an individualistic group, working alone for most of the time and regarded as low-status within the organisation, will pose an acute problem.

All of us are aware of some of the problems that the individual who is unhappy at work can cause whether it be college society or the multinational firm. The effects of the disgruntled individual will appear in a number of forms:

1. poor job performance;
2. expansion of minor complaints into major disasters;
3. development of other interests;
4. demoralising effects on other individuals within the group.

In a business these tendencies will lower morale, create disputes in the work-place and pressure for unionisation, and lead to poor timekeeping, increased illness or absenteeism.

Organisations therefore have to consider how the individuals within the group can best be persuaded to improve co-operation and performance. In primeval days the solution was fairly simple. Hunting man persuaded another hunting man to join him in his task by either offering him a juicy reindeer steak or threatening him with a blow from his trusty club. In more enlightened times this became known as the carrot and the stick approach, remaining even after the advent of psychology, the most highly used management technique to improve employee performance.

Our understanding of the forces that encourage good work performance have substantially improved even if there remain large areas of unpredictability. It is now clearly recognised that there exist a number of interlocking factors that influence the outcome of how well an individual will carry out a particular task:

1. The job content. That is the nature of the job, the variety of tasks, their difficulty, and how it changes over time.
2. The personality of the individual will be crucial; the degree of his commitment and involvement in the job, and how this will change over time.
3. Management will have a vital controlling influence.
4. The motivational input will include the methods which are used to stimulate interest in specific tasks.

These various elements can be arranged in diagrammatic form (Figure 6.1) and considered as a series of interlocking balloons. Low pressure in the job content area will require to be filled by the individual, management, or by motivational input, and pressures in other directions will have differing effects.

Once the training period is completed all organisations will face a common challenge in making sure that staff work as efficiently as

FIGURE 6.1
Job performance: the main interlocking factors

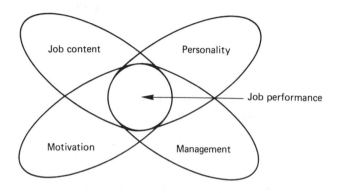

FIGURE 6.2
Differences in performance range

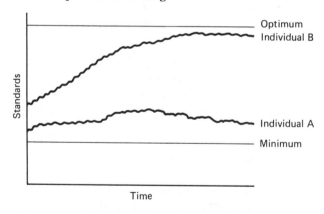

possible as the novelty of the new job or task wears off and repetitive elements begin to increase. The gap between what is theoretically possible and what is regarded as the minimum level of acceptable performance can be very large (Figure 6.2) and this repeated over many years will mean that the organisation is receiving a poor return on its investment. For example, an individual working at 60 per cent of efficiency earning a salary of £16 000 may cost an organisation hundreds of thousands of pounds in lost sales.

6.1   Job Content

There are a number of ways in which management can alter the level of an individual's performance:

1. changing the nature of the job;
2. by raising upper limits (supporting the job performance by the use of appropriate technology, for example);
3. by raising the lower acceptable limits (work study or some other approach);
4. attempting to move the individual onto a higher level of performance by personal motivation or additional training.

Increasing expectations of what a job should include lead the majority of surveys to conclude that there are fairly common attitudes towards what is regarded as a 'good' job.[1,2] These can be summarised as follows:

1. as great a variety of tasks as possible, but organised in a common pattern that provides overall direction;
2. the use of varied skills and abilities;
3. a fair degree of individual responsibility in decision taking, relevant to the level of task;
4. a reasonably clear path of personal development which need not necessarily include promotion;
5. an environment which is supportive of individual action and provides means of identifying success or failure;
6. the job should have some clear benefit to the organisation and ideally also to the community in which it operates.

Individuals tend therefore to prefer jobs where they can have an influence on their surroundings; where the task is integrated and varied; where there is clear direction to a defined goal.

Most firms will tend not to consider the possibilities of redefining a job task when confronted by deterioration in performance.

Certainly in large organisations with very clear-cut departmental objectives and manning the nature of the job description applied to a particular post will be seen as a definitive document, and individuals should not be allowed to break out of this organisational straitjacket, for otherwise anarchy would prevail. In smaller organisations redirection of the job can provide a very effective stimulus. Similarly, large organisations will tend not to investigate to any great extent the possibilities of developing the task by systematically applying technology. How the sales representatives' task can be improved by journey planning and control of documentation come into this category, but there are many other examples within the firm's ambit which are also relevant. The use of word processors by secretaries and support staff can for example remove a large element of mundane work allowing them to concentrate on other tasks, but very few organisations actively analyse the changes that such an introduction would make to overall job performance and job satisfaction.

A salesman will occupy a fixed position within the management hierarchy, with a defined job and reporting system. Progress for the individual in such cases will be seen as dependent on movement up the management ladder, and not something that can be achieved within the work task itself. Most organisations also find considerable difficulties in raising the minimum levels of expectations of job performance for a particular individual. Politically such moves will tend to be resisted within the organisation either by official organisations such as trade unions or staff associations, or by a combination of interested parties. The underlying logic will be that the policies relating to the group as a whole are more important than improved job-satisfaction for one employee and someone else's raised standard today will mean a raised standard for oneself tomorrow.

In consequence most organisations concentrate on the improvement of performance between two already clearly established and delineated upper and lower limits by means other than that of altering the nature of the job. Small organisations can very effectively stimulate employees by changes in job content but this becomes increasingly more difficult as the firm grows larger and relies more on tactical short-term methods rather than the broader strategy of altering job content on an individual basis.

6.2 The Nature of the Individual

We all react differently to a specific task – writing an essay for example will be seen as a medieval torture by some, others will regard it as a necessary chore, whereas a happy few will attack the problem with delight. In the Middle Ages mankind was divided into the 'four tempers of man' – sanguine, choleric, melancholy, and phlegmatic, and differences in human behaviour were explained in terms of variations in the mixture of the four elements. Modern psychology has re-invented this particular wheel, to see individuals varying between introvert and extrovert, stable and unstable.[3]

Some firms will perceive a specific type of individual as being more appropriate to a particular job and will employ aptitude and personality tests as a fundamental part of the selection procedure, in an attempt to narrow down the personality types that are being selected. There has been a considerable growth in the use of such techniques particularly in the United States.[4]

As the role of the salesman will vary both from industry to industry and from client type to client type, the selection of a particular personality type may be a short-sighted and dangerous policy, for whereas the extrovert sales representative may sell cleaning equipment very effectively in the town it is unlikely that such an approach will prove so successful when selling on the farm. In one large study on common psychological factors underlying the success of a sales representative only 'ego-drive' and 'empathy' were clearly identified.[5] Some organisations do claim that the use of tests has had a substantial impact in other areas, notably on lowering personnel turnover, but as these organisations are generally ones that have taken a greater overall interest in the selection process it will often be difficult to separate out the effects of tests within the overall recruitment process. Tests are often open to manipulation and individuals will generally have a clear conception of the type of answers expected from them.

The interaction between the organisation, the job and the individual's personality is unlikely therefore to be structured. They may be further complicated by group pressures which will be more important in certain cultures such as Japan than in others. Individual managers will know which of their staff would enjoy team-selling and which would not, but personnel planning is unlikely to extend beyond this.

In contrast to the vagueness concerning individual personality, most firms will have a clear view of how an employee will respond to pressure, accepting one of four possible explanations of human behavior as being most applicable to itself and tailoring the way that it perceives the task of stimulating performance accordingly.

1. *Rational man.* Everyone is regarded as being mainly driven by financial return or physical well-being, and when adequately compensated will perform well – when not, not. Many armed services operate this principle for the junior ranks, with weekend leave for those that behave and floor scrubbing for those that do not.
2. *Social man.* The group predominates. Each one of us is controlled by a need to belong and be accepted in the group. Team sports would tend to be a good example of this tendency, and it is interesting that companies following such an approach often encourage team games of all descriptions.
3. *Self-motivating man.* Each individual will set himself achievement goals by which he will judge himself. Many university departments attempt to use such a system.
4. *Complex man.* People will vary initially and over time in their reaction to organisational demands. In consequence the employee will acquire new motives over time by learning; simple motives such as financial insecurity will be replaced by others.

The use of a single approach will naturally pose problems especially when a group such as the salesforce are concerned, who both spend large amounts of time unsupervised and also away from the structured environment of the office, in addition to being temperamentally somewhat individualist as well.

It is interesting to note that the majority of firms tend to support the view of the sales representative as rational man. This can be seen in the three most popular methods used by employers to improve sales performance:[6]

Method	Ranking
Basic compensation plan	100
Competitions	62
Bonus payments	47

Much lower down the scale came informal appraisal and discussion systems, alteration in the nature of job content and the like.

Such an approach is significantly at odds with the traditional

findings of normal motivation studies which produce a totally
different picture. The classic study in this area shows the following
ranking of the importance individuals place on various elements of
the work in which they are involved:[7]

Element	Ranking
Achievement	41
Recognition	33
The nature of work	26
Responsibility	23
Advancement	20
Salary	15

Such studies identify salary levels as being important in the maintenance of employees within the system along with supervision,
working conditions, benefits, job security. Should these fall below
an 'acceptable' level the employees will become dissatisfied. It is
clear, however, that the reverse does not hold true – raising the
level of these items does not appear to dramatically increase the
level of contentment within the organisation nor necessarily the
level of performance. This in part contradicts the well-known
adage of paying peanuts and getting monkeys. An analysis of
corporate performance in the United States showed that if anything there was a negative correlation between salary and performance – that paying golden peanuts produced golden monkeys.[8]
More recent studies relating specifically to the salesforce and job
satisfaction find a similar picture – that salary is generally low on
overall factors influencing performance.[9, 10]

6.3 Management

Management's view of the relationship between subordinates and
authority will often determine how employees are generally classi-
fied – rational, self-motivating, or otherwise – and how performance should be improved. The expectations of each manager will
colour the relationships that he or she will have with his or her
subordinates, but overriding this will be an organisational ethos of
management. Thus some companies will have a rigid style of
authority and will enforce such an approach from managers who
left without guidance would adopt a relaxed management style.
Similarly the reverse will also occur, the less authoritarian com-

pany diminishing the dictatorial tendencies of the employed managers.

The nature of management style can be best seen as a graded scale from being entirely task oriented to entirely people orientated at the other extreme. Task orientation implies that the manager will be primarily concerned with issuing instructions, monitoring and regulating activities, controlling budgets. Socially he will tend to be distant, demanding the correct use of titles, and never exchanging jokes. One is left with the picture at this extreme of the classic dictator or Victorian mill-owner. The opposite extreme will be the individual who abdicates power, concentrates on the personal rather than the detailed work criteria of the particular task, who is socially close to his subordinates but who may nevertheless allow them to be authoritarian over others in the organisation. Several examples of such managerial styles can be seen in European monarchs – Tsar Nicholas of Russia, and Louis XVI of France. More effective yet using the same managerial style one can perhaps include Gandhi.

Some managerial styles will be more appropriate to certain types of job than others. Jobs that demand rapid decisions, have a fairly simple and straightforward range of tasks, operate within a stable and predictable environment, with a work-force with low expectations from the job, may be suited to a clear-cut authoritarian style. A good example of this would be a typing pool or an assembly plant producing simple standard items such as clothes or electronic components. When the task becomes more complex and unpredictable, where judgement is more important, and where personal achievement is of considerable importance to the individual, the managerial approach will need to be less clear-cut and more consultative. When one analyses the job of the sales representative in these terms it is fairly plain that a consultative style of management needs to be considered for the maximum performance of the individuals concerned.

6.4   Motivational Input

The final element in the interaction between the four factors influencing job performance is generally regarded as the major influencing factor in job performance. Most textbooks on sales

management devote a considerable amount of space to the description and evaluation of the major components of motivation or the 'motivational mix'.
Generally included are:

1. salary, commission and or bonus;
2. fringe benefits;
3. expenses;
4. competition within the group;
5. awards.

Occasionally included – but often considered to lie outside the mainstream 'financial' rewards – are items that are discussed elsewhere, namely:

6. promotion prospects;
7. information – meetings, conventions;
8. appraisal, managerial involvement in the job performance;
9. additional training.

Salary, commission and bonus

The development of the salary or 'compensation' package is generally considered to be of prime importance, indeed it is often regarded as the be-all and end-all of motivation. This is reflected in the majority of sales literature that concentrate almost exclusively on compensation levels.
   The overall aim of the salary structure will tend to be:

1. to control the activities of the salesforce;
2. to reward effective effort, and theoretically reward profitable business more than unprofitable;
3. to keep the established and trained salesforce;
4. to fit in with the overall company salary plans;
5. to be easily understandable and equitable;
6. to provide flexibility for rapid redirection of salesforce activities.

Several of these objectives can conflict with each other. A high level of commission will mean that sales representatives may easily be earning well in excess of their line managers thus upsetting any differential system that may be in operation; a high basic salary will not only keep people the organisation wants but also large numbers it does not; a low basic salary and high commission will mean that management will not be able to control the salesforce effectively. Commissions where paid may be gained on 'windfall' business for which the sales representative has not been responsible. Attempting to separate commission rates on differing types of product with differing levels of gross margin will often be extremely complicated; where more than one representative is involved with an account there will be difficulties of splitting the commission.

Finally and most important in the modern concept of the sales representative's role is the problem of what constitutes effective performance. With the sales representative increasingly being involved in marketing activities, developing new brands, administering distribution problems and the like, the issue of what is effective sales effort becomes more and more important, particularly when salary levels are tied to some pre-planned level of activity which may need to be altered during the year.

Because of these conflicting themes, the compensation plan in reality very rarely matches the underlying theory. A firm may claim that it wishes 'to reward effort' or 'maximise profitability' but rarely does this show in the reality of the compensation plan which is normally a result of compromise in the same fashion as the view that a camel is a horse designed by a committee.

The main elements that the company will tend to consider will be the nature of the job, the financial strength or otherwise of the organisation and general business conditions. In consequence, compensation levels for salesforces in the UK and elsewhere are generally set in broad terms by industry comparison, with each market having its own 'acceptable level of pay[11]':

Industry	On target salary (UK)
Computers	£20 000
Office equipment	£18 000
Insurance	£16 000
Drink	£14 000
Food	£12 000

These figures for salesforce earnings in various industries, in comparison with other countries, are very low particularly in relation to the United States although above average earnings in the UK. However, each country shows the same pattern with office equipment, computers, and insurance being the best paid, and drink and food at the base.[12] The similarity of the industry approach also extends to the structure of the salary plan. A greater and greater proportion of firms are using a combined basic salary and commission or bonus system; the numbers using either straight salary or straight commission have been steadily declining.[13]

A standard approach is to set an overall sales target for a sales representative and then to pay commission when 85 or 90 per cent of this target has been achieved. The commission can then either be open-ended; that is it will continue at the same rate for each additional piece of business or will show some form of gradation to encourage the individuals to either hit their targeted sales figure or to exceed it. Thus commission could be set at 5 per cent on sales value from 100–110 per cent of target achievement, 10 per cent from 110–120 per cent and 15 per cent on business above this level. Non-volume related activities can be allowed for by some form of points system which has the advantage that it can be changed fairly quickly. For example a company could direct a salesforce for a period to reopening old accounts in preference to new accounts by making the first worth 50 points and the second 10 points. Reversing the points will reverse the priorities. The administrative problems that such a scheme can cause will be seen to be immense; implementation and control demanding considerable documentation and day-to-day administration.

Another approach that is little used is to include the salesforce within a profit-sharing pool. One author proposes this as the most effective method of salesforce control directing it towards the development of the most profitable business while acting as a brake on the level of expenses.[14] Other authors dismiss such concepts because the salesforce 'does not have sufficient control over profits', an argument which applies one would consider to most parts of the organisation.[15]

Fringe benefits

Again, fringe benefits will tend to be set by industry comparison. Within the United Kingdom the status of the car that accompanies the sales job is often seen as an important recruitment tool. In the other countries of Western Europe there is a much lower provision of company cars and in consequence it is seen as less important when comparing one sales job with another.

The system of taxation is also relevant to any discussion of fringe benefits – whether direct pay or benefits in kind will be most cost effective for the organisation. Within the United Kingdom a standard company car worth £2000 per annum after tax (including depreciation, insurance, and the like) is only valued by the Inland Revenue at £144. For the company director with the Porsche, valued at £950 the after-tax worth may be well over £15 000 additional income.

Similar considerations will apply to health insurance, pension contributions, the amount of holiday provided, sick pay provisions and so on.

Expenses

How each organisation controls expenses will often be a major source of conflict and argument. The salesforce may for example develop the attitude, fostered and supported by one set of management that expenses exist to provide additional income. Changes in management with differing values will inevitably cause conflict. Unfortunately expense control is normally one of those 'grey' areas without clear guidelines.

Broadly, firms tend to adopt one of two approaches. The first entails the total refunding of all expenses, the other provides fixed sums by mileage, by day, and so on. In common with the salary plan, the organisation will have to consider the administrative problems that any scheme will involve, the nature of the job and the employee, the understandability of the scheme, and its fairness in application. In the author's experience disputes about expenses are one of the prime areas of discontent within a salesforce and it is vital that whatever system is adopted that the limitations of it are clearly defined. Can buyers be entertained and if so how often? What level of expenditure on hotel and eating out is acceptable? What happens when the sales representative is travelling with a senior member of staff? The list is fairly endless and opportunities for conflict will reflect this fact.

Competitions

Competitions are frequently used within salesforces to:

1. produce higher levels of overall performance or
2. to concentrate on a particular problem area.

It is a difficult technique to use effectively as competitions will often run into problems for a number of reasons. First, it may interfere with overall job performance by forcing the individual to concentrate on the aims of the competition. Second, unless it is very carefully structured it may be unfair to a large percentage of the salesforce, which may easily cause conflict and resentment within the organisation. Some organisations combine a yearly competition with prize-giving at the annual convention, which will again demand consistent planning and application.

Awards

The supply of awards on completion of a certain length of service, or an award for the best performance in the year can often be counter-productive, being regarded as patronising by the recipients. Properly handled it can be a very valuable motivational device. The German brandy company Asbach provides the employees of its overseas distributors with both a token and a dinner at which one of the Asbach family will be present on the completion of ten years service. The author found that this had been universally appreciated by all the recipients with whom it was discussed, building considerable loyalty towards the Asbach family for very little cost.

How the organisation approaches the use of various elements within the motivational mix will vary and will largely depend on the view of the management of how the employee should be treated, the nature of the management style, and how the individual regards his position within the organisation. Naturally each element will influence the other, and how the organisation's motivational system develops will be determined by the interplay of all three factors, the employees that it has recruited, and the nature of the tasks in which they are involved. Though the majority of studies indicate that job content is generally far more important in determining motivation that financial rewards, sales representatives will it appears continue to be considered as responding most effectively to the financial carrot backed by the evaluation whip. Only by detailed analysis of the effectiveness of various possible approaches will the organisation be able to define the most cost effective technique for improving sales performance, whether it be high commission rates, awards, training or competitions.

Maxim Ltd

Background

Maxim Ltd was a small supplier of control equipment and
replacement parts, which had recently joined the Unlisted
Securities Market after a fairly successful flotation. In the last
financial year sales amounted to £18 750 000. Of this 20 per
cent consisted of control systems used in speciality chemical
plants each of which sold for about £35 000. Remaining sales
were divided among replacement parts for the control systems, and gear and lathe control equipment sold not only to
the speciality chemical industry, but also to the machine tool
sector, and light engineering sector.

The market was made up of about 800 small and large
plants in England and Scotland. Maxim – with about one-
third of the market – was a major supplier but had two other
competitors one of which was considerably larger and supplied a wider range of capital goods. The capital equipment
portion of the business was cyclical, although the replacement parts and supplies portion of the business tended to
offset these fluctuations. Recently there had been dramatic
changes within the market. American, German and Japanese
equipment was starting to arrive in quantity. These units,
microprocessor controlled, showed greater reliability than
Maxim products. Over the last twelve months the Maxim
board had seen a gradual decline in profitability, and had
realised that substantial investment in research and development would be necessary to maintain market share. The
company was therefore faced with a period of retrenchment
and difficulty. Knowledge of these problems had filtered
down to the salesforce which viewed possible changes to
their salary structure with concern. Already the competitive
nature of the market and the fact that the Maxim products
were no longer superior was causing a drop in morale, and
the salesforce was starting to aggressively question company
objectives and strategy at area sales meetings.

The salesforce

A salesforce of eleven, assigned geographically, had all worked for the company for at least six years. Their backgrounds tended to be in engineering, and though some of them had moved from the factory floor, there was on the whole little movement between the salesforce and other areas within the company. The types of product sold and the market potentials varied substantially between territories. For example, there might be considerable potential for capital equipment in an industrial development area, but little opportunity to sell spare parts. It could be ten or more years before a piece of machinery required replacement so each sale of such a machine would decrease the remaining potential for that product. The salesforce was involved to an extent in the forecasting system that the company had put into operation by estimating the likely demand customer by customer for Maxim products in the forthcoming year. Though they were all technically qualified the salesmen had little impact on design or product development.

It was estimated that two-thirds of the salesforce time in front of the customer was spent in actually selling equipment, parts and supplies and in arranging the servicing of equipment; the rest tended to be given to investigating company requirements in discussions throughout the factory. The nature of their jobs brought them into contact with a very wide range of people: purchasing managers, production managers, plant foremen, technicians, machine operators, mechanics and accountants. At larger plants a sales representative of Maxim might have as many as 30 contacts. This informal contact had been quite important as the company previously did not advertise heavily. Considerable reliance was placed on word of mouth advertising which depended on customer contact. The salesforce was therefore expected to make a major contribution to the overall sales strategy, but this had become more and more difficult as foreign competitors advertising heavily in the trade press and at exhibitions had appeared in the market. The Maxim board had recently appointed a marketing manager as part of their product development strategy, who was already building up a direct mail list to support the product range.

The Maxim representatives travelled extensively and were expected to call on every potential customer in their territory at least once a month. The number of calls needed to make a sale tended to vary with the type of customer.

Salaries

Salesforce members were all currently paid a salary plus expenses. Salary was determined on a largely informal basis by:

1. the sales volume and gross margin contribution by each sales representative;
2. the comparative earnings of representatives in similar industries outside the company;
3. the earnings of others within the company.

Gross margin varied for each sales representative with sales volume and product mix but the average representative contributed twelve to fifteen times his salary.

Managers were strongly of the opinion that salary had to be comparable with the representative's opportunity for earning elsewhere because although the number of competitors were limited there were suitably attractive alternatives available, especially for the highly qualified Maxim salesforce.

As part of the payment scheme in operation, there was an annual review of salesforce performance. Pay increases were determined on the basis of these interviews. There were no definite yardsticks to determine the increases which tended to depend upon the individual's ability to negotiate successfully on his or her own behalf.

Although the scheme had operated successfully in the past, company managers felt that it called for high selling expenses, regardless of the volume of sales. Secondly managers were aware of the level of subjectivity in determining salary increases. The straight salary plan could restrict selling efforts because a representative's efforts on behalf of the company was not really reflected in take-home pay. This disquiet was heightened by the financial problems that Maxim was beginning to encounter, and management were looking for ways of more effectively controlling the substantial proportion of company expenditure that was channelled through the salesforce. However, the board were fully aware that salesforce disquiet would lead to increased labour turnover unless the company reappraised the way the salesforce was motivated and compensated. The recently appointed finance director felt that the over-reliance on monetary rewards had not worked in the past and was more interested in considering other motivational techniques.

Alternative schemes

The board of Maxim Ltd felt that a new pay scheme might help to achieve a better balance between capital equipment and other sales, directing sales more effectively and providing a greater control over the profitability of the operation. Some managers felt for example that representatives spent too much time trying to get a large order for machinery when there was no definite indication that such an order would materialise, and that this in the current climate was unacceptable – salesmen needed to concentrate on immediate business. It was hoped that a good pay scheme would also provide a measure for comparing achievement in the salesforce.

The board was considering a number of alternatives that had been put forward by a management consultancy firm brought in to advise on remuneration schemes:

Profit sharing

This envisaged the creation of profit targets, each of which when reached would mean a 2 per cent increase in pay. The scheme was to be introduced across the company and would not relate to individual performance but rather how the entire firm performed. It was felt that this would lead to an overall reduction in salesforce expenses if it could be shown that high expenses came effectively straight out of the sales representatives' pockets. This scheme had been put forward by the Amalgamated Engineering Workers' Union, the shop-floor trade union. It would mean that Maxim would need to freeze current salaries.

Share options

These schemes had become increasingly popular. Since changes in taxation policy and the entry of Maxim onto the Unlisted Securities Market, there had been considerable interest in share ownership amongst its employees. It was thought that linking performance with the ability to gain share options might have attractions to some of the long-serving members of the Maxim salesforce. The introduction of such a scheme was however so new in the industry that the board was hesitant in progressing with the concept.

Point scheme

This would involve a system of fixed basic salary and bonus/penalty points for various selling activities. The sales director would allocate points for various tasks and non-selling activities would earn the salesforce members extra income. Penalty points would be assigned for adverse reports such as customer complaints, and more importantly to a high level of expenses.

However, to assign points the scheme required more detailed reporting from the sales representatives about their jobs than they had hitherto had to prepare.

Salary and commission

Paying a salary, expenses, and a commission was another option under consideration. Salary would amount to 70 per cent of the representative's earnings, giving him security, while a 30 per cent on target commission would provide an incentive to do a better than average job. Commission rates could vary among the several products, depending on profitability, the degree of difficulty in obtaining initial and repeat sales, and the company's desire to promote certain items.

Closer examination of the proposal revealed that a commission plan along these lines would mean that most of the sales representatives would take a cut in salary so that the incentive payment could amount to 30 per cent of total earnings. Only in this way could the company hope to stop the ratio of sales expense to sales from changing drastically.

Certain questions also required further attention: whether the sales representatives would accept the reductions, assuming the relative efficiency of each representative to be the same; whether territory potential would affect the scheme; when incentives should be paid; whether there should be an upper limit.

Controlling the Salesforce: Analysing Sales Productivity

7

A key concern of the company employing a large salesforce is how to maximise their effectiveness and financial return to the company.

Typically, the amount spent on the salesforce will average three times the amount that the organisation spends on advertising – and sometimes it is even more. For example, in France the cost of maintaining a 35 strong hypermarket/supermarket salesforce for a distributor is 6 per cent of net sales price; the costs had been even higher for salesmen based in the major towns dealing with the traditional liquor shops.

7.1 The Problem

Two issues confront the firm:

1. what is required from the salesforce – (output); and
2. the constraints against which they are operating – (input).

7.2 Measuring Output

Output measurement will naturally vary with the sales task. For the van salesman delivering coal the level of output may be measured by the weight of coal removed from the back of the lorry. The traditional grocery salesforce might be measured on callage rate; for the computer salesman it may be sales volume, and for the evangelical organisation the criteria will be entirely different, consisting perhaps of redeemed souls.

The first stage must involve an analysis of the various tasks that the organisation expects of the salesforce as well as their relative importance. In many firms this is rarely approached systematically and in consequence conflict can rapidly develop between salesforce and commercial or marketing management.

Companies will also have different views about the elements of the sales achievement that are important. Nevertheless these will generally be included under:

1. sales volume achievement;
2. sales value achievement;
3. gross margin achievement;
4. callage rate;
5. repeat business;
6. new business development;
7. credit control;
8. merchandising/ test markets/ exhibitions;
9. public relations;
10. record keeping;
11. solving distribution problems;
12. providing information.

Sales volume

Sales volume tends to be the first measure that the majority of firms would choose for evaluation. The reasoning would obviously flow that the job of the sales representative, customer contact personnel, or whatever the department is named, is to provide the maximum potential inflow of work to maintain the existence of the organisation. It is particularly useful where the products are similarly priced, for differing values would make this an inappropriate measure.

Sales value

Where there is considerable variation in pricing between product lines the development of a value system will become more important as the number of product lines increases.

Gross margin analysis

Within the overall mix of products sold it is possible to combine the total gross margin and evaluate the salesforce on this basis. One factor that must be taken into account, however, is the cost of distribution. From the two extremes – that of the salesman who takes a small number of large orders and the individual gaining a large number of small orders – there may not be an overall difference in the margin received on sales but when the distribution costs are removed there will be a considerable variation in the gross margin. Many companies overcome this particular problem by some variation of a minimum order system. This can limit the client to either a minimum order, or the order can be delivered differently depending on size. This is at best, however, an approximation and within a company with a widely differing product range (very high margin products rubbing shoulders with low margin items) it is often not the most profitable route for the organisation to follow.

The type of account pursued by a salesman will have an important influence on the nature of the gross profit. A sale to a supermarket may net considerable gross volume but low margin as the discount provided would have to be considerable.

Callage rate

Many firms judge the fitness of their salesforce at least in part by the callage rate, the number of sales calls that are completed during the day. This can obviously lead to anomalies within the system with sales representatives filling the day with unproductive calls just to achieve the necessary quota.

Repeat business

The stability of the company obviously depends on the nature of its customers, how they are maintained over time, and the degree of repeat business that is achieved. In many industries this is regarded as a prime sales task though in some instances the repeat business generation moves away from the salesforce to some other section such as a telephone sales division. The loss or gain of accounts over time can be a particularly important element in the development of repeat business to give a measure of the account stability or the amount of business that can be reasonably relied upon in the next business period. Should there be a substantial loss of customer base from one period to another the degree of confidence in any forecasting process must be considerably blunted.

New business development

As a component of any sales representative's routine, the introduction of new products is frequently regarded as very important by certain sections of the organisation. Time spent in this area often, however, has deleterious effects on the repeat business achievement as the development of new products is time consuming.

Credit control

Many salesforces are used to determine and monitor credit within their areas, collecting overdue payments and acting as an agent for the accounting and finance function. This is especially true within the export sphere where clients are outside the home territory legal framework which can often accentuate the credit control problems.

Advertising activities: merchandising, exhibitions, test markets

One of the salesforce tasks in many companies is the control of local advertising activity. The salesforce is obliged to be present at national and local exhibitions, and control the work of sales demonstrators, and often maintain shelves, put up point of sale material and so on.

In addition regional sales representatives often have to supervise the activities of local distributors dealing with a different market sector, and control test marketing activity. All these tasks are obviously time consuming and must be included in any evaluation of sales performance.

Public relations

The sales representative is normally the first to receive customer complaints, acting as the front line individual between the organisation and the consumer.

Record keeping

Salesforces are expected to maintain accurate records not only of total business but also of mileage, expenses, callage rate, administrative time, competitive activity, pricing, merchandising and so on.

Distribution problems

As well as the standard tasks, the sales representative often also has to sort out distribution problems as a crucial element in keeping customers happy.

Providing information

As the first contact point between the company and its customers the salesforce will make an important contribution to the supply of information.

In addition to these largely quantifiable output criteria there may well be a number of more intangible aspects of the sales representative's job performance which could be regarded as important. Thus knowledge of the company and its products are factors difficult to quantify, as are attitudes (how co-operative the individual is and so on), and the ability of the individual to overcome objections and effectively conclude the sale. In some firms factors such as appearance and smartness may be regarded as important criteria for evaluating salesforce performance.

Anomalies in output criteria

Output criteria should be objective and attempt to provide a measure by which the firm can evaluate the return to the organisation related to the level of investment.

One salesforce statistic much misused in terms of output is the callage rate which is the number of calls performed over time. This can be divided by the frequency of success to produce the 'batting average'. In the opinion of the author and several other commentators these concepts are particularly meaningless for a number of reasons. The most important is that concentration on these criteria do not yield much usable data on the value of the sales individual to the organisation in terms of balance sheet return, which any control system should attempt to achieve. This approach is used by a number of companies to develop sales areas as profit centres whereby goods are 'sold' to the sales office at a transfer price. The office then controls the sales team as a distribution company, and is measured on the profitability that is generated. Most manufacturers would not be concerned if one of their overseas distributor's salesforce spent every other day playing golf *providing* they were performing effectively. Similar views are perhaps anathema when dealing with directly employed personnel, but surely what is important to any organisation is largely the end result achieved. Should this be obtained by working schedules regarded by the remainder of the firm as 'non-standard', so be it.

7.3   Input Factors – External and Industrial

Once the firm has determined the relevant output measure – be it profit or volume – the constraints against which the firm is operating need to be considered.

Industry potential

For any given territory there will be a total potential which will be arrived at by studying industry figures, available from government or commercial sources such as market research organisations.

An objective assessment of local potential will face the problem of how to allocate the volume that is dependent on nationally negotiated agreements, as these will need to be removed from any territorial assessment. Naturally the firm needs to be clear as to the way in which the statistics have been collated. Annual figures may hide substantial month by month variations if the product is highly seasonal. They nevertheless provide a standard benchmark against which annual sales performance can be judged.

For an analysis of return on investment the value of the potential sales should be considered as the relevant issue.

Market share

Again this would be available from rough calculation – company sales/ total industry value – or directly from market research data: retail audit for example. The level of market share will determine the total level of business that has historically been available to the company.

Total number of accounts

In many industries there will be a distinction between total accounts and total 'available' accounts. To take an example within the catering trade one could include all bars, restaurants and cafés within the account base for a liquor salesman, compared with selling to a small number of wholesale liquor outlets. The workload in each case may be very different. Similarly, should the smaller customers be dealt with by a distributor/wholesaler these should not be double counted within the salesforce territory.

Regional price position

The relative price at which the company's products are sold may vary with the region and this could influence the sales level achieved. Obviously for the majority of companies a standard national price will exist, particularly if there are major retailing chains throughout the country, but in some markets there may be considerable price variation. The effect of price will be seen through the price elasticity: the percentage drop in sales that occurs when the product increases its price relative to that charged by the competition. A price elasticity of 2 would mean a 2 per cent drop in volume for a 1 per cent change in relative price. Elasticities on butter for example are very high, around 10, whereas those on petfood are lower, around 5, and those on perfume lower still. Estimates of price elasticity can be gained from the use of audit data over time or by past experience of the effects of price rises in the market.

Company advertising

The ability of the company to carry out regional advertising to support local sales activity is becoming more and more important in the UK – it has always been important in large geographically diverse countries such as the USA. Regional television, radio, press and posters are being used increasingly to assist sales campaigns. High levels of investment in a regional area will obviously be relevant in relation to the level of expected return. Advertising investment will affect sales; in common with price elasticity there will be an advertising elasticity which will increase the effective market potential against which the sales performance will need to be evaluated. Within the consumer goods market there is some evidence that for major products elasticities lie between 1/3 and 1/8.

Competitive advertising

High levels of competitive advertising may well depress the market available for the sale of company products.

Company promotional expenditure

The amount of money that the company is investing in promotions will be another crucial factor affecting likely market strengths and weaknesses. In many consumer goods product fields, promotional expenditure is higher than the amount of money spent on media; with an increasing emphasis on couponing and promotional packs. In common with media advertising large promotional expenditures will also change the structure of the market, especially over a short time period.

Competitive promotional expenditure

Large scale investment in promotion by the competition will naturally reduce the market potential available for the parent company.

Together these eight factors will supply the total background against which the efforts of the local sales representative can be judged. Again it should be stressed that this analysis will be in terms of value and not volume.

7.4   Input Factors – The Salesforce

Next to be considered are those factors that pertain to the individual sales representative.

Training

Many of the output factors are thought to be influenced by training. Various psychological studies comment on the learning curve. They reveal that any individual in any new environment takes in data rapidly in the early days and this uptake of information levels off over time.

It is quite clear that a new sales representative will be less effective than one who has been long established in the job. This can mean acute problems in firms with high salesforce turnover as some of those operating in insurance/personal savings and office equipment.

The training component in any evaluation of salesforce ability is therefore crucial. One of the most valuable concepts in this area is the idea of *effective headcount*. This covers the area of salesforce development over time and provides for the fact that a newly joined salesman will be less effective than one who has worked for a period of time with that particular firm and that particular industry, often in a new part of the country. Management need to determine the length of time it will take them to fully train newly recruited individuals until they are fully effective. A number of studies suggest that upwards of 12 months is necessary for an individual to achieve maximum efficiency at a complex task. Though the rate of improvement is not linear the use of a training or effective headcount concept will provide the organisation with some form of in-built insurance to analyse salesforce productivity. This will be especially true in cases of high salesforce turnover, or salesforce expansion.

Days in field

This figure is naturally vital in any consideration of productivity analysis to yield a per day assessment of the individual's performance. To evaluate it some of the following calculations will need to be made:

Total days in year	365
Weekends (unless worked)	104
Public holidays	10
Company holidays	20
Sales meetings	12
Exhibitions	5
Varied support work	10
Illness	4
Total effective year	200

Total account base at analysis period

At the point at which the analysis is performed there will be a mixture of old accounts and new clients, details of which are important for the calculation of the stability of the customer base for the future development of the business. This factor has major implications for marketing policy. Should the account base be rapidly changing a considerable effort will need to be devoted to gaining new outlets; should there be considerable stability emphasis can then be placed on expanding business within already established outlets.

Customers lost in the accounting period

It will be important for the company in its analysis of sales productivity to consider the level of account loss against the overall account base and also to compare one sales representative against another.

Customers gained

Similarly, it will be important for the company to be aware of the number of accounts that have been gained during the analysis period.

Total value of orders obtained

A key factor in the analysis will be the value of the sales representative's orders. This will then need to be qualified by the gross margin of the product mix that is being sold to arrive at the overall contribution that the representative is returning to the company.

The concentration of the sales efforts in certain areas is naturally a feature of the overall company objectives, but nevertheless over-emphasis on one particular line could have significant effects on the individual profitability of sales representatives – those that are selling the more profitable product lines should be identified as those producing the greatest return to the company.

Expense levels

Expense levels are one of the standard input items that can show considerable variations due to working environment (rural/urban split, etc.). Ideally to calculate the exact costs of the sales representative the figures should include an allocation of the office overhead, in addition to the standard operating expenses, such as car costs, entertaining, and other travel.

Salary level/commission

This can vary considerably within the salesforce and is quite often not included in any consideration of salesforce productivity.

From the analysis of these figures the company should derive certain benefits.

1. Understanding of the industry background against which each salesman is operating; and of major regional differences which may affect performance.
2. An analysis of the costs to the company in relation to the return that is received.
3. An estimate of the daily effectiveness of the sales personnel.
4. Some measure of the effectiveness of the training methods in operation.
5. Insight into likely problems in areas of account management, and product mix in the market.

Appraisal and Discipline

8

When a company adopts plans establishing priorities and targets so as to operate in its markets as profitably and successfully as possible, people are an essential element of the equation. It is they who will ultimately control whether the plans will become a reality or remain a vision on a scrap of paper. Knowledge and understanding of its human resources are as vital to the company's long-term health as audits of its present and future strategy and physical resources. In arriving at an objective assessment of what is and is not feasible, a clear view of staffing matters, of the talents available and desirable is as important as financial and market considerations. This is the only way of ensuring that the correct team of individuals is available to cope with the future problems and opportunities. At the same time it should be said that clear-sightedness in dealing with personnel issues, in the carrot and stick areas especially, appears to be more elusive than in such matters as market trends or finance. Perhaps it is because it is an area where objectivity tends to be at the mercy of pragmatism.

An efficient organisation must therefore set out to ensure that it is aware of the essential human skills present and required and so develop its thinking on manpower planning. One study of 75 companies using regression techniques has shown that approximately 65 per cent of the changes in financial performance and productivity could be explained by analyses of the company's personnel policy within areas of decision making, the amount of information in the organisation, and the level of trust between management levels.[1]

8.1   The Case for Standardisation

The company has to deal with its employees both as individuals and as members of groups within it – whether they are managers, salesforce members, or secretaries. In seeking to reconcile this with financial, legal and moral obligations it will have to maintain systems designed to measure that it is giving, and getting 'an honest day's work for an honest day's pay'.

Any planning procedure will require a degree of formalisation with standard reporting structures in order to reduce bias and make it possible to reasonably accurately compare and contrast the past with the present, thereby developing a measure of what is happening within the company. Standardisation will help to identify the common ground that will have to be measured.

With capital investment projects, for example, a common approach is the return on capital employed with some assessment of the risk factors involved if the planned level of profit is going to be achieved. Since resources are scarce and ideas are not, the company will in all likelihood be evaluating the costs and benefits of several competing projects to decide which is the most profitable.

One can adopt a similar approach to the allocation of human resources or personnel issues within the firm. There always exists a gap, and sometimes a fairly substantial one, between the expectations of staff and the firm's ability to meet them fully.

Promotion

First, there have always been limited opportunities for promotion. For a number of reasons, however, it has become evident especially in the UK that promotions are increasingly difficult to secure: the decline in the economy springs immediately to mind but the situation has been aggravated by population factors – the children of the baby boom being ready for promotion at the time when the opportunities available to them had begun to shrink. As a result very few can see a clear promotion path ahead. This of course offers companies a much larger pool of talent on which they can draw for promotions providing that they chose to use the opportunity. Many do not. Since the issue of promotability tends to be sensitive many companies prefer to shed their talent rather than map out clear promotion paths. In addition, many use promotion selection procedures – seniority for example, or choosing as a first option an internal appointment – which severely limit their capacity to choose the best talent available. As a matter of efficiency it should be the case that where promotion occurs it should be to those people who are most valuable to the organisation as a whole, rather than a particular sectional interest.

Salaries and benefits

A second facet of the gap between employees' expectations and the firm's ability to meet them concerns salaries. The amount of money that a company can reasonably afford for salaries will also be limited and it is to its advantage to achieve the best rate of return to the investment made. While it may be comparatively easy to calculate an overall figure for salaries, how this is divided between groups and individuals within the firm can be extremely contentious particularly when it is linked with the notion of rate of return on the investment. A system which assessed this, when properly applied, could overturn traditional hierarchical reward structures. Yet in the area of salesforce management the system is hardly revolutionary in that a good sales representative can earn more than his manager when commissions and bonuses are taken into account. That personal merit will be recognised within the organisation, if promotion is not possible, by a degree of financial reward remains the key principle. The benefits may take the form of such management perks as company cars, subsidised health insurance and the like, rather than increased salary. It could also include foreign travel and training courses which are not normally regarded as classic 'fringe' benefits – except perhaps by the employee.

Indeed the development of non-financial rewards should be seen as a very important aspect of personnel planning, boosting the morale of the deserving employee. Where these operate, however, care should be taken to ensure that they are used in the proper manner. Many UK organisations, for example, operate a system of step increases within a fixed salary scale which is separate from the annual cost of living award. Frequently the rules require that the step increase is linked to job performance assessed via an annual job appraisal in the preceding year. In practice it is often only in very exceptional circumstances that the employee does not receive the annual step increase. The author has observed that those who do not deserve it by their job performance often tend to regard it as a length of service payment and on reaching the top of their salary scale begin to lobby for a continuation of annual step increments. Thus the system which could have been used to reward the good and exceptional workers, when no other perks and promotion prospects are available, serves to tell them that their performance is no better than average to below average.

8.2 Standardisation and Appraisal

The standardisation of an appraisal system will benefit on organisation by creating awareness of the short- and medium-term requirements of people and other resources. It may well reduce management and employee turnover levels. Though the research on this is fragmented there are indications that where formalised appraisal systems are in operation the level of employee turnover is diminished. On a practical level it is possible to see why this should be so. Individuals who are interviewed in depth at least once a year will have an opportunity to reveal at least part of their problems as well as their ambitions for the future. It departs from the mushroom principle often used by some firms as their main personnel tactic. This, for the uninitiated, is to keep everyone as much in the dark as possible occasionally opening the door to throw something unpleasant in.

The effective use of an efficient appraisal system which is continually searching for ways of improving the value of the personnel pool should also prevent the development of manpower stagnation which can often have serious effects on the long-term viability of the organisation. The failure, mentioned earlier, to map out a clear career/ promotion path for the more able will almost invariably mean that they will leave. The less able who remain tend to be promoted if seniority or internal appointment is the basis for the decision. Many of the problems of low performance in bureaucracies can be laid at the door of an unchanging personnel pool.

Properly applied, personnel analysis can determine job prospects (promotion or increasingly more relevant, redundancy) and the salary/benefit level of the employee. It should also increase the awareness about the employees' problems throughout the organisation. For example, it should encourage supervisors to take a more active interest in their subordinates: in how they can be encouraged and in how their performance can be improved by the sensible use of training schemes.

8.3 Appraisal Problems

As within other areas of management the operation of appraisal systems will tend to be subjective, for several reasons.

1. *Emotional reaction.* The personality of an individual will affect the assessment of his ability in his job. Frequently it is the informal structures in the work-place which can cloud the issue. Where, for example, working hours are flexible, a gregarious boss may think himself snubbed by a junior who is always at his or her desk before nine and after five especially if he or she also refuses to join the daily office gathering at the local pub because the party never breaks up until 2.30 p.m. The boss may well conclude that this behaviour indicates a less able worker instead of a more dedicated one because he will dislike the implication that his conduct suggests that he is less than fully devoted to his duties as a manager.
2. *Job content.* The nature of the job will vary often within very small areas of a firm's activity. For example, within the context of sales management, different sales representatives may have non-standard tasks such as training distributors and carrying out detailed promotional planning which others do not. The reaction of the individual salesforce members to this situation may vary greatly, some taking the view that it adds to the variety of the job; others that it costs time and money; still others will check whether the extra task is covered by their job description.
3. *Personal attitude.* Certain supervisors will tend to regard all their subordinates in a totally favourable light. Others might be wholly negative. Thus the same individual rated by the two extremes would receive differing evaluations.
4. *Policy effects.* The use to which the organisation puts the

appraisal system will obviously have a major influence on the nature of the process.

If the appraisal is being used primarily to determine the training needs of employees, negative aspects of performance may easily be magnified because there is no point in praise, as worthwhile aspects of the employees' performance will not be considered for training needs. These will be ticked-off on the list and most of the time will be spent concentrating on strengthening weakness. If salary is at stake, the positive will be expanded as negative findings will rebound in the supervisor's evaluation by senior management. The tendency will therefore always be towards the middle ground where the supervisor cannot be criticised by his superior for poor personnel management or asked to support the high ranking of a subordinate.

Furthermore the rights of the emploee to have access to the appraisal is a source of further limitations. The manager may also find it easier from the point of view of staff relations to simply provide the type of assessment required by the staff member. In such cases the appraisal becomes little more than a useless time-consuming part of annual management routine and there is a tendency for everyone to forget that the exercise costs money.

5. *Halo effect.* Within the actual assessment itself, the ranking of one characteristic can often influence another. Thus the employee will tend to be given more or less the same mark throughout the appraisal regardless of a possible variation in many areas of job performance.

8.4 Personnel Appraisal Techniques

Provided suitable allowance is made for them, the various methods used can still be valuable. The majority of the failings appear to be related to the inability of each supervisor to cope with a variety of personal reactions to the individual reporting to him or her, and the problems imposed by the standardised measurement of performance. These shortcomings can be seen in the variety of systems commonly used for job appraisals which are described next.

Employee comparison

Under this system the immediate supervisor of a particular department ranks staff in order according to their job performance and importance to the organisation, producing a division into the top, middle and bottom third. The problems encountered are that the method makes it impossible to compare across departments and does not identify clearly individual training needs – a fundamental requirement of any system of job analysis. The tendency to mark all staff equally can be overcome by specifying that they should be ranked in a particular way. This causes further problems in that those within the organisation will already be an atypical sample due to the selection procedure and any attempt to force a standard distribution onto a non-standard sample is unlikely to be successful.

Critical incident or attainment

In this system the main points of an employee's performance are measured either in an unstructured or structured fashion. For the unstructured approach each major decision/action is recorded together with a comment as to how the individual coped with the problem. With this approach the individual is assigned targets in each of the main areas of job activity. Achievement is then measured and compared with the goals set at the previous appraisal period. The advantage of this system is that it is highly attuned to the needs of the individual and can be very useful for identifying training requirements on a personal basis. As a method of salary assessment and for overall company manpower planning it poses certain problems. First, the tasks set will be extremely varied. Second, the fundamental strengths of the employee will tend to be ignored. Thus his performance in record keeping or his ability with foreign languages will be masked under the cloak of task-oriented target setting. Lastly the high performer or the unpopular employee will be given harder jobs than the others, again invalidating the testing procedure.

Check-list system

The use of a check-list containing a large number of statements
about the work can accurately measure the level of performance as
seen by the supervisor. Each job will contain a different specific
series of checks. In consequence the evaluation will again be
limited to the stated tasks and will also require a considerable
length of time to prepare.

Rating scales

This, the most commonly used appraisal system, assigns scores to a
number of qualities. For the production employee the attributes
could be items such as dependability, quantity and quality of work.
For the managerial grade the criteria could be decisiveness, attitude and creative ability. This method obviously suffers from the
defects mentioned elsewhere, the lack of objectivity of the supervisor, and whether a high score in one attribute can offset a low
one in another. If properly structured, it does offer an approach to
the standardisation of appraisal systems across a wide range of
managerial and non-managerial grades. It provides the ability to
break down widely differing jobs into common elements, determining the importance of these various elements, and then rating
each person on this basis

The group approach

The main hazard of most appraisal systems, the effect of one
individual on the evaluation of another, can be improved by the
introduction of a supervisory pool into appraisal systems. Here a
group of three supervisors each in charge of five or six individuals
would jointly appraise the 15 to 18 individuals beneath them.
Where employees have been appraised by a group system with a
supervisory pool evaluating all their subordinates, the anomalies
of personal assessment largely disappear and the training programme mapped out is often more imaginative than would otherwise be possible. This can only be developed as a company wide
method, however, if the performance evaluation is sufficiently
broad and comprehensive. It has other advantages to an organisation faced with a steady turnover in employees, as managers apart

from those with direct line responsibility will have a clear impression of the individual's skills and weaknesses, which will greatly strengthen the overall management team's awareness of personnel strengths. Such a system will also ensure that personal conflict between line manager and subordinate is reduced, as there will be a degree of external supervision on promotion prospects and re-grading exercises. For the subordinate it provides additional points of contact within the organisation for any grievance that may arise. It will also minimise the risks to the organisation from any accusation of constructive dismissal occurring when line managers over-step the grounds of disciplinary procedure.

8.5 The Job Description and Appraisal

A detailed job description has the advantage of providing an objective method for appraisal purposes.

Performance can be judged against the various criteria that have been laid down:

- Target achievement. Has the individual met the required targets both for callage and for volume laid down in the job description? How does his sales productivity compare with other individuals?
- Selling skills. Does the subordinate show the correct level of skills for the task? Are there gaps that need to be filled, such as product information?
- Record keeping/administration. Has the record keeping met the desired level of performance? Are there any shortfalls in vehicle maintenance or expense claim forms?
- Promotional activity. Does the individual show a full understanding and correct application of promotional techniques as required by the job description?
- Physical. Has the individual maintained the necessary standards as laid down in the company instructions? Has the performance been adequate, superior or excellent?

A grading system on the various aspects of the job can then be developed to show the highpoints and weaknesses of the individuals appraised:

Performance: Sub-standard   Average   Good

Skills:
Physical
Selling
Intelligence
Knowledge

Tasks:
Administration
Callage
Volume achievement
Promotion

This will clearly identify areas where further training is needed; will the sales representative require further practice at sales techniques; does administrative skills need further improvement and so on.

It is useful to generate a formal *short* report based on these findings to become part of the personnel record to be reviewed the following year to ensure that any remedial training that has been put in hand has proved satisfactory.

8.6 Implementation of the Appraisal

The importance of the employee to the organisation has already been stressed: the role of the manager in *managing* is often ignored. The lack of effective contact between line management and subordinates is starkly apparent in most organisations. Managers everywhere are prepared to spend weeks developing sophisticated plans and are often unwilling to spend the occasional hour to ensure that the human resources will be there to ensure their success in the long-term.

It is central to effective management that sufficient time is laid aside to develop the individual's skills in an effective way; to ensure that the individual is aware of how the firm regards him or her (positive features being far more important than negative) and what changes would need to be put into effect to meet the firm's requirements in areas of weaknesses.

It is in the interests of both the supervisor and the subordinate that areas of strengths and weaknesses are clearly identified in some form of documentation which should also include training needs and promotional prospects. Such procedures put the relationships on a firm footing and minimise likely problems that can arise if disciplinary procedures are necessary.

8.7 The Background to Discipline

Discipline can be defined as the procedure necessary to develop those forms of conduct that the company regards as highly desirable in order to achieve its objectives through improved job performance; it should not be seen as purely punitive.

Such considerations are emphasised in the Code of Practice that accompanied the UK Employment Protection Act of 1975:

In any undertaking management needs to use its resources efficiently, while employees look for continuity of employment, security of earnings and satisfaction in their work. Both have a common interest in the company's success because without it their aims cannot be achieved.

The Code gives guidelines as to how potential conflict should be minimised:

Management should ensure that fair and effective arrangements exist for dealing with disciplinary matters. There should be a formal procedure except in very small establishments where there is close personal contact between the employer and his employees.

According to the Code of Practice management should make known to each employee: its disciplinary rules and the agreed procedure: the type of circumstance that can lead to suspension or dismissal. The procedure should be in writing and should:

(a) specify who has the authority to take various forms of disciplinary action, and ensure that supervisors do not have the

power to dismiss without reference to more senior management;
(b) give the employee the opportunity to state his case and the right to be accompanied by his representative;
(c) provide for a right of appeal, wherever practicable, to a level of management not previously involved.

Where there has been misconduct, the disciplinary action to be taken will depend on the circumstances, the Code of Practice says, including the nature of the misconduct. But normally the procedure should operate as follows:

(a) the first step should be a verbal warning or in the case of more serious misconduct, a written warning setting out the circumstancces;
(b) no employee should be dismissed for a first breach of discipline except in the case of gross misconduct.
(c) action on any further misconduct, for example, final warning, suspension without pay or dismissal, should be recorded in writing; details of any disciplinary action should be given in writing to the employee.

Minimising conflict

Conflict can be minimised if the employee:

• is informed of the exact nature of the requirements of the job. This requirement will be fulfilled if the job description is detailed and precise;
• is given every opportunity to obtain the knowledge and develop the skills required in the job;
• is regularly informed of progress.

8.8   Disciplinary Problems

The entire range of disciplinary problems that a company may encounter is considerable but it is possible to identify the underlying causes.

• Lack of effort. The able individual who fails to succeed because of lack of application is a common feature of most organisations. It appears in various forms including for example the unwillingness to call on minor customers in out-of-the-way locations; poor administration and record-keeping. Close supervision is essential to improve performance: substandard administration may easily reflect the effects of sub-standard supervision.

- Lack of ability. Employees who fail to perform well through lack of knowledge or selling skills will need training; those who fail continually from lack of basic intelligence or aptitude will pose a far more serious problem for the organisation, requiring eventual dismissal.
- Alcoholism. The level of alcoholism in certain professional groups, including salesmen, is often considered to be higher than the general level in the population. Late starts on Monday mornings, and long lunch breaks are often held to be warning signs of incipient drink problems. Different companies have differing policies on alcoholism; for the salesforce continually on the road this will often need to be more rigorously enforced than for Head Office personnel.
- Psychological problems. A number of studies have shown that factors such as divorce, death of a spouse or close relation, and moving house, can cause considerable psychological problems such as depression or other neuroses. Often such incidents will put the company in a serious dilemma, as the job performance will be adversely affected over a long period. Some companies treat such issues as they would serious accidents; the employee is retained on sick pay until matters have improved. This provides the support the individual requires while accepting the reality for the company in that the individual is unable to perform effectively as would be the case if the representative had suffered a physical injury.
- Personality clashes. No employee be he manager or not is perfect, and it is a foolish system that expects perfection. There will be instances in all organisations where supervisors and subordinates clash over what most outside observers would consider to be mundane issues; because of the personal chemistry involved these can escalate into a war of nerves fought out at long distance by memo and telephone call. Discipline in this context is often self-defeating, as the individual is often highly competent in other aspects of job performance, and often

merely requires the transfer of the subordinate from one district to another.

8.9 Grievance Procedure

The possibilities of personality clashes especially when they involve two highly competent employees makes the existence of an appeals procedure which is clearly understood by staff to be particularly important. Regrettably in most companies the grievance and appeals procedures are almost always seen as a sham with senior management always supporting the view of junior management – the 'Them and Us' syndrome. The use of the appraisal panel system discussed earlier to arbitrate in disputes can have an effect in reducing employee reservations about an effective grievance procedure.

8.10 The Disciplinary Process

The various stages that make up the disciplinary ladder can be listed as:

- counselling;
- verbal warnings;
- written warnings;
- dismissal (or demotion).

Counselling

The initial step will be central to the training and discussion process to ensure that problems are identified early, and speedily corrected without creating a raised level of anxiety or animosity between the supervisor and the subordinate.

Verbal warnings

These should be given if the initial counselling sessions fail to achieve their required effect. They will be the first formal step in the disciplinary procedure, ensuring that the subordinate is aware of the standards required and what changes are necessary to achieve them. The existence of a verbal warning should be confirmed in writing to senior management as it may have future legal implications.

Written warnings

The reasons for all warnings should relate to a failure to meet the standards required for job performance. It should state clearly:

- the reason for it being given with specific details of the poor performance;
- the standards required for correct performance and how rapidly they should be achieved;
- the period during which the warning will be valid;
- the disciplinary action that will be taken if the job performance is not improved.

Dismissal

(a) Should the job performance continue to fail to meet the required standards after the process of counselling, oral and written warning, the organisation may feel that it has no alternative but to dismiss the individual.
(b) In certain instances, such as fraud or theft, the company may consider that it has grounds for immediate dismissal.

The legislation currently in force in the United Kingdom does, however, stipulate that an employee who is forced to resign or is dismissed by a manager acting unreasonably has suffered 'constructive dismissal' against which there are legal grounds for appeal under various employment acts.

Channel

Background

Tim Grange, sales director of Channel, a company specialising in the sale of electronic equipment for sailing boats, each
year received the annual job appraisals of salesforce members. Usually he glanced quickly through each appraisee's
report giving more detailed attention to the 'best' and 'worst'
achievers in each area manager's batch. This time around he
was concerned about seeming inconsistencies between the
'best' and 'worst' appraisals submitted by the area manager
for the south-west, Robert Crawley. Grange felt that the in-
congruities between the two reports were sufficiently important to arrange a special meeting with the area manager to
discuss the matter.

The two appraisal reports

In the batch of appraisals sent by Crawley to the sales director
he had selected Bernie Sands as his 'best' salesman and
Norbert LeBlanc as his 'worst'.

Bernie Sands' appraisal

Here is the appraisal of Bernie Sands' achievements as a
member of the Channel South-West salesforce in the year to
March 1982.

Target 81/2	Actual 81/2	%	Target 82/3
620 units	400	(50)	350
£150 000	£105 000	(45)	£98 000
1000 calls	820	(18)	850
20 000 miles	25 000	25	25 000
120 accounts	110	(10)	115
Expenses:			
£1500	£2000	33	£2000

Performance:	Poor	Average	High
Selling			x
Intelligence			x

Knowledge		x
Promotions		x
Physical		x

In the appraisal Bob Crawley stated that it had soon become apparent that the targets set for Bernie Sands for the year to March 1982 were unrealistic. The recession had hit parts of his territory – Devon and Cornwall – particularly badly and an estimated 25 per cent of his best and most loyal customers, mainly small racing yacht concerns, had either closed down or severely reduced their operations. Against this background, Sands' achievements of 70 per cent of the target set was a tribute to his outstanding selling skills and his dedication to Channel. He remained committed to the company and had not allowed the poor prospects in his territory to erode his morale.

Norbert LeBlanc's appraisal

Here is the appraisal of Norbert LeBlanc's achievements as a member of the Channel South-West salesforce in the year to March 1982.

Target 81/2	Actual 81/2	%	Target 82/3
700 units	920	30	1050
£220 000	£265 000	20	£300 000
1100 calls	1220	10	1200
15 000 miles	19 000	30	20 000
160 accounts	180	12	200
Expenses:			
£1500	£1000	(50)	£1000

Performance:	Poor	Average	High
Selling		x	
Intelligence		x	
Knowledge		x	
Promotions	x		
Physical	x		

On LeBlanc's appraisal Bob Crawley wrote that sales achievements in the territory – Dorset, Wiltshire and Hampshire – were largely due to the Channel Area Sales' Offices promotional efforts in fairly easily defined, compact, locations which were enthusiastic about boats. LeBlanc's territory included the Isle of Wight. At his appraisal LeBlanc had admitted having a somewhat negative attitude towards promotions and had offered no comment when it was proposed that he might benefit from an intensive re-orientation training course.

The meeting to discuss the appraisals

Tim Grange, the Channel sales director said that he was somewhat startled by the area manager's choice of the 'best' and 'worst' achiever's among his salesforce.

Crawley: Why?

Grange: Well, if you just assess these two men on the figures in your appraisal alone, that is on what they're achieving for the company, the situation should be reversed. LeBlanc seems more of an asset to the Channel than Sands: he's selling more, his callage patterns seem more effective and the mileage he puts in on behalf of the company seems well organised, and the benefit of that appears in his expenses – they're lower as you'd expect if a salesman is using his time effectively.

Crawley: But you can't go on figures alone that's the whole point about allowing managers to add comments to the appraisals. Bernie's been having a very difficult time and he's been marvellous about it – the distances he has had to travel are much greater in Devon and Cornwall and you can see he's been putting in more miles looking for business for us. That's why his expenses have gone up. He has also been extremely co-operative with the Area Office about promotions and has given us a lot of help with stands and the Cowes' week, and with surveys and so on. That's one reason why his callage rates have gone down. I can tell you he's done a lot to make the work of my office a lot easier.

LeBlanc on the other hand seems to have his own method of organising his travel. As he's always saying that he detests English food and thinks that its 'quaint' – that's his word, not mine – that people should like spending hours standing around drinking beer in a pub without food, he never spends a night away from home if he can help it. That's why his expenses are lower and he's lucky in having a territory which allows him to do that.

Grange: You say LeBlanc has a negative attitude towards promotions even though you believe that his area has benefited from them rather more than Sands has. Why are you so sure?

Crawley: Simply that we've had a much better response from customers in LeBlanc's area.

Grange: And LeBlanc from these appraisal figures is clearly succeeding in turning these leads into business for Channel. How does Sands' compare for the leads you have managed to generate through promotional activity?

Crawley: It really is very difficult to get a clear-cut figure for the sake of comparison. You know as well as I do how carried away people get at exhibitions. A lot of the time they're interested in our products but haven't got the money. Bernie's been doing his best, he hasn't given up on a lot of the leads. People are still interested but they're not ready to buy at this moment. I have spent a lot of time with him because of the problems and I have seen it quite clearly myself. Businesses in LeBlanc's territory seem to have a more optimistic outlook added to which he seems exceptionally astute at so enchanting secretaries that they see to it that the boss gives him every attention. He's French you know.

Grange: You don't feel that LeBlanc's attitude towards promotions and manning stands may be because he's now getting rather busy and I see that his targets for next year are substantially higher, Sands' interestingly are lower? Since the Area Office is in his territory he may well take the view that these matters can be left to them.

Crawley (hesitantly): I'm not entirely sure because he can cope with a lot of work – he's amazing in that respect. It could be that he feels out of place and I know that some of the other salesforce staff would prefer him not to be at exhibitions because he is disorganised and simply won't help to keep the stand looking tidy. You should see his car. Of course I have to make sure that he is aware of the important role of these events. But LeBlanc does stand out rather. He says pin-stripes remind him of school uniform and opts for lighter coloured, Continental style suits and his shirts range from Indonesian batik to crêpe de Chine. A lot of the time he prefers a blazer and trousers, a cravat instead of a tie. That's why I feel that he could benefit from some sort of re-orientation training. He always seems to be on the borderline of what is acceptable to Channel as regards appearance.

Grange: LeBlanc gets no extra help from sales support staff during promotions whereas I believe Sands does?

Crawley: There has been some confusion and disagreement about that in the past year but I have clarified the rules regarding that. LeBlanc had drawn attention to the discrepancy but the situation is that any support that he needs in this area will be given by the Area Office.

Grange: You're saying that the Area Office staff will provide support identical to that coming from sales support staff from an outside agency?

Crawley: 'Er no. Two entirely different forms of organisation are concerned requiring different inputs. In the case of Sands' area the job is relatively more simple because we can simply tell the sales support agency what we require. When it's the Area Office there's more of an element of bargaining between ourselves and LeBlanc. We have other things to do as well.

Grange: Let me just summarise the picture that is emerging. Sands' you say is your best achiever but is working in a stagnant or declining market. This made it difficult for him to achieve the past year's targets and those for next year reflects this. He is getting extra support in the form of increased expense allowances and extra sales support staff help during promotions. His involvement in promotional activity has reduced his callage record in the past year and you expect this to continue into the next year despite the sales support.

LeBlanc, your worst performer, owes his selling achievements mainly to the promotional activity provided by the Area Sales Office. He has exceeded the targets set for the year, selling more than twice the volume achieved by Sands despite his higher initial target. He has underspent on his expenses which will remain at the same level for the next year. Targets set for him for the next year all show significant increases. Should he need additional support this will come from the Area Sales Office and he will have to negotiate with you about the support he wants and gets.

Crawley: Yes, I think that is a fair summary.

Burrow's Toys

John Buckley the personnel manager at Burrow's Toys had just received the notice of the monthly meeting of Burrow's directors which also asked for items for the agenda. Buckley had not yet made up his mind whether he should ask for a discussion of the company's disciplinary procedure and the setting up of a working group to review its operation and consider alternatives. He was inclined to think that he could let the matter rest if a satisfactory solution could be found to the controversy currently surrounding salesforce member James Philips and Robert Brown, the sales and marketing manager.

Background

The first indication that anything was amiss had arrived three months earlier in the form of a letter to John Buckley from the branch secretary of the Association of Scientific, Technical, and Managerial Staffs (ASTMS). The letter stated that an ASTMS member had expressed serious and convincing doubts about the safety of the new 'Cuddly' novelty soft toy range. Enclosed with the letter was a copy of the sales promotion leaflet emphasising the Burrow's Toys reputation for manufacturing safe, quality toys. Buckley re-routed the letter to the director of marketing, Ben Hall.

Buckley's reaction to the letter was that it represented a recruitment ploy by the union. Over the past two years the ASTMS membership among the clerical, junior management and salesforce members had crept up slowly but steadily and the union was now within a stone's throw of the situation where the company would be legally obliged to recognise its right to negotiate on behalf of its members. Moreover, to those teetering on the brink of union membership the 'Cuddly' novelty soft toy range touched a sensitive nerve.

The 'Cuddly' range represented a fundamental change of direction for Burrow's Toys to which, as Buckley saw it, some of its employees had yet to adjust. It was the first of its new soft toy products to be entirely manufactured abroad. For some years the company had struggled to maintain its share of the quality soft toys market in competition with cheaper imported items with outdated plant and ever increasing costs in the UK. The same problems had not affected the Burrow's range of board games which had been manufactured in Hong Kong at a factory owned by the company. The contribution of games to overall company profits had increased as had market share since Burrow's had successfully introduced a number of very popular new board games and up-dated some of the older ones. The company had agonised over the path it should follow. Ben Hall, the marketing director, had successfully resisted arguments that the company should enter electronic games on the grounds that Burrow's had no experience in this area and that the market was fragile and cut-throat. When he was subsequently proved correct, Hall was able to carry through the proposal to close down the Burrow's UK manufacturing operations transferring them to Hong Kong thereby allowing the company to better exploit its growing markets in the Far East.

Reaction to the ASTMS Letter

A week after he had re-routed the ASTMS letter to the director of marketing, Buckley was somewhat surprised that Bob Brown, the sales and marketing manager asked him for a meeting to discuss the matter. At the beginning of the interview it became clear that Brown was extremely angry. He asked immediately whether James Philips, a senior member of the Burrow's national salesforce had anything to do with ASTMS.

Buckley: Can't say. As the union isn't recognised keeping a track record of who is and isn't a member hasn't been relevant. There's also the fact to consider that some fairly senior managers do not want it known that they are members of ASTMS. What I know from office gossip is that the union is only four or five recruits away from achieving bargaining rights. As for James Philips, I do know that he is a local big-wig of the Consumer's Association. His wife was telling me at the last office party that they test things out for the CA surveys. Anyway there's this on his file.

Buckley handed over a press cutting with the headline 'Working Together'. It showed the Burrow's managing director shaking hands with Philips after the latter had commended his company's record of service to the consumer at a Consumer's Association symposium which Philips had attended during his spare time.

Brown: Yes, I remember this and I know that at the time the MD wasn't too happy about Philips dragging his hobby into his work – blurring the lines was how he put it. I think you're going to have to speak to Philips.

Buckley: I'm only too pleased to help but you know you still haven't told me what this is all about.

Brown: Well it started a few weeks ago at the monthly salesforce meeting. This was the first after we'd handed out the promotional material and Cuddly sample. That was a good meeting all round. The salesforce were pleased that the range was getting substantial advertising, that we'd together tried to foresee and deal with the usual distribution bottlenecks, and for once they seemed to like the product. I always think that makes a lot of difference to the sales effort. There was a roomful of pretty hard types being amused by a soft toy with a lot of play potential: hair that grows, a tongue to pull out, a nose that can be squashed. We've spent a lot of money getting that product right. For once everything seemed to be looking up for an about turn with our soft toys and then at the next meeting along comes Philips and says that he doesn't think the product is safe; in a full meeting as well. Then he points to the promotion leaflet and says that it gives a misleading impression about safety.

Buckley: What did he say was wrong?

Brown: He said that a child could pull out, and swallow, the pop out eyes. They're mounted on a wire spring and if they are pulled off that would leave quite a piece of wire sharp enough to cut the skin. I countered that by saying that the eyes were made in exactly the same way as the Super Ted's, first produced some 20 years ago, and as far as we know there'd been no reported accidents. Philips replied that that was no reason to continue with something that was potentially harmful especially when people nowadays expected higher standards. Then he mentioned that if the fabric of the tongue absorbed even a little moisture, the dye ran and was it poisonous.

Philips has been here so long and is so highly regarded by his colleagues that his reservations completely altered their attitudes to the toy. I of course said that the toy had undergone fairly rigorous safety testing even to the point of being flame proof. At that point Philips intervened to say that he had thrown one of the samples on to a fire and that although it didn't catch light it did give out some very nasty fumes once the temperature got high enough. Was I prepared to say that those fumes were harmless.

I kept Philips back at the end of the meeting and told him that Burrow's were of the view that the Cuddly range was entirely in keeping with the company's high standards of quality and safety. I said that if he had any further doubts he should first raise the matter with me in person and that under no circumstances should he bring the matter up in the presence of third parties. I gave a verbal report of the meeting to Ben Hall and he fully supports my stand.

Buckley: Are you saying that Philips has ignored your advice? Legally we may act if it is 'more likely than not' that he disregarded it.

Brown: Well isn't it clear from that ASTMS letter that after my warning he is unwilling to let the matter rest. He really has to come to a decision whether his first duty is to his employer or to the Consumer's Association. I think that this is the line you should take with him. I have also prepared for you an outline of a reply to ASTMS. It basically reaffirms what I said at the salesforce meeting and since we're not answerable to them I don't think anything else should be said.

The interview with James Philips

Before meeting with James Philips, Buckley had tried to see the marketing director, Ben Hall to discuss the matter with him. The latter had been too busy. Instead he sent Buckley a memo saying that he had been fully briefed by Bob Brown and was entirely in agreement with the line taken by the sales and marketing manager.

The file on James Philips recorded that he was an exceptional employee and an excellent salesman. Over ten years, his job appraisal reports consistently showed him to be a star performer who was reliable, even-tempered and liked by everyone. If he had a fault it was that he took his job too seriously, was constantly trying to please and to improve his performance. Buckley asked Philips whether he regarded himself as a perfectionist.

Philips: I think that if I do a thing I should do it as well as I possibly can.

Buckley: Do you never find that being a perfectionist in one area might conflict with being a perfectionist in another. In other words that working with Burrow's might affect how you look at things for the Consumer's Association.

Philips: I've never found it so, until now that is, and I've been involved with both for about the same length of time. It's been very useful to Burrow's knowing what the CA people are thinking. If you doubt me go and ask Oliver Bird, the production manager. I always keep him abreast of any new thinking about materials and processes that we use and he always finds it very useful. He says I'm a mole. I don't think its ever occurred to him to say that I'm stepping beyond my job or being uppity.

Buckley: But you think that's how Bob Brown feels?

Philips: Well it is, isn't it. Otherwise I wouldn't be here today.

Buckley: Wouldn't you say that ignoring the advice of your manager about discussing the safety aspects of a toy range was being uppity?

Buckley handed the ASTMS letter to Philips.

Philips: I see. You think or at least you accept the view handed down to you that I am responsible for this letter because I raised the issue about consumer responsibility in the first place. Take a look at my file and then do your worst!

Epilogue

Shortly afterwards Burrow's Toys was obliged to grant negotiating rights to ASTMS. Buckley subsequently received a
request from the union that the disciplinary procedure should
be reviewed. Complaints had again arisen that the existing
procedure was not impartial as it was biased in favour of the
line manager. ASTMS cited the case of James Philips a
salesforce member with an exceptional record. Steps to discipline him had been initiated on the unfounded suspicion of
the line manager concerned that he had acted contrary to
given instructions against the best interests of the company.
The union could prove that the safety aspects of the Cuddly
soft toy range had been brought to its attention by another
member of the salesforce. At the time that the letter was
written Philips had not been a member of ASTMS but he had
subsequently joined the union.

ASTMS demanded that Philips should receive an apology
from both the director of marketing and the sales and marketing manager.

Defining Sales Structures 9

The structure of any organisation must be closely related to the goals that it is trying to achieve: this is especially relevant to the salesforce that is one of the prime executive arms of the firm. Its activities should be reflected in the way that the salesforce is organised, in the quality of the salesman employed and in the way in which his work-load is organised.

9.1 Reconciling Tasks and Objectives

In examining the diversity of tasks confronting a salesforce it becomes apparent that the work-load and the strategic objectives of the organisation can differ considerably between one type of company and another:

1. salesforce involved in physical delivery such as the van sales-men of frozen food for example;
2. salesforce mainly acting as a repeat order taker – for example, sales staff in shops or sales representatives for chocolate firms calling on small retail outlets;
3. salesforce acting as a 'persuader' – influencing potential pur-chasers but not taking an order. Illustrations are technical representatives for government contracts, pharmaceutical com-panies' representatives calling on doctors;

4. salesforce acting to secure initial non-repeat orders as in computers, cars, double glazing, insurance.

Although there will be variation in the actual tasks associated with the job, and in the level of expertise of the sales representative the issues faced by each firm will be remarkably similar:

- how should the salesforce be organised to be most effective – management considerations?
- how many salesmen will be needed to effectively fulfil the defined task – work-load considerations?

9.2 Effective Organisation

To survive, all forms of social organisation must adapt to changing environments and circumstances. As the firm grows, there will be an increasing need for formal structures to cope with the larger number of people working within the firm otherwise employees will lack a sense of direction and become uncertain about what exactly they are trying to achieve. At the same time there is the danger that formal structures become an end in themselves causing managers to believe that reorganisations alone will solve any problem. This often leads to the development of frameworks that do not function effectively.

Ideally, the organisation should have taken account of a number of factors.

1. Its structure should reflect market conditions.
2. The firm should concentrate on the channelling of activity towards the actions that it wants, and not the individuals that it employs, to ensure that the long-term stability achieved is not dependent on the individuals filling certain roles.
3. Responsibility and authority should be closely related. In other words if an individual is expected to achieve a given task he must be allowed the authority to carry it out. For example, if a sales area is set up as a profit centre, the manager will be expected to achieve a certain profit level – in return he will need the authority to take decisions about pricing and manpower levels.
4. The extent of executive control should be reasonable. The

number of people that any individual can supervise will naturally be an amalgam of the variety and complexity of the task, the nature of their physical separation, and the level of training that is required. Effective supervision of routine work on the shopfloor will obviously make considerably different supervisory demands than the management of a field salesforce. Commonly in the United Kingdom the sales manager will be supervising six sales representatives. Complicated, or highly technical products, widely spread sales territories, or a large number of new sales representatives may increase – or diminish – the extent of control that is necessary. In addition, the number of levels in the hierarchy can have an important influence on the flexibility and possible speed of change within the organisation.

5. The organisation should attempt to achieve the maximum flexibility within the constraints of the formal structure.

Organisational considerations and the salesforce

Fundamental to the effective implementation of these structural concepts regarding salesforce management is how the task is divided into manageable proportions. This is commonly regarded as the first step in a systematic approach to salesforce organisation and a number of authors identify a series of discrete steps.[1]

1. Determine the control unit. How should the sales area be measured – by county; province; trading area (major town and surrounding area)?
2. Analyse work-loads. This encompasses the effects of the actual sales job; the product type; the distribution channels – wholesalers or retailers; strategic considerations – whether or not the organisation is prepared to invest in extensive market coverage; and competitive activity.
3. Determine basic territories. This is achieved either by 'building up' from current and prospective customers, determining callage patterns and from there matching the work-load factor derived in item (2); or by a 'breakdown' method which divides the market so that each sales representative will have the same potential cutomer base and then consider the physical problems

that this can produce – for example, distances that need to be travelled in rural areas compared with urban areas.

4. Assign representatives to territories. Management has to take account of regional problems and the skills of the individual to ensure that there is the best possible match between individual and area.
5. Determining nature of the callage cycle. Consider how frequently accounts should be called upon, and whether the firm should route the salesforce rigidly.
6. Revise sales territories if initial objectives are not being achieved.

Normally, the salesforce functions within the confines of an organisational structure which will have line authority down from the sales director to the sales representative. In small firms this may consist of the owner or managing director being directly in contact with the salesforce. As the organisation becomes more complex other departments within the firm will start to have an influence on the sales department, notably accounts and marketing, in a staff capacity, with no direct authority over the salesforce. A third approach is team management with a group of executives having responsibility over the salesforce for their particular discipline (see Figure 9.1). In large organisations the line and staff structure is most commonly found, as team management where tried has been generally unsatisfactory owing to the conflicting claims of various management groups.

9.3 Work-load Factors

The reality of salesforce management has little if any relevance to this academic consideration of structural and organisational efficiency. Companies first consider how they are going to reach their required customers. This will lead them to certain conclusions about the physical nature of the sales organisation that they create. The next step is to consider elements of work loading either in a systematic or more commonly an *ad hoc* basis to arrive at the total numbers required within the sales organisation.

FIGURE 9.1
Various approaches to sales management structures

(A) Line responsibility

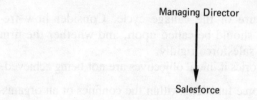

(B) Line and staff responsibility

(C) Group responsibility

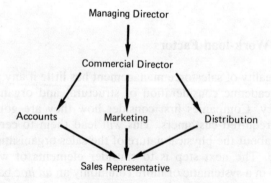

Geographical divisions

This was the traditional method of salesforce organisation. The sales representative was allocated a territory and was responsible for all selling functions within that area, reporting to a territorially based sales manager. Such a structure:

- minimises cost by reducing travel time;
- provides a method of concentrating sales effort throughout an area;
- enables the company to respond to regional needs and develop local knowledge;
- provides an easily understandable method of control over achievement and profit.

However, there are drawbacks to this approach:

- it reduces the level of specialised knowledge that the sales representative will have, requiring him or her to handle all the company's products to all the company's customers;
- it may create a conflict of loyalties in long established sales representatives taking the 'side' of the local community against the company;
- it may restrict the company's development as representatives may not plan their work-load to coincide with the company objectives calling more frequently on the easier accounts.

Product divisions

When a company such as a wholesaler, for example, has either a wide range of products or a number of unrelated ones, the division of the salesforce can be on a product basis, with two or more sales representatives covering the same area with responsibility for different lines.
Such a system has the following advantages:

- that the sales representative's product knowledge is likely to be substantially greater;
- that the company can direct the salesforce more accurately by determining the product ranges that will be handled.

However the disadvantages are considerable:

- it will increase the distances that have to be covered inevitably causing costs to rise, and will need a higher level of both supervision and administration;
- it will decrease the knowledge that the salesforce will have of each individual customer;
- two or more sales representatives from the same company may be calling on the same individual buyer often causing confusion, as the buyer is unlikely to perceive the same neat divisions between products that drove the company to introduce the scheme.

Customer divisions

Here the salesforce is organised on the basis that each industrial or retail sector has specific problems that require specific solutions. This is the 'systems' approach, particularly appropriate with: clearly identifiable customer groups; reasonable geographic concentration; complicated equipment; and a management philosophy that emphasises problem solving rather than the sale of specific product.

ICL, the computer company for example, divides its sales organisation into specific categories with specific problems – health, defence, education, office services, and so on.

The advantages of this system are that:

- it enables the company to provide a very effective service to the customer by developing an understanding of their problems;
- it can eliminate conflict between product areas – the representative will be selling the entire range of items to the customer such as a hospital;
- it can provide a more rapid information service about competitive change;
- the salesforce can be more easily integrated into specific promotional activity.

Disadvantages largely centre around the area of cost. As the salesforce in these areas will need to be highly trained their expense will be considerable.

National account division

There is an increasing trend towards industrial concentration in all
major sectors.

Number of firms holding 50 per cent of total assets in the sector:

	End 1957	End 1967	End 1986
Drink	12	4	3
Wholesaling	21	14	3
Clothing	3	1	1
Textiles	8	3	3
Retailing	6	6	3

Such considerations have suggested to a growing number of firms
that they should develop a major or national accounts department
that deals with the majority of the firm's business, integrating
sales, promotional, marketing, manufacturing and financial considerations.

The advantages of such a system are that the major accounts
receive detailed treatment – all elements of the company can be
involved in the decision-making process. The disadvantage is that
the system is costly, and that the sales representatives outside the
national accounts department can resent the attention that is given
to them. In addition the development of a specialised national
accounts department may reduce salesforce mobility – national
accounts personnel cannot be transferred to 'field' nor vice versa.
Some of the problems that this creates can be overcome by
allowing the individual sales representative or sales manager to
handle regional major accounts, enabling a pool of expertise to be
developed to handle the problems of negotiating with major
accounts.

9.4 Approaches to Estimating Work-load

When approaching the problem of work-load it is necessary to first
clarify the exact nature of the work. Second, there will be – in
common with many management problems – difficulty in obtaining
adequate historic data to evaluate the relationship between salesforce numbers and performance.

Intuitive approach

Because of the difficulties in data acquisition and evaluation, many firms base their salesforce numbers by comparison with the numbers employed by competitors or as a result of the qualitative sales strategy adopted by the firm. This would build up the workload from the job description and percentage of time spent on various activities, and together with an overall evaluation of the market potential determine the ideal level of sales representation. This level is then qualified by the financial resources of the firm.

Sales productivity approach[2]

In this approach the total gross profit on the sales for a given area minus the costs of attaining them is combined with the area's potential as a percentage of the total. Dividing the one by the other gives a figure of sales value by percentage potential.

$$\frac{\text{Net profit}}{\text{Percentage total potential}} = X$$

For example the greatest sales would occur with 100 salesmen each dealing with 1 per cent of the total. However, the net profit figure would be lower and in consequence X would be worse. With a number of points on a graph, the firm will be able to derive the optimal salesforce loading (Figure 9.2).

This method will provide a reasonable management overview where potential can be accurately measured and the sales territories are homogeneous, as it is rapid and easy to calculate. If these conditions are not met (for example a geographical concentration of major accounts), problems will arise. Obviously, the nature of the market potential will always be judgemental – is the entirety of the market open to the firm?

Contribution to operating margin (COM)

The profitability approach has been further developed into a concept of 'operating margin' by certain authors.[3]

COM = Gross margin − selling expenses.

FIGURE 9.2

Sales productivity: optimum profitability analysis

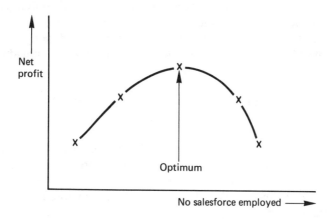

This of course is identical to net profit except that Head Office overheads have not been included. The optimisation process that is then envisaged concentrates not on total market potential but on corporate potential within that market.

$$Z = \frac{(pw)}{m^*n^*f^*\,(nn) - cn}$$

m = profit margin per unit,
n = number in salesforce,
c = cost per salesforce,
p = total company potential,
w = total company work-load,
Z = variable to be optimised.

The accuracy of this system makes similar demands on the sophistication of data that is available, for unless the data is reasonably accurate it is unlikely that the results of the evaluation will give a clear indication of salesforce numbers.

Evaluating work-load[4]

This approach concentrates on grouping customers on the basis of annual sales volume and determining the length of time that each will demand annually for the determined level of service. The total number of calls divided by the average number of calls per year for the salesforce will determine the total number of individuals required to service the total area.

$$\frac{\text{Total number of callage hours}}{\text{Normal work-load}} = N$$

This approach cannot allow the established company to fine tune the salesforce levels, because of the circular arguments that are built into such an evaluation. It is useful for a new venture to rapidly determine the likely level of salesforce required for market penetration at the required level of service.

Sales effort

An approach which relies on the studying of changing distribution effects[5] has been suggested as taking most account of the personal effort involved in the selling process.

$$T = Xc\ Nc + Xh\ Nh$$

T = time available for sales effort,
Xc = optimal sales effort to achieve conversion,
Xh = optimal sales effort to maintain customer base,
Nc = number of new accounts per individual,
Nh = number of current accounts.

The values of Xc and Xh can be obtained from:

$$Nc\ \text{Pr}(C) = \text{Pr}(H)Nh$$

$\text{Pr}(C)$ = probability of conversion with optimal sales effort,
$\text{Pr}(H)$ = probability of maintaining current customers with optimal sales effort.

Practical sales management considerations would make the implementation of such an approach impossible demanding as it does changes in the level of attention that customers receive and the size of the salesforce.

Simulation systems

In common with other management problems a simulation of salesforce levels can be carried out in relation to a number of factors:

1. number of sales calls made;
2. sales potential;
3. number of customers;
4. level of training;
5. sales achievement;
6. geographical concentration or otherwise of the sales territories.

Using computer modelling techniques the effects of changes in various levels of service can be determined. Currently such simulation systems are preserves of large companies but it is inevitable that commercially available computer software packages will be shortly available that will make such simulation approaches more widely applicable.

'Callplan'

This approach which again demands computerisation for its fullest implementation considers the marginal return on either additional effort or additional salesforce (Figure 9.3).

1. A decision is taken as to how many calls should be made on each account and prospect in order to achieve maximum profit contribution.
2. From that assessment an analysis of what could happen if time was either added to or taken away from the territory can be generated. There will be a point where increasing time spent lowers the marginal contribution per hour.
3. If the time planned to be spent in the territory produces the best marginal contribution then the analysis will be complete, if not, not.

184

FIGURE 9.3
'Callplan' approach

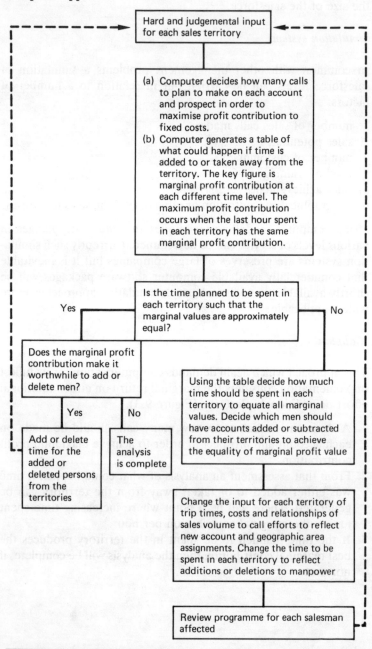

4. Management can decide to either increase the numbers of salesforce or to change the work-load on a territory by territory basis and then rework the calculations.

The advantages of this approach are those of simulation models with the additional benefits:

1. it provides a method of integrating profitability with costs and investment;
2. it is simple and direct in its approach, usable for the vast range of companies with different sales problems;[6]
3. it attempts to deal with the difficulty of lack of data by requiring assumptions to be built into the analysis, thus speeding up the entire evaluation process.

Naturally any system that demands the making of assumptions about the likely level of sales performance and the possible contribution of new accounts will always produce results that will not be wholly accurate. Nevertheless the role of models should be to aid the manager towards reducing the areas of uncertainty and not to eliminate totally the need for judgement in any area.

Return on time invested (ROTI)

A technique available for the analysis of callage patterns of established salesforces is the return on time invested.[7]

This divides accounts on the basis of time spent and profit achieved into those that produce high ROTI, medium ROTI and low ROTI. The calculations are simple and straightforward:

CPCH = DC/CH.
BEV = DC/GMP
ROTI = GM/CTI
BEV/CHR = GPCH/GMP
CPCH = cost per call hour,
DC = direct costs,
BEV = break even volume,
GMP = gross margin percentage,
GM = gross margin on sales obtained,
CTI = cost of time invested,
ROTI = return on time invested.

Analysing accounts in this fashion may produce valuable pointers as to the real underlying relationship between the company and the buying organisation. Thus many sales organisations will rank calls on the basis of potential, without considering whether the potential is realisable or not. What this system does is to concentrate the sales management on those accounts that are *actually* generating money for the organisation. By annually evaluating each account in this fashion, a far greater control over the level of salesforce investment and return to the organisation can be achieved.

HandyMan Ltd

Background

Larry Smythe, the Midlands area manager of HandyMan Ltd, was examining the possibility of recommending the replacement of the company's existing policy of allocating sales territories on a geographical basis in his area. He was instead considering the potential in reorganising the salesforce either by product type or category of customer.

A family-owned maker of hand-tools founded at the end of the nineteenth century, HandyMan Ltd had been taken over some two years earlier by Webber and Blackitt – one of Europe's largest industrial hand-tool manufacturers. The group had previously allowed HandyMan to retain its autonomous salesforce but spiralling costs was leading it to reappraise the situation with the help of area managers like Larry Smythe. The area managers as well as senior management were being asked to seriously examine the current organisation of their salesforces with a view to maximising efficiency and cutting costs wherever possible. In his brief to the group's salesforce managers the Webber and Blackitt sales director also suggested that in considering the possibilities for improving sales performance through a reorganisation of the salesforce, they should also give thought to the proposal that what the group needed was a single salesforce, finance department and managing director and common production control. He proceeded to ask the area managers of the operating companies to look at the possibilities of integration of the company's product range in their particular areas and what problems or opportunities would arise.

Webber and Blackitt and the Hand-tool Industry

For a decade beginning in 1960 Webber and Blackitt had experienced a period of phenomenal and acquisitive growth. During that time it acquired control of various companies producing files, spanners and wrenches, precision measuring tools, and pliers. Its manufacturing output is currently about

155 million items across 3500 product lines with certain specific areas of strength:

(1) *Hand-tools*. These included saws and saw blades, punches and magnets, nippers and files, spanners and wrenches.
(2) *Measurement tools*. Micrometers and chucks.
(3) *Hydraulics*. Jacks and hydraulic conveyor belts.

Strategy

The company had not been over-concerned with plant modernisation and until quite recently production of hacksaw blades was so backward that they had to be hand moved from machine to machine eight times and hand shuffled on five other occasions. For the previous five years turnover (apart from acquisitions) in the UK had remained at about £50 million. Of this £36 million came from hand and torque tools, £5 million from measurement tools with the rest coming from welding rods, cutting wire, hydraulic tube coupling and magnets.

Webber and Blackitt had also stuck to its old customer base – the engineering industry selling products without a brand name across its range. Of the total UK hand-tool market, including agricultural needs, imports had grown from 27 per cent in 1973 to 47 per cent in 1980. Webber had similarly seen its share of the files market eroded by Portuguese imports to about 25 per cent.

A halving of the Webber and Blackitt work-force formed part of a programme of cost-cutting, rationalisation, and modernisation initiated in 1980. Sales per employee, estimated at £25 000, however remained at half of that of some of its foreign competitors. The product range was under investigation and it was inevitable that major changes would take place especially in the rationalisation of the number of lines produced.

HandyMan

HandyMan had seen its slice of the British spanner sector eroded from 30 per cent to 16 per cent by 1980. The company also made wrenches, pliers and precision tools and acted as distributors for a substantial part of the parent company's product range.

In the Midlands, Larry Smythe's salesforce sold products to four types of customers: engineering contractors, engineering distributors, small specialist shops and DIY superstores.

Engineering distributors

Engineering tool distributors, the company's traditional major market, now accounted for 35 per cent of sales giving Handy-Man access to what had in the past been large industrial markets. Purchasing agents for these customers usually ordered equipment directly from the salesman assigned to that customer. Since HandyMan had become part of Webber and Blackitt and handled the distribution of some of its products the task confronting the sales representative dealing with engineering tool distributors had grown to marathon proportions. Some 500 product lines were now involved. In the area of specialised machine tools especially in the hydraulic sector, a substantial level of technical knowledge was required. Handy-Man management were increasingly concerned about where this steady increase in product range was likely to lead.

Engineering contractors

Engineering contractors, another important market in the past, accounted for another 20 per cent of HandyMan sales. The size of engineering contractors operations had decreased substantially over the past decade. They were now mainly small organisations run by self-employed individuals who provided work for perhaps one or two others. Because of their small size, the contractors were often very difficult to contact. Despite this, selling to them also required a good level of technical expertise.

The importance of the engineering tool distributors and engineering contractors as customers had begun to alter. Sales to them of highly specialised equipment remained stable. But their share of sales in other product areas had begun to decline. In the case of specialised tools they were mainly concerned with the quality of the HandyMan products, particularly reliability and durability. In the past, the price overall of the products bought by them had not been a major issue. As customers, they would continue to require the services of sales staff able to handle technical information.

Specialist shops

Diverse, independent, local stores throughout the area provided another most important market accounting for about 30 per cent of the total volume. The shops varied substantially in their interests – some were builders' suppliers, others were general hardware shops giving a small amount of space to hand-tools, still others were do-it-yourself operations and there were one or two specialist shops. These outlets typically also stocked competitors' products and were generally interested only in a comparatively limited range of items – their requirements being quite different from those of the engineering specialists: spanners, pliers, saws. As customers they did not demand a high level of expertise from the sales representative but were concerned about other matters. There was an increased awareness about price and sales staff were finding that where there was a significant price difference between a HandyMan product and that of the competition, the retailer would opt for the latter particularly if the shelf-space available was limited. Retailers were generally reluctant to give shelf-space to any new brand especially if it was not supported by advertising. They complained that the recent introduction of brand names by Webber and Blackitt and the streamlined packaging, unsupported by advertising, had only served to confuse customers.

DIY Superstores

About 15 per cent of HandyMan's sales in the area was with two DIY Superstores. Their share of sales in a number of product areas was increasing at 5 per cent a year.

It had become increasingly clear to the West Midlands salesforce that increasingly the engineering contractors were buying tools from these two DIY Superstores. HandyMan's competitors had already established a strong presence in these outlets. However, the extensive HandyMan and Webber and Blackitt range provided good bargaining counters when dealing with the stores' buyers. The group could offer products which did not overlap substantially with those of competitors.

Major engineering outlets

Traditionally HandyMan had not sold direct to major engineering customers relying on the distributors to provide this service. Increasingly a number of major firms particularly in the motor manufacturing sector were buying direct and bypassing the classical distribution systems. This could become a major problem if more of the highly technical Webber and Blackitt range was handled by the HandyMan salesforce.

Salesforce Personnel

The HandyMan salesforce in the West Midlands area were currently geographically assigned. There were eight salesmen and one area sales manager, Larry Smythe.

Over the years Smythe had consistently pressed management with the problems of the growing DIY sector and the changing purchasing pattern of the major engineering works. Previously he had been the most productive and far-sighted salesman. He had managed to get the two DIY superstores to open accounts with HandyMan and his good technical knowledge of the company's products had helped to maintain the level of specialised equipment sold to industrial customers and develop close links with contractors.

Basil Home, Smythe's most senior sales representative also thought that there were greater opportunities for Handy-Man products in retail outlets, superstores in particular, than the salesforce realised. His area included the medium sized supermarkets and DIY stores bordering on housing estates. He had discovered that retailers were increasingly responsive to lower prices as a major influence on stockturn and was optimistic about the future. He had worked for HandyMan for over eight years and had moved territory twice within the West Midlands area.

Dennis Skinner's inner city territory was dominated by small retail shops which had been hard hit by the recession. To survive some had been forced into offering special trade price deals to contractors and Skinner found himself occasionally competing with the retailers for business from the contractors. The whole area itself was in decline, although there was talk of a special development programme. As a relative newcomer to HandyMan, young Skinner found his task a tough one.

The territory of Desmond Wilkins was a mainly rural one and his customers had changed little over the seven years he had worked for HandyMan, though Larry had tried several times to make him more active in other sectors. Self-employed contractors remained the bulk of his customers. Large amounts of his time was spent travelling as a result and his expenses were high. Many of the major engineering works had relocated themselves in Desmond's area but he had been unable to make any progress with them.

Before becoming a salesman, John Eliot had worked as an engineering distributor in his allocated sales area having been a good customer of HandyMan in those times. A significant part of his sales were to friends and contacts he had established earlier in his career. He was openly contemptuous of the move towards selling to the retail sector which he regarded as selling shoddy goods.

James Grant had been very successful in developing the industrial engineering customer base in his territory. His technical expertise was often commented on by major customers including the army ordnance factory with which he had started to build up business.

Nigel Conradi had on many occasions just failed to win national sales competitions. He had aggressively built up his territory sales particularly to the retail sector and the large DIY superstore that had become established in his area.

Alessia Brown had recently joined the salesforce from the parent company. She was part of the management training scheme in operation at Blackitt and Webber which had recently been introduced by the new personnel director. Development of other sales expertise after a successful stint selling complex hydraulic equipment in the south of England to major clients was seen as a preliminary step to sales management.

Salesforce Organisation

Larry Smythe considered three different organisational plans. First, a specific geographical territory would be assigned to each salesman, with the salesman in each territory being responsible for the entire range of HandyMan products and other products of the Blackitt range. Larry thought that this would cut down journey time and improve representatives' knowledge of the area. It would demand a considerable amount of retraining and increased product knowledge.

Plan 2 involved the specialisation by customer type. Two salesmen would cover all the retail stores, two to contractors and two to industrial outlets, with a geographical division within the product specialisation. Some Blackitt tools could be included also in this reorganisation.

Plan 3 involved specialisation by type of product divided into hand-tools, measuring equipment and the hydraulic sector. This would have the advantage that the salesmen would be able to concentrate on the new range of Blackitt products that would be introduced.

Larry was also concerned that the changing nature of the products and customers might necessitate the development of a national or major accounts function. This had not initially appeared as part of his brief and he wondered what the implications within the rest of the Blackitt and Webber organisation might be if he put forward this as another avenue of possible development.

Sales Budgets and Forecasting 10

Central to the design of productive salesforce structures and control over costs and profits is the generation of accurate predictions or forecasts of the likely trends in the business environment in which the firm will be operating.

The development of forecasts is rightly regarded as one of the most difficult aspects of the business manager's job, particularly in a climate which is rapidly changing. Thus in the hypothetical environment of one company selling, to one end user, one product with no competition or other variation in the environment, the problems of forecasting are largely minimised. In this situation the firm will be able to ask the end user what the likely demand for the particular product will be: indeed the supplier may easily be able to enter into a contract with this single customer which to all intents and purposes will remove all the uncertainty in the business plan as the supplier will know the quantity, the price, when the goods should be delivered, and when they will be paid for. At the other extreme is the company facing rapidly changing political, economic, legal conditions, and having to cope with continuing alterations in technology and the customer base. Consider for example, the problems faced by a firm in the electronics sector protected for many years by tariff barriers. These happen to be removed following a change in government and subsequently the firm has to compete with manufacturers several generations ahead in the application of technology. All the assumptions on which the business had been based would have to alter to enable it to cope with the dramatic change in its circumstances.

10.1 Two Key Issues

One can isolate two key issues that confront management when examining the future plans of the company:

1. the level of uncertainty (or risk); and
2. the potential return if the forecast is accurate (the level of reward).

The level of the firm's investment in forecasting techniques will depend heavily on assumptions related to these two factors – low levels of risk and/or reward will mean that little investment will be required, and where the survival of the organisation is at stake considerable time and care will need to be taken in the forecasting process. If we return for a moment to the two contrasting companies mentioned earlier, it is fairly clear that for the second definition of how the market will develop will be crucial; for the first it is largely unnecessary.

10.2 The Need for a Structured Approach

In common with many other activities the use of a structured approach will ensure that where gaps or weaknesses exist, they will at least be identified and the shortfalls of the process or system realised and allowed for.

The following steps must be considered in any forecasting system:

1. Identifying the forecasting problem. A key question relates to the importance of the forecast to the organisation and the level of the resources involved. From this it will be possible to develop an evaluation of the cost/benefit of various approaches including the problems of data collection.
2. Forecast structure. This will show how various elements of the forecasting system interact as well as identifying whether data has to be collected to fill in gaps – the commissioning of market research for example. Another important decision will be the

FIGURE 10.1
The interaction of cost and accuracy: various forecasting systems

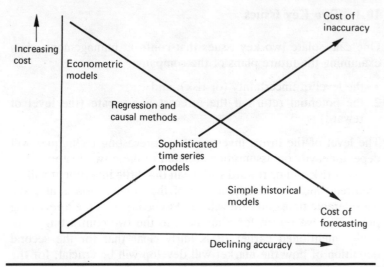

cost of the forecasting technique necessary to produce accurate results, balanced against the level of investment hanging on the decision. This can be summarised diagrammatically (Figure 10.1).

3. Collecting the data.
4. Model construction and analysis. The main important factor in any data evaluation is that a predetermined hypothesis should be tested against the available data, and not that the data is tested for possible correlations, as this will tend to produce numerous spurious interrelationships.
5. Preparing the forecast. The assumptions underlying the forecast can now be checked against a 'reasonableness' test – whether the data is within the bounds expected.
6. Evaluation of the forecast. The accuracy of the forecast will need to be updated on a regular basis and should the estimates differ significantly from the actual, the forecasting system should be re-evaluated.

Though forecasting will be a difficult exercise the more accurate the picture that is obtained the smaller the area of uncertainty that the business will face. The forecasts will aim to reduce the risk element through a system bounded by knowledge controlling success and failure.

10.3   Handling the Less Predictable

The broad areas which can impinge on the business are quite often those over which the organisation has no control and in consequence has not developed sufficient expertise to evaluate. These problems will include political, economic and technological factors the impact of which has already been described in one limited case.

These general issues need to be resolved before detailed 'number crunching' – the building up of the page after page of numbers that the modern large business requires. These can be separated into political, economic, and technological.

Political

The extent of the political problem will naturally vary from company to company. For a firm engaged in the aerospace business, the nature of the conflict between East and West will be of overriding importance in determining the growth in demand. In recent years, however, the operation of a high technology embargo on East-West trade has restricted the activities of Western computer and even construction companies. On a more mundane level, is the case where a change in formula by a leading UK detergent manufacturer eliminated the protection from skin irritation given by the old product formula to eczema sufferers. The result was an outcry from various interest groups and politicians leading to the reinstatement of the old product.

The political equation becomes relatively even more important when the company ventures outside its home base. The problems that firms can face are as complex as they are numerous ranging from the general attitudes of governments towards investment by foreigners to specific regulations about products. In a number of countries difficulties may extend from straightforward sequestration of assets to the restricted ability to expand or remit profits. In others like the People's Republic of China special taxes on foreign investors may increase the already high cost of maintaining the export operation; still others may simply change the method of calculating the country of origin.

Economic

The basic economic problems that the firm faces will also vary. Where an organisation is actively involved in overseas trade the movement of the exchange rates over time will be vital, especially where the ability to raise prices is limited. The level of inflation is of general importance to all firms but especially to those which are subject to an overall policy of price control. The level of interest rates will have extremely important implications not only for its effects on demand but also for its effect on the firm's finances including its ability to borrow, so that forecasting changes in this can have important implications in two spheres of company activity.

These major or macroeconomic trends have proved practically impossible for governments let alone small to medium sized firms to determine. There is always dispute, for example, about future levels of inflation and overall economic growth. In recent years the issue has become something of a game: the government releases its own predictions which triggers off competing views from the models favoured by other prestigious institutions. Despite their efforts the exact interaction of the amount of money in circulation and the level of price rises remains uncertain.

Technology

The impact of technology is another area that historically has eluded prediction. There are several examples of conferences of 'futurist experts' coming up with a practically blank sheet of success, predicting the arrival of the currently impossible (anti-gravity, commercial nuclear fusion) while omitting the attainable (hovercraft, lasers). In common with major political and economic factors, all that the overall consideration of the impact of major technological change can do is to set a series of broad limits to any forecast.

While it may be impossible to foresee the technological future there are dimensions of the issue that are less unpredictable and worthy of consideration. How quickly, for example, are other countries entering the high technology market? Will their products be more advanced or competitive in terms of price, quality, quantity?

The area of uncertainty will widen as the time horizon lengthens. Thus the impact of the 256k silicon chip on the computer industry can perhaps be predicted with some degree of accuracy. Looking forward two or three years, the introduction of the one megabyte chip will surely introduce entirely new problems and opportunities each with their influences on demand.

It is therefore possible to develop a series of ground rules for the credibility that can be placed on any eventual trend that can be established from the most simple to the most complex. The key is in the simplicity of the information and the degree to which the data bears a steady relationship to other factors. Taking our example of the single product sold to a single end-user the buyer will obviously be the best source of information on the likely demand for the product in the forthcoming period. Where a limited number of outlets is involved this method is easily achievable and produces the best estimates for future demand. The salesforce could also be used to develop estimates from their contact with the buyers; a particularly appropriate method when the number of end-users remains small and the product faces considerable competition with a high technical content.

Once this simple level of product and market interaction is passed the problems of forecasting become more acute and a variety of techniques are brought into play each of which has advantages and disadvantages. All forecasting systems will be subject to a number of caveats:

- the more checks that can be made on the projections by using other approaches the better;
- no forecast will ever be wholly accurate; it should produce maximum and minimum levels of likely outcome;
- each product will show slightly differing patterns of demand that will further confuse the forecasting problem.

10.4   Forecasting Techniques

Historical analysis

This involves the comparison of records of similar products both within and outside the company. The data required is several years' sales records of one or more competitive products in their respective markets.

The value of the use of historical analyses is largely in the forecasting of margins and perhaps new product sales. It generally fails to identify short-term and very long-term trends with its greatest accuracy on the medium-term horizon (three months to two years).

The main shortcoming of historical analysis is that it fails to identify likely changes in product usage, the turning point should this be likely to occur. Take for example the case of the skateboard manufacturer and the importance of determining when the popularity of the item would start to decline. Most failed to do so and collapsed with the declining market. However, this remains a very commonly used technique in a large number of companies and when translated into the development of sales quotas becomes the 'beat last years' sales' syndrome.

Visionary statement

The visionary statement can occasionally be extremely successful consisting as they do of a leap in the dark usually by the chief executive. In general terms, however, the visionary statement can be regarded as suspect failing in accuracy either in short-, medium- or long-term success.

Panel consensus

This system – in operation for example at the Lockheed Corporation[1] – works on the assumption that the combination of a team of experts will produce a more sophisticated and reliable forecast than one produced by an individual. Psychological studies would suggest that the group will be heavily influenced by generally one, occasionally two individuals.[2] The data required is similar to that needed for the historical analysis. The accuracy of the information can as a consequence of the nature of the group decision be regarded as suspect for all time periods.

The development of the panel consensus method using the salesforce is to produce a salesforce composite of all the major customers and from that to derive overall market demand. Such an approach has advantages in that the salesforce is closely identified with the final forecast which will be immediately available on an area by area basis for this was how it was built up, but will tend to produce inaccurate results when the economic or technological conditions are rapidly changing, and because the salesforce will be judged on the outcome the targets set will tend to be conservative.

Delphi method

This system attempts to remove the dominant personality effects seen in the panel consensus. It involves the development of questionnaires to which the relevant individuals are required to produce answers in isolation from others. The process is time consuming requiring a whole series of questionnaires and in consequence only has relevance to the medium- and long-term problems that the firm may be encountering, such as technological changes. In the development of trends it tends to be an accurate evaluation of the particular problems though there may be problems identifying the turning points in the product sales.

Cross-impact analysis

With the use of large-scale technical assistance it is possible to assign values to the interaction of each major factor on another and then to determine the probability of it occurring. The data required for this analysis are extensive and time consuming, though the results appear to be able to provide information on the likely decline of the product range in the medium- to long-term. One of the major drawbacks of this method is that it often needs extensive market research to establish the underlying interrelationships, which often have to use regression techniques for correct evaluation. As a consequence of this the method is largely irrelevant once the underlying interactions have been exposed by regression calculation.

These qualitative methods suffer from the fact that they largely do not sufficiently analyse the past data nor do they identify effectively the causal relationships inherent in any changing business environment.

The analysis of the changes that occur over time are particularly important when in addition to seasonal changes there may be significant changes in long-term demand.

Exponential smoothing

This technique develops a moving annual or bi-annual total which is then weighted to give more credence to the more recent elements of the record. It has the advantages of speed and data collection but in common with the qualitative methods, the long-term value of the predictions will tend to be small.

Box-Jenkins

A development of exponential smoothing, this technique involves the use of a mathematical model which accurately describes the past history of the data. The value of this system is particularly strong in the short-term enabling accurate definition of problems such as inventory control and production planning. It does, however, require more detailed mathematical analysis than the majority of forecasting models.

X-11

A further development of the exponential smoothing system, it consists of the division of historical data into a series of sub-components.[3] It removes all seasonal fluctuation to short-term data and can, in consequence, produce accurate short- to medium-term forecasting showing whether growth trends are in reality declining or reversing. The data required for the evaluation is more than three years' sales history and in consequence its main application is in the areas of forecasting sales in the short-term and evaluating budgets.

The problem with all such trend analyses remains that the change in the sales level over a period of time may be heavily dependent on a particular factor which, if it changes significantly, will lead to considerable changes in sales levels unpredicted by any smoothing or extrapolation system.

In consequence causal forecasting systems are regarded as the most valuable method of developing an understanding of the business environment. They all attempt to derive an interrelationship between a company factor (such as sales) with an independent data element in the external environment (per capita income).

Index systems

With these a 'basket' of economic or social indicators is developed which allow an index to be produced from which the sales performance or other company data can be derived. These indexes suffer from the fact that the real underlying causes of company performance are not identified making long-term projections highly questionable.

Life-cycle analysis

There are many companies that use the concept of product life-cycle – that all products go through a period of growth, maturity and then decline – to derive forecasts of new introductions, separating the socioeconomic divisions of innovators, early acceptors, and so on to derive the overall progress of the particular item. The problem with life-cycle analysis is that no product is sufficiently predictable: they will all show differing time scales in all phases. This will be more marked between product types – fabric conditioner versus bar soap for example – than within a particular sector, such as fridge freezers. Companies with considerable experience of a *specific* business area may find life-cycle analysis a useful forecasting aid providing they accept its limitations.

Econometric analysis

The development of an econometric model is an attempt to develop a predictive system for one or more economic variables which affect the particular business. Relationships that have been defined for various industries are:

Automobiles: disposable income, relative price, unemployment, credit.
Services: disposable income, consumption of non-durables in previous time periods.

The further development of econometric models enables simulations to be developed through which 'what-if' problems can be evaluated. The problem with econometric analysis is that it becomes divorced from the management responsible for the implementation of the results flowing from the analyses, and because the relationship is statistical in nature the results will often be viewed with scepticism.

Regression analysis

The use of a regression analysis technique appears to offer the line manager the best forecasting system available, as it provides functional analysis of the underlying variable interactions, by the use of statistical techniques which can best be calculated using computer methods. The relationships obtained provide accurate indications of short- and medium-term trends within the business environment.[4]

10.5 Integrating the Forecast with Budgetary Control

Once the overall business forecast has been calculated and its interaction with the overall corporate and marketing strategy determined, it has to be integrated into sales budgets for implementation.

In common with the forecasting systems budgets can be as complex or as simple as the business environment merits. Complex budgets demand complex controls and allocation of time so that all personnel are fully briefed as to what is expected of them.

There are in consequence a large number of factors that can be used to set budgets:

1. sales volume;
2. sales volume by product line;
3. sales value or gross profit;

4. net profit (after salary, commission and expenses);
5. sales value by account type.

The criteria against which any system should be judged must be:

(a) Whether the quota is attainable. All those with experience of salesforces are too well aware of the effects of unobtainable goals on the performance of the salesforce. This is particularly acute when the quotas are used to assess commission or bonus rates. The quota will also need to take into account the amount of experience that individual sales representatives possess.
(b) Whether it accurately reflects market conditions, differences in price, promotional activity, and market share.
(c) Whether it can be easily administered – will it be comprehensible by both management and representative?
(d) Whether it is flexible: will it cope with the inevitable changes that an annual plan will face?

Any budgetary control procedure that is put into effect must obviously also be closely integrated with other aspects of the organisation's financial planning. Variations in both the level of sales revenue achieved and the level of costs within the salesforce will have a substantial and obvious effect on the overall profitability of the organisation.

Pilgrim Paper

Background

Pilgrim Paper executives were reviewing the company's sales forecasting system. Estimates of potential sales were used not only in production planning but also in the preparation of sales budgets and regional and area selling quotas. The quotas were used as a compensation yardstick against which commissions were paid. Managers were particularly concerned about the effects of this aspect of the forecasting system on salesforce morale.

The company

Pilgrim Paper sold a wide range of paper products to over 120 different industrial sectors. Over the past 15 years the paper industry had shown steady growth in line with increased sales of newspapers, magazines, increased consumption of tissues, and a great expansion of office and school use of paper products. Recently, the market had shown further dramatic growth with the advent of new technology in offices and shops. The new thermal printers used to label produce in the superstores and the rapid spread of dot matrix printers associated with computerisation in offices were changing the pattern of demand for paper products throughout the entire industry. The market was in a state of flux and Pilgrim Paper were unsure of long-term trends particularly in the area of computer paper.

The company had divided its operations into a number of product areas in the early 1970s. The main divisions were Print (dealing with the newspaper industry); Consumer (mainly for the provision of tissues) and the New Technology Section (which dealt with the office and industrial sector for such products as computer paper). Each division had its own sales force and marketing teams. The divisions remained in close contact with each other as part of the overall company policy. The salesforce though split on a customer base continued to meet regionally as management believed in maintaining an overall company awareness within the organisation. This policy extended to transferring sales representatives from one division to another as part of a promotional pathway. Though generally the product division worked well, there were obvious occasions when two departments were actively involved in dealing with the same consumers, same market.

As a result of the continued expansion in the industry the paper market had grown in size between 1975 and 1983 from 180 000 tons to 410 000 tons, a year on year growth of just under 25 per cent. The NTS (New Technology Sector) which had started to be identified as a clear market sector in 1979, was by 1983 accounting for 50 000 tons, though there had been considerable fluctuation in growth over the four years. Annual growth rates had in fact varied between 252 and 14 per cent. Part of the reason for this variation had been the fact that production capacity had failed to match demand and in consequence the underlying trend was difficult to establish. By the end of 1983 Pilgrim were making an increasing percentage of their profit from this sector as they had been one of the earliest companies to appreciate the potential that was available.

Market trends for paper and NTS by year

	Paper (tons)	Growth (%)	NTS (tons)	Growth (%)
1975	180 000	22	—	—
1976	230 000	28	—	—
1977	264 000	15	—	—
1978	278 000	5	—	—
1979	300 000	8	7 000	—
1980	320 000	6	14 000	202
1981	325 000	1	35 000	252
1982	340 000	4	40 000	14
1983	360 000	6	50 000	25

Pilgrim Market Share/Profit 1981/1983

	Paper	Total profit (%)	NTS	(%)
1981	15	88	30	12
1982	15	70	25	30
1983	16	63	26	37

The forecasting system

During the middle of the year the marketing department collected data for the next year's sales forecast. Each Pilgrim Paper salesman provided an analysis of likely volumes by each major account. This was reviewed by the district manager and the general sales manager and forwarded to the production plant managers as a detailed break-down on an item by item basis. This would include size and style of paper, pack size requirements, grade of material, and so on.

The corporate planner prepared a separate forecast based on the growth rate of the industry, Pilgrim Paper market share and major changes in customer business. This approach had previously proved extremely accurate up to the late 1970s when major shifts in demand had caused considerable differences between sales achievement and forecast levels of demand.

Of crucial importance to the Pilgrim Paper planning process was the need to decide where the plant investment should be made; errors in this area had led to some of the wide fluctuations seen in the NTS market.

Due to the problems in defining demand in the NTS sector the error in the forecast had increased from 1.5 to 25 per cent over the last four years which was creating major concern at board level, with its impact on factory planning and cash flow.

The sales budget

Once the forecast had been agreed an income statement was developed for each division which included any additional expenditure for an increase in sales – including changes in the number of salesforce and expense levels.

This was then used to develop the sales quotas for particular territories taking into account the business transferred to other divisions and likely price and competitive changes. The sales quota did not include those changes in the market brought about by competitive activity but did take account of underlying growth trends.

There were a number of sales incentive bonus schemes tied to the performance against quota. Should the salesman reach 85 per cent of his sales target an additional 1 per cent of his salary would be payable. This had been an open-ended commitment which had recently led to wide-scale anomalies between the divisions. While certain salesmen in the Paper and Consumer Divisions were only receiving their basic salary of £11 000 a year, certain individuals in the NTS Group were earning over £20 000. The company faced a serious dilemma: the salary structure that had been devised was enabling them to increase their profitability substantially in the main growth area of the paper market, but this was having the deleterious effect of creating internal conflict within the company. Fourteen of the 40 strong combined Paper and Consumer products salesforces had applied for transfer to the NTS division; three had already resigned because of the differences in earnings between the two groups.

Sales Strategy and the Marketing Mix   **11**

Companies must cope with different market, customer and competitor structures and are therefore obliged to develop strategies and tactics that will enable them to deal successfully with these challenges. These strategies will have implications at all levels of the firm; from manufacturing to finance and from personnel to sales. At all stages the company will strive to achieve a balance between the level of investment and the expected achievement relating to the overall company strategy; market share, return on capital employed, sales volume, or whatever criteria is deemed to be central to those objectives.

11.1 The Development of a Sales Strategy

Certain general criteria will need to be examined as part of the process of development of a sales strategy:

- Cost. First and foremost will be the issue of cost. What are the cost implications of employing the salesforce and what is the likely rate of return? How will the costs of alternative methods of distribution compare?

  Employing a large salesforce will naturally imply a considerable investment, using wholesalers or middlemen considerably less. The vast majority of firms receive 80 per cent of their business from 20 per cent of their customers, what is called the 80/20 rule, and therefore investment in marginal customers needs to be carefully considered.

- Coverage. What percentage of the market will need to be covered; is it necessary for example for the company to provide a service to all outlets, and if so at what frequency of call? A company that decides on universal coverage will need a considerable increase in salesforce numbers. The Frito Corporation in the United States demanding a 99 per cent level of customer service needs a huge salesforce: comparisons of the Mars salesforce and that of Cadbury reveals similar differences in service commitment.
- Control. What level of control does the company need over the manufactured goods or services it produces? The decision to limit the outlets in which the product appears, or reduce the selling price will also affect the number of sales representatives that the company employs.
- Competition. The nature of the competition will often determine the investment requirements of the company in the salesforce. This can be clearly seen in the television rental market with the rival companies determining the number of outlets by reference to each other: if Radio Rentals has 90 outlets in London, Granada should have 85–95, and so on.
- Custom. Different markets have different constraints as a result of custom. When one compares the role of the sales representative for consumer goods in the Japanese and European markets the effects of custom can be clearly seen. Thus in the Japanese market the wholesaler must be approached because of the structure of the trade, whereas in the European trade the majority of the trade will be done on a direct basis.

11.2 The Impact of Product Strategy Factors

Firms will also have to give detailed consideration to products or services. Various approaches to product planning are used including the product life-cycle concept mentioned in Chapter 10, ideas based on the systems advanced by the Boston Consulting Group, or other analytical systems.[1] From such analyses one of five basic options may emerge for the product's future:

- abandonment,
- market penetration,
- product development,
- market development,
- diversification.

Each will have implications for the way the salesforce is structured and managed. The more extreme the changes that are proposed in the product policy the greater the structural alterations necessary in the salesforce. Phasing out a marginal product from an extensive list will for example require far less co-ordination than the introduction of a completely new range of different items.

Abandonment

The involvement of the salesforce will be important for the smooth withdrawal of a product from the market. The salesforce will be able to advise whether the product, though unprofitable, is regarded as an important element of the service that the company provides. Secondly they will be involved in the selling out of the final stocks to ensure that the level of obsolescent material will be minimised.

Market penetration

This strategy aims to increase the usage of the current product within the current market. This will either consist of finding new customers or developing the product usage with the current customer base. Though this route is generally one of low risk, in that the customers and the market are well understood, the rewards in the form of dramatically improved market position will tend to be more limited. Options available will include:

- Increasing salesforce representation. Reducing territory size will mean that more time will be spent with each client and effort concentrated on getting new customers.
- Changing promotional policy. Increases in either above-the-line (media) expenditure or below-the-line (promotional) expenditure will involve the salesforce in either increasing the number of clients or the offtake per client. Alterations in the balance of

expenditure between the various elements will also have effects on salesforce utilisation.

- Changing distribution policy. Changing the distribution system will radically change the nature of the selling task. It can mean an increased need for training to overcome the problems of the new sector; recruitment procedures will need to be altered if the selling skills are radically different. For example, changing from specialist shops to national accounts will require different negotiating skills. Development of new distribution channels will naturally also have implications on the percentage of time spent on repeat business and the development of new accounts.
- Changing pricing policy. Alterations in pricing policy should be carried through smoothly if they coincide with the customers' buying pattern. For example mail order catalogue buyers will react to price changes at only one time of the year, and pricing changes should accept the reality of the sales environment.
- Changing product identity. The development of branding of the firm's products may be seen as an important means of establishing a strong position within the market. Again such changes will demand that the salesforce spend more time explaining the benefits of the brand to buyers and its advantages over the competition.

Product development

This policy involves the selling of modified products to the same customers. Product development strategies will enable the firm to continue to maintain and extend a position of strength within the market.

- Product modification aims to achieve new usage by changes in the product formulation. For example, increasing the strength of a detergent could be considered if the current product was only being bought by a limited number of consumers with light wash-loads. The salesforce will need to be fully aware of the new consumers that the product is trying to reach and its likely impact on the distribution, pricing and promotional strategy.
- Product addition. After an initial success many companies attempt to establish a firmer grip on the market by offering a

broader 'package' of a single product. The car companies for example, provide L, GL, GLS, SR, SRi versions of the same model. The implications for the salesforce is the likely confusion between the various models (or pack sizes when put in the consumer goods context). Where there is an increasing variety of this kind, the salesforce needs to be clear as to the benefits of each of the models/sizes and where sales effort is best targeted.

- Line extension. This strategy involves the development of a variation of a basic model or product: Bisto gravy granules from ordinary Bisto gravy mix; Batchelors mushy peas from tinned peas; estate versions from saloon cars. Such changes in the product range may lead the company into areas where they lack specific selling skills; policies of product addition and line extension will continually expand the number of items that are maintained on the sales list, reducing the time given to each individual product.

Market development

Policies to promote the sales of the current product range in new markets require a change in emphasis. The sales representatives in the new territories must turn their energy towards developing new accounts but this will need skills different from those of the salesforce selling to established outlets.

Diversification

Diversification policies involving the sale of different products to different consumers can place severe burdens upon the salesforce. There are three options:

- Production integration. This entails developing a range from current production expertise such as the flour manufacturer developing a range of animal feed from the by-products of milling.
- Market integration. A range of new products are produced to sell to the same type of customers, such as the IBM personal computer.
- Opportunity diversification. Here the firm develops a totally new concept which is removed from current production and

marketing skills, such as Spillers entering the cook-in-sauce market from a base in flour.

Most companies will see the need for the establishment of a totally new salesforce for such ventures; attempting to integrate a very different product range and customer base with one currently established is often a recipe for poor progress as neither management nor the field salesforce are clear as to their real priorities.

11.3 Salesforces and the Marketing Mix

Surprisingly, there is little discussion of the implications of the interaction between a firm's salesforce and its marketing strategy and tactics. In many companies there is often the feeling that 'marketing' and 'sales' are unrelated functions. Passing from the rarefied atmosphere of the marketing department to a negotiating session in front of a client can produce the impression of two different companies rather than two differing departments.

Management on both sides of the divide tend therefore to be unaware of the potential contribution of the salesforce in considering the issues relevant to the development of marketing policy and so fail to maximise its effectiveness.

Classically the marketing mix considered the interaction of four elements called the 4Ps; price, promotion, place (distribution) and product. The substantial growth in the service sector has led certain authors to identify further factors; people (the nature of the people employed in the organisation), process (the way in which the service is carried out), and physical (the environment in which the service is performed).[2]

The salesforce will have important influences in almost all these areas, though for the traditional industrial and consumer goods sales representatives the impact that they will have on the nature of the people employed and the physical surroundings will be minimal.

Price

A major study has identified the level of gross margin as the most important influence on the long-term survival of organisations.[3] Crucial to the achievement of adequate levels of gross margin will be the discount policy that is followed, and the proportion of the product range that is sold under various levels of discount.

- Reducing discounts. A simple example illustrates the importance of discount policy. Consider two companies selling 10 000 units with the same discount structure; company A selling far more at larger levels of discount dramatically reduces overall profitability.

	A	Profit	B	Profit
List price (%)	10	5 000	30	15 000
10% discount	30	13 500	50	22 500
20% discount	30	12 000	20	8 000
30% discount	10	3 500		
40% discount	20	6 000		
Total profit		40 000		45 500

High levels of discounting will have a major impact on profitability. The freedom of the salesforce to grant discounts will be extremely important for the achievement of the required level of profitability. Most company experience suggests that for the majority of salesforces in the consumer goods sector the flexibility on pricing should be minimal as otherwise pricing policy will be difficult to sustain and product will be sold on a higher and higher level of discount.

Credit levels will also need strict control, as the company's ability to manage its cash flow will be vital for small organisations and have significant effects on the profitability of larger firms. It has been suggested for example that one of the reasons why the retailing sector has become more profitable than manufacturing is that the average number of days credit given by a supermarket chain will be two or three days, while they demand from their suppliers over 60 days. Manufacturers have been forced to provide longer credit terms thereby lowering their level of profitability.

- Problems of standard discounts. Similar problems exist when discount rates apply across a product range when it will be necessary to ensure that the proportions of the product type sold will not affect the overall level of profitability. For the national accounts salesforce dealing with large volumes such considerations have become so important that sophisticated financial control methods are deemed necessary to cope. A regionally based salesforce can allow the company to increase prices in those areas which are potentially more profitable or have higher distribution costs. This may naturally conflict with any national price agreements with nationally based end-users or retailers. An interesting example of such a system has been developed by the retailer Colruyt in Belgium. This store group determines the level of retail pricing by the proximity of competing stores. Should these stores be at a distance the prices in the Colruyt outlet will be higher than when competing stores such as Delhaize or GB are nearby. The degree of control that such a system demands is considerable but it nevertheless ensures that Colruyt is extremely profitable.

- Pricing flexibility. The presence of a salesforce enables price changes to be more rapidly introduced than where a company is dependent on middlemen. It also enables the firm to react locally to confuse competitive test market activity. Nestlé for example will reduce prices locally in the coffee market to confuse any test market activity of the competition.
- Transaction nature. In industrial markets, the proportion of business that is sold on lease or long-term financial bases will also have major effects on company cash flow. For firms in the vending industry – like Autobar or Klix – changes in leasing policy will inevitably affect the salesforce sales techniques and the company profitability.

Distribution

How the company evaluates the various distribution objectives and deals with the issues involved is discussed in Chapter 12. The salesforce will be important in identifying the type of customer with whom they deal and the product range that is concentrated upon.

- Regional coverage. The integration of the salesforce in the marketing mix enables the company to sell regionally: it can focus on selling certain products to certain customers or in certain regions. Take for example two products with a regional appeal – mushy peas and salt free butter or margarine, the one with higher sales in the north of England the other in the north-east. Directed effort with these products within the national marketing strategy will greatly depend on salesforce involvement and enthusiasm. Krona, the leading margarine brand, introduced a non-salted variant to compete with Lurpak the leading non-salted butter with its largest market share in the north-east of England which historically had always had the strongest links with Denmark. Effort during the national launch of non-salted Krona were greatest in this area as it provided a much larger potential than the remainder of the country.

• Store coverage. Combined with the ability of the salesforce to concentrate geographically, separation by client type may be an extremely important element of marketing strategy. For example IBM follows the policy of selling computers through dealers unless the sales turnover on a single deal is more than £50 000, at which level the salesforce becomes actively involved. This is an instance of setting service levels for the salesforce; the percentage of the customer base that will be covered by the salesforce and the consequences of market coverage by middlemen. The proud boast of the Frito Corporation in the United States is to provide a 99 per cent level of service, unmatched by other snack manufacturers.[4]

The extent of customer coverage will need to be determined partly as an issue of policy, and partly on financial grounds. Customer turnover will follow some form of standard distribution (see Figure 11.1) and the firm will need to determine the percentage of stores which will be called on direct.

• Inventory levels. A problem facing all companies with a large distribution network is the level of inventory required to provide a certain level of service, maintaining a buffer stock which allows for peaks and troughs of receiving production and orders (see Figure 11.2). Reducing the level of service can significantly reduce the inventory levels and improve the company balance sheet. In consequence the salesforce should be involved in determining the ideal level of service that is required by the end-users or retailers.

• Differential selling. Though there are legal barriers to restrictive sales practices in the majority of European countries they do often occur on an informal basis. The Argos discount chain has over the years taken a number of manufacturers to court to attempt to clarify such problems as the supply of electrical

FIGURE 11.1
Frequency distribution of outlets by turnover

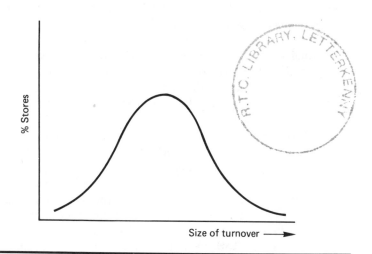

FIGURE 11.2
Effects of fluctuating supply and demand on inventory levels

equipment. Discount chains like Makro often prove major problems for the supplier attempting to maintain a standard pricing structure in the market and informal sales agreements can be established between the retailer and supplier for the maintenance of price levels in the market.

- Overseas problems. These are more important when multinational companies are involved with single overseas distributors of well known consumer products. The maintenance of high margins both for the supplier and the distributor can be threatened if product can be bought into the market from some lower priced alternative source. Thus the company has to try and maximise its control over the final destination of such products by either supplying wholesalers with limited quantities (restricting their ability to supply container loads of product for export markets) or for other overseas customers only shipping on Carriage, Insurance, Freight (CIF) terms which minimises to an extent the chances of product disturbing the planned sales schedule in any overseas territory. Distillers, for example supplied orders in Rotterdam for Scotch whisky ostensibly for Eastern Europe. This product then appeared in the Middle East reducing margins substantially for six months. Toys ordered at substantial discounts for the Yugoslav market reappeared on Woolworth shelves in the United Kingdom at substantial discounts, causing similar confusion and trade discontent.

Product

- Product extension. The salesforce will be critically involved in the success or failure of product extensions; the introduction of new sizes or grades of a single product. Certain products will appeal more to certain store types, and the salesforce will be central in persuading the store to carry as much as possible of the sizes available.
- Product diversification. The commitment of the salesforce to product diversification is a frequently overlooked factor in sales success. Part of the inability of Airfix Toys to expand away from their base in the construction model kit market was the fact that the salesforce were not convinced of the benefits or the quality of the additional range of board games, sports equipment and plastic toys that they were asked to handle.

- Test markets. To evaluate the potential of a new product or to consider the effects of changes in product or promotional policy, the company may carry out a test in a limited area. Normally it wishes to achieve the greatest possible distribution and maximum level of consumer trial possible. The first will often involve the salesforce calling on non-traditional outlets, administering the involvement of wholesalers' or special 'commando style' salesforces. The second will often mean the salesforce organising product demonstrations. Should either of these elements be important in the test market it will be crucial that both sales and marketing management consider the implications both for training and for allocating the correct amount of non-selling time to such activities.
- Quality control. The salesforce will often be first to be aware of any quality control problems that may arise, and management should ensure that there is a simple, easy to administer path by which product comments will pass back quickly to central management. Such an issue must again be viewed in relation to the amount of time the salesforce has available for non-selling activity. The salesforce will be in the best position to comment on the effectiveness of packaging – whether it stands up well to distribution methods, whether display stands are effective, and so on.
- Competitive information. The salesforce can be a major source of competitive information, with details of promotional activities, pricing and distribution changes.
- New product ideas. Many companies find that the salesforce is a very fertile source of new product ideas or new service concepts. Including discussion of possible new product ideas at sales meetings can also be a valuable means of improving motivation. Such ideas have led to the concept of 'quality circles'.[5] The author is not aware of any company that has introduced quality circles systematically into the salesforce, but it would be an interesting area of experimentation.

Promotion

Sales promotion (or below the line advertising) has become a more and more important part of the total promotional expenditure, and it is now estimated that the total money spent in this area is now greater than that on media.[6] Examples of promotional tools include: coupons – offering discounts on future purchases; competitions; gift offers; banded or premium packs – two products combined at a reduced price or a larger pack containing 10, 25 or 30 per cent more; advertising allowances and incentive items for industrial customers.

Sales promotion is often regarded as tending to encourage short-term shifts in purchasing behaviour, with media expenditure developing longer term brand loyalty.[7]

The salesforce will be closely involved in the development of promotions in a number of areas:

- Timing. Major consumer goods companies operate a promotional cycle system whereby goods are promoted on a rotational basis often coinciding with media expenditure (see Figure 11.3) to ensure that the salesforce will concentrate on selling the appropriate product while the advertising campaign is in progress.

FIGURE 11.3
Simplified media/promotional plan

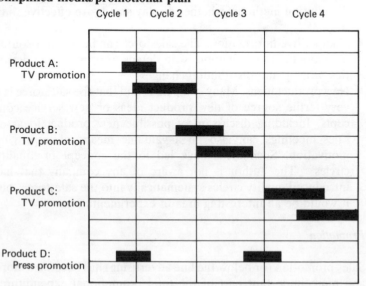

- Budgets. The level of promotional expenditure that is necessary to achieve sales levels should be decided as part of the overall sales budgeting process. The ideal process of:

    1. establishing objectives;
    2. selecting the correct promotional technique;
    3. pre-testing the promotional plan;
    4. controlling the introduction and continuation of the sales promotion,
    5. evaluating effectiveness,

    is rarely, if ever, followed.

    Sales management will generally be able to accurately define the promotional system most likely to work; they will be closely involved in any testing procedure, in-store merchandising, and reporting on effectiveness.

- Field marketing. With the continued growth of large accounts in both the retail and the industrial sector the involvement of the salesforce in local marketing activity is more and more important for major suppliers in both sectors.

    This has led certain companies to introduce field marketing, with local sales representatives co-ordinating local co-operative advertising in the regional newpapers to promote the product and the store.

- Public relations. As the local representatives of the company, the salesforce will often be involved in developing publicity for the company, either by promoting the interests of the product or supporting the broader interests of the company.

- Trade catalogues. The salesforce should be closely involved in the development and design of any trade catalogue that is under consideration, as they will be among those with first-hand experience about buyer needs and preferences in the presentation of information.

- Exhibitions. Central to the planning of exhibitions will be the necessary assessment of the likely number of buyers as well as their information and follow-up requirements so that the company can evaluate the likely effectiveness of the expenditure. The majority of this information will be received through the salesforce, who may also be involved in the day-to-day administration of the stand.

Process

Most sales roles can be seen in part as a service – providing goods
or techniques which will make the buying organisation more
effective. How the supplying company can best persuade the
organisation to initially purchase and then continue to use the
supplier will demand an assessment of the level of service that
must be provided.

A vending company for example found that the policy it had
been adopting of using a tele-sales system for repeat orders once a
new account had been opened led to a steady decline in the
number of accounts kept by the company over time. It was found
necessary to use the salesforce to maintain a level of repeat
purchase.

Brights' Cutlery Test Market

During October/November 1982 Brights', a producer of high-quality cutlery, scissors, knives and other kitchen and gardening accessories launched a limited advertising campaign, in the form of a test market, as part of a reassessment of company advertising support for the Brights' cutlery range. The company expected that the test market, organised in two areas – one, Yorkshire where the cutlery range was historically weak, the other, Tyne-Tees where the range was rather more popular – would provide a measure of reassurance about the overall impact of advertising, and would supply a long-term formula for a national advertising policy for the brand.

Background

With the exception of a £130 000 television campaign in 1980, there had been no advertising support given to Brights' cutlery since 1978.

Since the 1950s Brights' had been a household name in cutlery. Throughout the 1970s the cutlery market had grown steadily, due largely to investment by Brights on behalf of its brand. However, by the end of the decade the company's share of the market had begun to stagnate although research indicated that the overall cutlery market was in fact growing still but cheaper imported cutlery was beginning to erode the company's market share. Brights' share for its three cutlery lines, Exclusive, Efficient, and Economy, had declined from 80 per cent in 1978 to 60 per cent at the time of the test market in 1982.

The Brights' range, including the Economy, was between 30 and 60 per cent more expensive than competitors' and the difference was maintained in the price to the trade. Research also indicated that the Brights' cutlery had a traditional old-user profile. Younger buyers of cutlery tended to be more concerned about price. Overall there had been over the past four years a general erosion of brand image, and a decline in the numbers of distributors especially among independent retailers and hardware shops.

The advertising campaign

With a budget of about £100 000, the advertising campaign sought to achieve maximum coverage of the target market in the two areas. Further support for the advertising effort would be provided through a drive to improve distribution and promotional material.

A television commercial supplied the basis for the campaign in the two areas and aimed to reach 90 per cent of all housewives, who were expected to see the commercial an average of seven times. The theme of the TV advertisement was further developed in the other media used. Four-sheet size posters were placed in shopping precincts at 150 sites in Yorkshire and 200 in Tyne-Tees during October and November. Trolley advertisements were used by one department store chain which had not sold the Brights' cutlery range for some time.

Sales presenters prepared for the salesforce were designed to help sell the campaign to retailers. They included such information about the campaign as media expenditure and coverage; storyboard and posters; and point of sale material. The latter were also supplied to multiple grocers, independent stores, cash and carries.

ISS, an independent sales support service, helped to provide total sales coverage among independent operators in the test areas, and to improve distribution. Some 10 ISS operators would make about 20 calls a day over two weeks selling stock to retailers at trade prices and supplying a free set of cutlery to retailers with every order obtained. They would obtain stock from cash and carries.

ISS operators were also responsible for demonstrations at 22 cash and carries over two weeks. During two days of demonstrations on key trading days, operators would offer the whole Brights' cutlery range assisted by point of sale material, money off coupons, and a free set of cutlery with every dozen sets.

The campaign was reported in the trade press and a 'mail shot' was sent to independent suppliers in the test market areas.

Organising the campaign

It was the Brights' marketing department that initiated the test market proposals. With the help of an advertising agency it had designed the campaign and was directly responsible for its planning and implementation. Although the exercise centred around the Brights' marketing department, collaboration with other sections of the company was essential to its success. Sales data collection and co-ordination before and after the test market involved both the advertising agency and the Brights' research department as well as marketing. The sales department with responsibility for the salesforce and the Brights' distribution depot were brought into the exercise as was the company's Head Office, since it was responsible for distribution. An efficient method of communication was also important for the ISS operators.

A special effort was made by the marketing department to provide a focal point to facilitate co-ordination of the test market effort. During the two weeks of ISS operations a temporary office was set up in the two areas which was manned at all times by a member of the marketing team in order to deal with any immediate problems which should arise.

The role of the salesforce

As part of the marketing department's efforts to ensure a successful test market operation, a special salesforce conference was organised. At this meeting the special contribution expected of the salesforce in the Yorkshire and Tyne-Tees areas was outlined in detail.

The budget for the operation was very restricted the marketing manager explained. It had therefore been decided that certain essential information and communication tasks would have to be undertaken by salesforce staff. They would have to prepare their areas for the forthcoming test informing retailers about the pending advertising boost; advising them to order stocks of the cutlery range; and ensuring that retailers used the point of sale material. To help them, sales presenters had been specially developed for these tasks the marketing manager said. They would also have to spread the message to the cash and carries and, because the ISS operators had been told to get their stock from these bases, it was particularly important that they were well stocked. Cash and carries would also have to be informed of the dates of the demonstrations by the salesforce after it had secured the agreement of site managers to the demonstrations.

Crucial to the determination of the success of the test market was the collection of accurate data about the impact of the campaign the marketing manager continued. In order to monitor more efficiently the campaign's effects, but also because of the high cost of alternative methods, sales data would have to be obtained by the salesforce from the retail chains directly. This was cheap, more accurate, and quicker as co-ordination would be done at Head Office. The salesforce must therefore ensure the regular return of the weekly sales off-take form to Head Office.

The salesforce's response

To the Brights' salesforce the end of the year was a particularly fraught period. Under their terms of employment the salesmen received a 10 per cent bonus on all orders once they had achieved more than 90 per cent of their annual sales target. At the time that the test market was organised, not long before Christmas, most of them had achieved their targets and were dedicating themselves to earning an incentive bonus. Moreover none of them expected to earn anything from the Brights' cutlery range. The price of other Brights' products were much more competitive and the generally accepted trade view was that the cutlery was too expensive. The test market they said offered no attractions as regards price. There was to be a gift incentive to retailers but no incentive was offered to Brights' own salesmen. Moreover, the salesforce was being asked to implement measures to back up the ISS part of the programme. Why should an independent sales support agency require support and why could this not be given by the marketing department which was responsible for involving ISS.

A few days before the test market was due to begin the Head Office sales department informed the marketing department that there was insufficient stock at the cash and carries which were to supply the ISS demonstrators with stock. Arrangements for special deliveries to the demonstrators had to be made and some had to delay the start of their work. Many of those demonstrators who could start work found that they were without the point of sale material required for the independent retailers; others found that there was not enough stock available for display, never mind selling. Permission to hold the demonstrations had not been obtained from a number of store managers who were surprised to be suddenly confronted with demonstrators wanting floor space which was unavailable on that particular day. As a result, extensive reorganisation of demonstrations at the cash and carries had to be undertaken at short notice and at a high cost.

The Yorkshire and Tyne-Tees salesforces were also less than diligent in returning the sales data. As a result, sales data was inadequate and inconclusive for the purpose of testing the effectiveness of the campaign and alternative sales data collection methods had to be used.

Breaker Radio

Background

Breaker Radio had been founded by Ernest Bent, an ex-employee of Thorn EMI, in the mid-1960s, in a small industrial unit on the outskirts of Bradford. Growth had been slow over the years until the market for CB (citizen band) radio had finally mushroomed in the late 1970s.

Yr	Sales £000 000	Profit %
1967	1.2	10
1968	1.4	11
1969	1.5	10
1970	1.6	11
1971	1.6	12
1972	2.0	14
1973	3.0	12
1974	4.0	13
1975	6.0	14
1977	8.0	15
1978	12.0	16
1979	16.0	17
1980	24.0	18
1981	31.0	22

Staff had been steadily recruited over the period to meet the increasing demand. The factory employed 33 people on the shop-floor, and by 1981 there were four salesmen, a commercial director who dealt with all the marketing aspects of the firm, and a sales director together with the founder Ernest Bent.

The product range had changed slightly over the years and now consisted of a radio and power pack for the CB market, and a specialised short-wave radio for home enthusiasts which also was increasingly bought by yachtsmen and small commercial boat-owners. The growth in this area of the business had been swamped by the increase in demand for the CB radios which had gained ready acceptance throughout the country particularly with the car and lorry owning of socio-economic groups B and C.

Year	% CB sales	% short-wave
1978	50	50
1979	65	35
1980	70	30
1981	75	25

Prices and competition within the CB market were generally more acute than the short-wave radio sector, but Breaker managed to make more or less the same percentage margin in the two product areas. The main competition was as follows:

CB

Company	Brand	Retail price
Amstrad	Freeway	£29.99
Thorn	Roller	£32.00
Breaker	Breaker	£31.50
Decca	Sonic	£28.50

As the units were all solid-state technology there was little servicing involved and Breaker models had shown themselves to be particularly robust. Though there were only four main brands in the market there were a host of smaller brands put together from Japanese components which were sold through the large number of small wholesalers and distributors that operated within the market. The retail outlets varied from electrical stores such as Comet to numerous specialists in each large and small town. It was estimated that in 1981 there were approximately 1500 outlets stocking a variety of citizen band radios. Installation of any unit was fairly straightforward requiring the use of standard components.

The short-wave radio market was far more specialised both in respect of outlets and the amount of information purchasers required for installation. The main manufacturers and brands in the market were:

Company	Product	Price
Racal	Wavemaster	£350
Grundig	Global	£500
Philips	Mainstream	£470
Breaker	Worldwide	£550
Sony	Chieftain	£570

There were a number of wholesalers that dealt with parts of this market: ships' chandlers tended to be restricted geographically, as were the hobbyists radio distributors. There were in contrast to the CB market certain geographical concentrations – London and the south-east were particular areas where the Breaker product sold well, whereas sales near their northern factory were disappointing.

1981 onwards

1981 showed the first sign that the dramatic growth that had been seen in the CB radio market was coming to an end. Breaker showed a sales decline for the first time with turnover declining to £2.8 million and profit margins also came under pressure. Ernest Bent responded by increasing the promotional expenditure that Breaker were putting into the market concentrating on exhibitions. Sales in the next year remained static, but profit margins were further eroded, and the company only made a profit of £50 000 for the year. There were clear signs in the market that the demand for CB radios was dropping dramatically and Breaker could only maintain its position by deep price cutting, reducing the retail price of its unit to £24.99. Amstrad were showing signs of pulling out of the market totally by continuing to dump their remaining stock. Certain major multiples had indicated that they would no longer stock CB equipment and this would decrease the number of outlets nationally to around 900, mostly small independents. The salesforce commissions fell and the four Breaker salesmen had become collectively more and more unhappy with the progress of the company. At an exhibition at York, Ernest Bent accompanied by the teetotal commercial director Melvin Weatherall, found all asleep on the exhibition stand after a long and liquid lunch. After consultations with the sales director it was decided that they should all be dismissed for gross misconduct.

The meeting

The board of Breaker met in early 1983 to reappraise their distribution policy. The current salesforce was costing the

company around £100 000 and in the present financial position of the company this could obviously be an area of
potential savings. Melvin Weatherall, the commercial director, was strongly of the opinion that Breaker no longer required a direct salesforce and should concentrate on selling
their CB product via direct mail, and their short-wave products via middlemen, and prepared a paper for the meeting
supporting these views. The sales director, Raymond Stubbs,
was firmly of the opposite view. He considered that there
were large areas of the market that currently had not been
developed for the sales of short-wave radios and considered
that future growth areas such as local community services
would require direct sales representation and could not be
handled on an indirect basis.

The WXY Field Market

The UK convenience food giant WXY had a long history as an innovator in sales promotions. Its current marketing director had built up a reputation as a pioneer in field marketing using it as a highly efficient strategy for promoting the company's brands in superstores. He had found field marketing a flexible and cost-effective technique but was looking for further refinements. He had just received back the comments of the sales director on a report containing his proposals for improving the field marketing operations which could be tested out with the planned promotion of 'Mmmm' sauces.

Background

WXY's field marketing strategy basically involved a series of tailor-made promotions run in conjunction with specified superstores and the local Press. To date the company's experience was that the process, although efficient, could become over-complicated.

An earlier campaign had involved 175 out of 350 UK superstores to promote speciality ready meals. Two competitions were available to superstores and appeared in the Press as well. Competition entries were posted within the superstore where the competition had an in-store display. Entries to the competition were used as a measure of awareness and the 5 million circulation achieved through the involvement of 55 local newspapers.

The company had employed a public relations agency working with the marketing department to negotiate with local newspapers free space for competition details in return for advertising the paper's involvement in the competition on superstore in-store displays. This had proved both difficult to co-ordinate as well as time consuming especially since negotiations with the newspapers were being handled by letter because of the scale of the promotion. Publication dates for newspapers varied; some did not advertise superstores; others wanted to run the competition themselves, disliked the prizes, or wanted the competition entries through the paper rather than the store. There were timing difficulties with the superstores as well – many had to juggle with other promotional commitments.

The marketing director's proposals

The marketing director's proposals for streamlining the field marketing technique stressed the need for a degree of devolution. The problems to date had arisen from over-centralisation in dealing with the media. This function should now be handed over to the salesforce which would negotiate directly with the local Press.

Because the salesforce is already in contact with the superstores and within easy access of the local papers attached to the superstores, this change would make the field marketing package very efficient in its use of time. By using the salesmen who were already on the spot in locations throughout the country, communication would be speeded up and the impersonal approach of using an agency eliminated.

By using the entire strength of the salesforce, the burden of contacting such a large number of superstores would be more equitably shared between a larger number of employees. By contrast an agency could allocate far fewer staff to such a task.

Previously negotiation with the Press had been by letter or telephone. There were distinct advantages to be gained if the salesforce was to negotiate face to face for 'free' space in return for the competition and advertising in a superstore. The salesman could ensure that no selling points of the field marketing programme were overlooked or ignored. Moreover, the astute representative could concentrate on the aspects of the field programme which were most relevant to the situation. One local paper might like the flexibility of the programme so the seller would emphasise that point in the negotiation. The salesman could also use the superstore competition posters to good effect if he were bargaining directly with the local Press.

During the previous field market the salesforce had been responsible for arranging the competition with superstore managers and ensured that point of sale support material was available throughout the promotion. It was also responsible for making the draw for the competition. The salesmen knew when the competition would start and finish, and when the couponers would be in-store so there would no longer be any ambiguity.

In sum, the marketing director concluded in his report, the streamlined field marketing programme would give the opportunity to expand the salesforce marketing skills as well as their negotiating skills, extending their duties into new fields of activity. Furthermore, the field marketing package had a lot of unique selling points attached to it, and if the salesman is aware of them and can communicate them, he should have few problems.

The sales director's views

The WXY sales director had a number of reservations about the marketing director's proposals.

He was concerned that negotiating with the Press was not an area in which most salesforce members would be skilled. The proposal represented an extension of duties for the WXY salesforce and lack of skill in the area could well limit the results attainable.

Because of their lack of expertise in negotiating with the Press, the salesforce would require more time to buy 'free' space from the local Press; the failure rate would be higher than if negotiation were undertaken by experts. The time a salesman spends negotiating must be taken into consideration with regards to the cost-effectiveness of the programme. Using figures supplied by the WXY's promotion agency the sales director calculated that it could cost £100 for every 'free' newspaper insert if negotiated by a member of the salesforce.

In some cases the extra work could be a burden on the salesforce the sales director noted. Although on average, four stores and regional papers were to be allocated to each salesman, this figure would vary according to the area the salesman worked in, and his seniority. Salesmen in heavily urbanised areas, and more senior salesmen tended to be allocated a figure above the average.

The sales director mentioned the likely attitudes of the

salesforce to the marketing director's proposals. The WXY salesforce clearly defined its job as selling, and did not feel that 'marketing' should be brought into its job. The time consumed by the field marketing activity would also be another area of concern.

Circus Records

Background

Circus Records had been founded by David Smith in the mid-1960s. For the first three years the operation had not been a success but since then the company had shown substantial overall growth. Management style had always been individualistic and with the steady growth in the company formal structures had largely been ignored. There had been a very rapid turnover of personnel.

Year	Turnover £ mill	Profit %
1966	0.2	—
1967	0.24	—
1968	0.3	5
1969	0.6	10
1970	1.2	15
1971	1.8	18
1972	5.0	19
1973	12.0	20
1974	20.0	18
1975	30.0	17
1976	35.0	16
1977	37.0	16
1978	42.0	19
1979	45.0	20
1980	55.0	18
1981	50.0	16
1982	47.0	14
1983	42.0	10

From the early days the company had concentrated on developing popular talent. The first discovery that of the ballad singer Henry Harrison had led to the company's dramatic growth in the early 1970s. A move away from this traditional music had led them to capitalise on the progressive music boom of the late 1970s particularly with their lead group

Drum Beat. Recently the decline in these groups fortunes had severely affected the overall group profitability, especially as the company had diversified into a number of other areas.

1983 structure

Area of operation	Turnover £ mill	Profit £ mill
Records	35	5.4
Entertainment	4	−0.6
Travel	3	−0.6

The records division was mainly concentrated in 40 shops which provided the bulk of the Circus turnover employing 240 staff. There was a small telephone sales staff which handled the sale of the record label to other outlets and dealt with overseas enquiries. Overseas sales were handled through overseas distributors. Market share had been always a worry overseas. Whereas Circus had 12 per cent of the UK record market, share in the US which was eight times the size of the UK market, was around 0.5 per cent, and other major markets also showed very small shares.

One worrying feature of the market was the fact that the department stores and multiples were gaining increased market share within the record sector, Boots, Woolworths and W. H. Smith showing particular strength in this area but others such as Debenhams also gathering momentum. It was possible that the supermarket chains such as Tesco, Asda and Sainsburys might also become more active in this area.

Circus Records own market research estimated retail market shares as follows:

Market share	%(UK)
Boots	15
WH Smith	13
Our Price	10
Woolworth	5
Debenhams	4
Circus	12
HMV	3
Others	38

Analysis of sales of Circus store by store showed that there were wide scale variations in profitability.

Shop	Site value £ mill	Sales £ mill	Profit £ mill	Employees
London 1	0.3	0.6	0.24	8
London 2	0.5	1.2	0.3	10
London 3	0.2	0.6	0.18	6
London 4	0.1	0.45	0.09	5
London 6	0.15	0.6	0.21	5
London 7	0.1	0.3	0.03	5
London 8	0.2	0.15	0.03	5
London 9	0.05	0.45	0.06	5
Birmingham 1	0.07	0.6	0.3	8
Birmingham 2	0.03	0.75	0.15	6
Birmingham 3	0.03	0.9	0.21	7
Birmingham 4	0.02	1.2	0.09	8
Birmingham 5	0.02	0.9	0.06	6
Manchester 1	0.03	0.9	0.18	6
Manchester 2	0.02	0.45	0.12	6
Manchester 3	0.03	0.9	0.18	5
Manchester 4	0.02	0.75	0.21	6
Liverpool 1	0.01	0.75	0.12	7
Liverpool 2	0.02	0.60	0.09	7
Leeds 1	0.01	0.45	0.09	8
Leeds 2	0.02	0.6	0.12	6
Sheffield 1	0.01	0.9	0.18	5
Sheffield 2	0.02	1.2	0.15	4
Sheffield 3	0.01	0.9	0.06	4
Bristol 1	0.02	0.6	0.03	4
Portsmouth 1	0.01	0.9	0.06	4
Southampton 1	0.02	0.6	0.03	4
Coventry 1	0.02	0.45	0.06	4
Coventry 2	0.03	0.3	0.03	5
Reading	0.02	0.9	0.09	6
Windsor 1	0.01	0.45	0.03	5
Brighton 1	0.01	0.3	0.03	8
Dover 1	0.01	0.6	0.09	6
Stoke 1	0.01	0.9	0.09	4

Hull 1	0.01	0.6	0.03	5
Newcastle 1	0.01	0.3	0.03	6
Newcastle 2	0.01	0.3	0.03	6
Wigan 1	0.005	0.02	0.001	6
Glasgow 1	0.04	0.6	0.12	4
Glasgow 2	0.03	0.9	0.06	6
Telsales		10.0	1.2	9

Recently a number of branches had been closed following a reassessment policy; the Wigan branch was under notice of closure in addition. Redundancy costs for the staff were running at about £6000 per head, and it was worrying that market share would be steadily eroded as the less profitable stores were closed.

The entertainment division produced films and ran some betting shops and pubs. The total staff employed were 64.

The newest venture, that of ethnic arts, had so far proved a considerable loss-maker but Smith hoped that his policy of providing specialist holidays for the specialist music lover would eventually be successful. Circus 'Soul' tours around the Southern states of the USA had run into difficulties and the 'Reggae' tour of the Caribbean had run for two years at a loss.

Total staff in this area were 52.

The problem

Circus management were becoming increasingly aware that the company was heading for financial difficulties and had spent some time in considering various alternatives mainly concentrating on further closure of the stores and the development of a salesforce. Currently, Circus through its shops made about half its profit from Circus label records at an average price of £4.30 per long playing record. The production cost of these items was around 90p per disc, producing a gross profit per unit of £3.40. It bought in other records at around £2.80 reducing the profit margin on these items to £.60. One problem with moving away to a direct sales policy would be a considerable loss of profitability. Furthermore the current policy of the major groups such as

Boots was to discourage discounting – this had been a major element of the Circus strategy over the last five years to maintain market share.

The costs of introducing a salesforce would therefore be high – would the benefits outweigh the risks? Circus management considered that they could achieve around 5 per cent market share at wholesale prices if the shops were either totally closed down or curtailed. The total number of record shops in the country was estimated at 2000 out of which 800 would be nationally negotiated – W. H. Smith, Boots, Woolworth and Debenhams. Regionally the stores were quite evenly spread.

On the costing side, Circus were aware that a sales representative would cost around £15 000 for the UK – export representatives would be more expensive at £25 000.

Selling Overseas I: The Problem of Distribution **12**

For the company growth, or the expansion of its markets, can be approached in a number of ways. It can embark on a programme of product development which would enable the firm to maintain its regional base while it introduces new products. Geographical expansion is another option with local firms changing into national organisations; national companies becoming international; still others prefer a mixture of the two. Each alternative will pose problems, the greater and more rapid the degree of change the more severe the demands.

In order to expand the firm will have to carefully consider the impact of such a decision on the organisation and its products. For example it will have to evaluate the marketing problems that such a development will cause – product acceptability, media problems and the like, as well as the adjustments to distribution organisation that will be required. Distribution bottlenecks will naturally occur when a local firm extends out of its regional base, a fact particularly important in large countries such as the United States.

Geographical expansion in the European context is generally taken to mean the development of an export business and though the comments that follow in this chapter largely refer to this; the concepts are also relevant to any firm deciding on a policy of geographical expansion. Recent surveys do show that the proportion of turnover that small firms achieve overseas is very limited, in the range of 0.5–5.0 per cent of turnover, as many see the problems of exporting as being too severe.[1] The most serious obstacle is distribution, with credit availability, pricing, tariff barriers, and high selling costs high on the list.[2]

12.1 Distribution

For many firms there may be a variety of distribution channels used for different areas and different products. As the ensuing discussion will highlight, a distribution method suitable for one type of product will not do for another. In common with many business decisions each avenue carries with it risks and rewards. The risk factor is the amount of investment that is involved in the distribution channel and the level of control that it allows the organisation. This will be balanced against the profitability of the sales achieved. The effect of distance from the manufacturing point merely serves to compound the same basic problems. A firm based in say France will have to satisfactorily resolve various matters whether it is selling in England or New Guinea, with the minor difficulties in one market becoming the major headaches in another. For example transport problems within the country may be more satisfactorily resolved in England than in New Guinea but unpredictable weather may cause more distribution bottlenecks in England. One method of distribution that works in the home market which is generally excluded in overseas territories is the use of direct mail, as customs and postal regulations will generally make this a very difficult proposition.

12.2 Choosing a Distribution Channel

The method of choosing a new distribution channel is rarely clear-cut or systematic, varying with both product and market factors. However, the interplay of these produce a number of standard direct and indirect approaches.

Direct approaches

1. Manufacturer direct to consumer.
2. Manufacturer to retailer.

3. Manufacturer via salesforce to retailer or end user.

Indirect approaches

1. Manufacturer to wholesaler.
2. Manufacturer to agents/franchisees or contractors (in the case of industrial goods).

Examples of each pattern are fairly clear. The first is best illustrated by the large number of firms that operate by mail order, particularly strong in the household and fashion sectors but also strong in many industrial component areas. Organisations producing commodities such as grain and potatoes fall often into the second category. Fast food outlets are frequently good examples of franchised operations and many industrial companies operate through a network of agents – computers and office equipment being particular cases in point.

The final possibility is the classical one of the direct salesforce used to generate national distribution between manufacturer, end user or retailer.

12.3 The Criteria Involved

In general, there are a number of universal criteria which can be applied in selecting a distribution channel regardless of whether the market is at home or overseas.

In order to evaluate these factors the company can weigh each factor for the importance that should be placed on it within the particular market or area that is under consideration and then assign a probability of achieving satisfactory results using (1) direct (2) indirect sales methods. Any evaluation of these factors must always be placed within the boundaries of the firm's strategic objectives. A firm, for example, may take the view that to become established in a highly competitive market it needs to develop its own salesforce though logic would suggest that it would be best to use middlemen when judged on other grounds.

Unit price

Very high levels of unit price – military aircraft, for example – will inevitably imply a direct sale, as financing and lengthy negotiation will be involved, and will tend to exclude agents or intermediaries. Products with low unit price, on the other hand are ideally handled by agents or wholesalers.

Degree of flexibility

Where there will be a high level of negotiation and argument about pricing levels and financing arrangements, it is obvious that the supplier or manufacturer will have to become involved as only it knows the implications of various pricing levels. Should the product be clearly defined in the range of prices that are acceptable to the manufacturer, agents or distributors can be more suitable.

Frequency of purchase

Items that are rarely purchased require detailed planning by the manufacturer. An example would be the supply of analytical equipment to hospitals, whereas supplying them with cleaning fluid on a regular basis would ideally be handled by a distributor.

Standardisation

Products that do not require customisation can be more readily delegated to middlemen than those that are specific to each order – the intermediary is unlikely to have the technical back-up necessary to handle the necessary changes to the standard product whereas these can be integrated into the production line by the manufacturer.

Technical content

Similarly agents are unlikely to be able to provide the level of knowledge to deal with highly technical products. A good example of this is a Dutch producer of chromatography equipment being forced to establish a local salesforce in England even when sales levels were low as only in this way could the benefits of the product be fully developed in a highly technical field.

Installation requirements/servicing

Should there be a high level of servicing required or complicated installation procedures it is likely that the manufacturer will have to provide them. Technical specifications tend to change slowly over time – new components are added as the product becomes more refined – and it is unlikely that an agent can maintain the continuous high level of knowledge required, especially as the service he provided would probably not be restricted to one manufacturer.

Number of customers

Should there be a limited range of customers for the product the economics of direct sales contact are more positive than if the product has a wide customer base. Providing computer equipment for colleges would be a fairly restricted market, for example, whereas the catering market would not – the first might be suitable for the development of direct sales whereas the second would rely heavily on the development of links with wholesalers.

Geographical concentration/order size

Should the amount of travelling time between customers be small, this would also favour the development of a direct sales approach. Where distances are considerable the economics of employing an individual solely for one particular product or product field become more questionable. The effect of the order size on this problem is obviously crucial: large distances separating customers can be offset by large orders. Some form of ratio such as sales value/miles can therefore be developed to help in this area.

Speed of delivery

The problems of delivery are obviously another area where major investment decisions have to be taken. If the manufacturer has to provide rapid national delivery, major investments in warehousing, inventories and transport fleets will have to be made if a direct sales distribution route is chosen. Using intermediaries to hold stock at a distance from the production point is one way of decreasing this sometimes massive investment. Should delivery timing be more flexible, local stock holding will be less necessary, allowing a direct sales method to become established at a lower level of investment.

Financial strength

The nature of the firm's finances will of course affect its distribution choices. The strength of a company's financial position is often crucial in determining the proposed sales strategy. A firm that has cash flow problems may chose to factor its invoices, handing over its sales invoices to another company that pays out immediately a large proportion of the face value.

The establishment of an overseas sales subsidiary will be a very expensive venture which is unlikely to immediately pay for itself, however profitable it may be in the long term. An organisation with strong financial backing may choose this route as part of its strategic objectives – the firm less well placed will need to consider less costly alternatives in the short term.

Legal problems

There are many instances in overseas markets where legal barriers can have important influences on the nature of distribution. First is the degree of local control that is demanded by the host country. This can vary from a minority stake to a stipulation that a majority local shareholding is obligatory. Secondly there may be laws governing the nature of employment – for example, that the firm must employ the racial mix in the community, or that beyond a certain number of employees there must be a trade union or similar organisation. Both these factors are relevant to the investment decision that the firm needs to make to achieve the required level of distribution. A complex legal environment suggests that the development of a local sales subsidiary may be faced with too many problems to make the exercise worthwhile, and the use of agents or distributors to be the better option.

Currency problems

In addition to the various legal difficulties that selling overseas faces, there is the crucial issue of transfer of funds. Many countries totally block the transfer of funds out of the country unless certain very stringent conditions are met; in others the transfer is limited and complicated. The transfer of funds to the parent company is naturally paramount in the evaluation of profitability – it is of little value to an international organisation to have a highly profitable local subsidiary in which there has been considerable investment if the firm cannot enjoy some at least of the benefits of that invest-ment. In consequence currency restrictions will again affect the distribution channel decision that the firm takes.

Culture

Communication between cultures is discussed in Chapter 1. In certain areas it is very difficult for a 'foreign' company to become established because of the differences in local culture. This may be no less true of companies expanding say from the north of Italy to the south as it is for European companies selling in Africa or Japan. Religious differences are an obvious example with differing festivals and feasts having a fundamental effect on sales seasonal-ity. Apart from these major differences minor facts such as the number of public holidays may also influence the market condi-tions.

A cultural factor that should not be ignored in any market is the barrier to entry posed by informal contacts within the community. These extend from who gets the contract for the refurbishment of the community hall to who is the main supplier of tinned food to the local army barracks. The marketing of contraceptives in some countries for example, could not proceed without the co-operation of religious, traditional and community leaders. Culturally distinct communities may resist very effectively the arrival of a foreign organisation, however attractive the goods may be. The English language contains the legacy of one such encounter – the ousting of a certain Captain Boycott from Ireland. Such a process can extend to outright corruption which can be found in all societies at one level or another, and though every sales representative and manager would claim to be totally pure from any such taint the reality of these constraints is often hard to ignore. The use of a locally-based sales organisation in certain circumstances may therefore be far more appropriate where there are strong cultural barriers than direct sales from the home base.

Climate/physical factors

Major differences in climatic conditions can be very important in the structuring of sales effort, and how the product will perform. Extreme heat in the Middle East in summer for instance will require additional investment in food distribution, which local organisations will understand, whereas overseas principals who have not experienced the often appalling conditions will not.

12.4　Indirect Distribution Methods

There are a number of possible choices open to the firm to decrease the risk that development in a certain overseas market may cause, through the use of indirect distribution methods.

Export houses

There are certain intermediaries that can be classed as export houses. They form a distinct group enabling the supplier to be paid in his own country minimising currency/distribution problems, and removing the necessity for the establishment of an export department estimated at around £60 000 for the medium sized firm.[3]

Wholesalers

Similar to wholesalers within the home country, and occasionally the overseas arm of the same organisation, they provide either a pick-up point for foreign buyers or have overseas subsidiaries providing the same service.

Buying offices

Several countries with centralised economies maintain overseas buying offices to deal with all state purchases. Some large store groups, notably the Japanese, also support a similar system.

Confirming houses

These are independent trading companies that act on behalf of overseas principals providing shipping and financial services.

Specialist export firms

These are organisations that have particular links with the trade in one part of the world – for example the Caribbean where the low turnover on each individual island often poses problems for firms with limited product portfolios. They will purchase product in the home territory and act as the export distributor for that country or group of countries.

Though the financial risk is minimised the use of these export houses does not permit the principal to develop any confidence in either the stability of pricing or the continuity of supply that can be achieved through these channels. In every case other suppliers can easily supplant the initial manufacturer, though the reverse of this is that the manufacturer is also able to change the method of distribution quickly due to the lack of contractual obligations.

Agents and distributors

The development of a contractual framework with an overseas representative demands a more long-term commitment, certainly from the supplier, and is the means by which substantial proportion of overseas trade is carried out.

In these contractual agreements the supplier guarantees that all sales for a given market over a period of time will pass through the local exclusive representative. There are broadly two main options: the agent who works on commission on orders received, without holding stock; or the distributor who holds stock and provides a higher level of service to generally a larger market. Both of them may employ a salesforce – the distributor being most likely to do so. Payment terms will be more complex – the supplier will receive payment in foreign currency with all the risks that this can imply – but in return the principal improves the control he has over the market to an extent.

The degree to which control is actually improved will vary as there are a number of general characteristics of distributors and agents which have important implications for the supplier and which must be understood in any consideration of overseas expansion.

Of most importance to the majority of firms will be the way in which distributors and agents tend to operate.

First, the nature of ownership is critical to success or failure. Many distributors are subsidiaries of large firms or will be family run and backed by considerable private finance.

Second, the management team is usually very small with a much smaller management turnover than is found in direct sales organisations – quite often one will find that the managing director has worked in the organisation since leaving school or university.

Third, the distributor frequently has a wide range of products to deal with – generally the longer the distributor has been established the bigger unless a conscious decision has ben taken to limit the product range. The majority of distributors tend, however, to be great believers in the philosophy of marginal profitability: once the overheads are covered each additional line will further increase profitability.

Finally, the business horizons of the distributor are often limited. Options that are open to the majority of manufacturing firms are rarely considered – expansion abroad, changing drastically the nature of the product portfolio by acquisition or product development, or diversification into other areas of business. The distribution company by the nature of its business tends to be more interested in a quicker return on capital employed than the supplier.

These organisational trends have certain effects upon the job that the distributor performs in the market.

Concentration on key products

The distributor will tend to concentrate on the most profitable products, often to the detriment of the supplier's views on new product development. One problem that frequently occurs is the clash of two new products within the distributor's range of brands. Companies A and B with widely differing product ranges appoint the same distributor 15 years previously. As time progresses, the product ranges diversify and become very similar. The distributor then is faced by two principals insisting on effort being placed behind two closely competing lines.

Profitability criteria

The distributor will have specific profit targets to be achieved which may well conflict with the principal's view of the correct volume and pricing relationships within the market. This may also have an effect on the level of stocks or the level of service that the distributor is prepared to consider, which again may be at variance with the views of the supplier.

Distribution policy

The distributor will have a fairly clear view of his own distribution policy in the market whether he is selling to the broadest base or concentrating on key outlets.

Promotional timing and policy

The distributor will also have his own priorities for promotion. Combining promotional expenditure across brands may be necessary for large retail outlets which will interfere with the principal's plan for concentration of activity at a certain time of the year, or other commitments may make it impossible for the distributor to be present at an appropriate exhibition for one of his suppliers. Further, the use of point of sale material and the proper use of explanatory manuals will be difficult to achieve.

Some of these problems may be overcome by the careful selection of new agents or distributors when a new market is explored and a decision taken to use this particular distribution method. Here the disciplines required in the recruitment of individual salesmen are no less valid, with the creation of a job description followed by an evaluation of how well the chosen company performs against these requirements. The criteria on which the majority of British firms judge distributors are financial strength, distribution methods and length of time they have been established in the market. French and German firms tend to look more for marketing expertise as their main selection criteria.

Modern Sales Management

However, even with the best planning and evaluation problems will still arise over time and the sanctions that the supplier has to ensure compliance with the original agreement are frequently limited. Obviously, the agreement between the distributor and supplier can be terminated, though in many countries, in the Middle East for example, this is no longer possible without the distributor's agreement. The ending of the contract will tend to lead to a fairly lengthy interregnum causing confusion in the market and often severe drops in market share.

Plasty Case Study

The toys and games company Plasty had grown tremendously since its foundation in 1957. By the late 1960s it was one of the most important toy companies in Europe and had an international reputation for its construction kits of all sizes, though a large proportion of its turnover was derived from die-cast vehicles, puzzles and pre-school toys. The range of construction kits had grown steadily larger over the years and by the late 1970s there were around 550 moulds in existence divided into 20 kit sizes. The product range was made up of a backbone of 40 per cent aircraft, 20 per cent ships, 10 per cent figures, with natural history, space and military vehicle kits making up the remainder. Only a limited number of these would be in production at any one time. The basic production cost in the United Kingdom, the minimum production run and retail prices relating to the mid-1970s are given in the table below.

Series	Production cost	Run	Retail
1–2	£0.25	10 000	£0.6
3–5	£0.40	6 000	£1.8
6–9	£0.80	3 000	£3.0

The market

The world-wide market was made up of around 50 per cent series 1–2, 20 per cent series 3–5, 15 per cent series 6–9, and the remainder of the larger model kits.

The international market had been slowly changing over the 15 years since the company had been founded. First, the number of competitors had vastly increased from a total of four to 26. Secondly, there had been a substantial growth in demand in Japan which was now by far the largest market in the world for construction kits, and a steady increase in interest in the United States as the following table shows.

Market	Size[£m]
Japan	70
USA	23
UK	14

Germany   10
France   6

In Europe, the declining birth-rate and the enormous growth in competing leisure time activities particularly television and video, meant that the market had shown little growth since the mid-1970s. Plasty had attempted to diversify into industrial plastics and other ventures without great success and was now looking towards a re-vitalisation of its overseas activities.

Plasty and overseas expansion

One of the main barriers to overseas expansion was that the costs of freight were extremely high for plastic kits, consisting as they did of large amounts of air, and this together with local duties made a number of Far Eastern markets very difficult to penetrate, even though sales had been achieved in the majority of markets. Generally, retail and wholesale margins throughout the area were 50–65 per cent on retail price.

None of the overseas distributors had proven particularly satisfactory except for those in Hong Kong and Singapore. Senior management were confident that local manufacture together with changes in distribution would bring substantial benefit to the group.

The problem

The company carried out research on the markets in the Far East to ascertain the various factors that would be important in developing the new sales structure. The initial conclusion reached from this analysis was that the method of distribution and sales of the kits would have to be changed to enable the Japanese and other markets to be profitably exploited. Management were also unsure about how this might affect the development of the United States market. The major factors to be taken into consideration in exploring the possibility of local manufacture in the Far East were presented to senior sales management in table form.

Malaysia
Population: 14 million
Market size: £0.1 million
Current sales: £0.025 million
Political stability: Moderate
Import duties: 15 %
Advertising media: All
Locally produced competition: Nil
Plastics/paper skills: Moderate

Distribution method: Direct to store via local distributor
Legal considerations: All investment must have high local stake and large local labour content. Investment level required for establishment £0.1 million
Warehouse costs: 15% on manufacture
Production index: [production costs compared with UK] 125
Retail price index: [UK price translated into local currency] 130

Singapore
Population: 2.5 million
Market size: £0.2 million
Current sales: £0.05 million
Political stability: High
Import duties: 8%
Advertising media: All, except TV
Locally produced competition: Nil
Paper/plastics skills: High
Distribution method: Direct to store
Legal considerations: None, investment level necessary £0.05
Warehouse costs: 25% on manufacture
Production index: 90
Retail price index: 115

Philippines
Population: 42 million
Market size: £0.1 million
Current sales: £0.02
Political stability: Low
Import duties: 100–150%
Advertising media: Press/magazines
Locally produced competition: Nil

Paper/plastics skills: Low
Distribution method: Via commission agent and government monopoly
Legal considerations: High minimum investment required around £0.25 m, and the company would only be allowed to establish in inconvenient duty-free entrepôts.
Warehouse costs: 10%
Production index: 115%
Retail price index: 225

Australia
Population: 14 million
Market size: £2 million
Current sales: £0.3 million
Political stability: High
Import duties: 30%
Advertising media: All
Locally produced competition: Two brands produced in New Zealand (import duty only 8%)
Paper/plastic skills: High
Distribution methods: Via distributors and wholesalers
Legal considerations: Nil, with low minimum investment costs £0.1 million
Warehouse costs: 12%
Production index: 130
Retail price index: 120

New Zealand
Population: 2.5 million
Market size: £0.3 million
Current sales: £0.08 million
Political stability: High
Import duties: Imports on quota system with 50% duty
Advertising media: All
Locally produced competition: Two
Paper/plastic skills: High
Distribution methods: Direct to store via distributors
Legal considerations: Local manufacture allows quota restrictions to be eased on product range. Very low investment costs.
Warehouse costs: 10%

Production index: 130
Retail price index: 205

Hong Kong
Population: 5.5 million
Market size: £0.5 million
Current sales: £0.04 million
Political stability: Short-term (until 1997) high
Import duties: Nil
Advertising media: All
Locally produced competition: Nil
Paper/plastics skills: High
Distribution methods: Direct via distributors
Legal considerations: Nil, with very low investment costs
Warehouse costs: 15%
Production index: 80
Retail price index: 105

Taiwan
Population: 18 million
Market size: £0.1 million
Current sales: £0.02 million
Political stability: High
Import duties: 150%
Advertising media: Limited
Locally produced competition: Three
Paper/plastics skills: High
Distribution methods: Via distributors
Legal considerations: High minimum investment around £0.3
million, with plant restricted to duty-free zones
Warehouse costs: 10%
Production index: 85
Retail price index: Local (70) Imported (180)

Japan
Population: 110 million
Market size: £70 million
Current sales: £0.1 million
Political stability: High
Import duties: 8%
Advertising media: All

Locally produced competition: 20
Paper/plastics skills: High
Distribution methods: Via primary secondary and tertiary wholesalers to stores. Distributors do not hold stock, attempting to pre-sell all production.
Legal considerations: Minority stake in joint venture only practical route with a high level of investment required, around £0.5 million.
Warehouse costs: 30%
Production index: 100
Retail price index: 90

USA
Population: 220 million
Market size: £23 million
Current sales: £0.1 million
Political stability: High
Import duties: 15%
Advertising media: All
Locally produced competition: 3
Paper/plastics skills: High
Distribution methods: Via specialist wholesalers or direct to major store groups
Legal considerations: None
Warehouse costs: 30%
Production index: 160
Retail price index: 180

In addition to the country by country analysis freight costs were provided on a grid form:

	UK	Jpn	Aus	NZ	Spr	Ph	Tw	M	HK	US
UK		25	30	30	20	25	25	20	15	22
Jpn	25		15	20	10	10	10	15	6	12
Aus	30	15		5	8	10	10	10	8	20
NZ	30	20	5		10	12	15	12	10	26
Spr	20	10	8	10		6	8	3	6	18
Ph	25	10	10	10	6		8	10	8	16
Tw	25	10	10	15	8	8		10	3	22
M	20	15	10	12	3	10	10		6	18
HK	15	6	8	10	6	8	3	6		
US	22	12	20	26	18	16	22	18	14	

TSC – Bahrein

Background

In the early 1960s TSC, a major American food and toiletries company, was considering the possibilities of improving distribution within the Bahrein market. Bahrein, halfway up the Arabian Gulf on the eastern coast of Saudi Arabia then had a population of 250 000 concentrated in the north of the island in two towns Manama and Muharraq. The local inhabitants were employed in the oil industry, aluminium smelting, shipyards, telecommunications, construction, and airport work. The standard of living rose steadily from the early 1960s with the new affluence showing in the rise in household ownership of fridges, air conditioners, and cars. With the greater affluence came a taste for Western goods which because of the low import duties were well within the purchasing power of the bulk of the population.

Distributors in Bahrein

Higher living standards had been accompanied by a steady growth in the level of Western investment in the banking and offshore services sector. This had further fuelled property values in Bahrein and made the merchant class extremely wealthy and independent, distributors especially. It had been the law in Bahrein that no foreigner could own property and there was increasing pressure for foreign firms to accept large minority Bahreini shareholdings. Recent changes in the law had also made it increasingly difficult to dispose of a distributor once appointed without paying enormous compensation after lengthy legal proceedings; the reality was that a distributor once appointed could only be changed with the owner's consent.

The structure of the distribution trade for consumer goods was fairly straightforward. The Arab markets or *Suqs* contained the local wholesalers who dealt with the small shops in the outlying areas, the supermarkets and their associated interests accounted for the remaining 40 per cent of grocery turnover.

Five main supermarkets were operating at the end of the 1960s:

1. Moon Stores associated with the Gulf Hotel;
2. Al-Jazira Cold Store supplying the oil commissaries and the construction camps;
3. Jawad Cold Store supplying the bulk of the ship chandler business;
4. Motiwallah supplying the Indian community and business interests;
5. Al-Hasameh supplying many government contracts including the Bahreini army.

Each of these supermarkets had followed a policy of trying to develop their own agency lines acting as distributors for overseas principals. They tended not to stock products competitive with their agency lines. The supermarket groups in contrast to the other local distributors were not particularly effective in sales development. These local distributors, none of whom had cold store facilities, were also limited in number:

1. Bahrein and Middle East Trading acted as agents for Oakridge Chemicals one of the major TSC competitors;
2. Arab Traders acted as agents for Allied Food and Drug;
3. Ibrahim Fazweh acted as agents for Ikonand BTT, the major European multinational;
4. Peninsular acted for TSC particularly in the distribution of its detergent range.

In the late 1960s one Peninsular salesman handled the 28 different packs of the TSC range with approximately 40 packs of other products including tea, tinned fish, rice and pasta, selling to approximately 75 customers. Peninsular also acted for the international confectionery company Home Pie maintaining a cool store for chocolate storage. They did not have a cold store for frozen goods. Cold store costs would probably have been in the order of £100 000 though normal warehousing costs were fairly low. Expatriate staff were a major expense for all distribution companies. Housing costs were at that stage around £12 000 a year, and this was combined with generous education allowances and high salaries.

The problem

TSC saw that the rapidly rising consumer spending power would increase the demand for more Western style products and was determined to introduce the products of its other subsidiaries which were as follows:

1. Toiletries, shampoos, toothpaste (60 packs).
2. Tinned vegetables, dried soups, and dehydrated meals (40 packs).
3. Industrial detergents and cleaning systems (130 packs).
4. Margarines, cooking oil (30 packs).
5. Tinned meat, fruit and fish (45 packs).
6. Industrial fats (40 lines).
7. Frozen vegetables, desserts, cooked meat (250 lines).
8. Frozen sausages (30 lines).
9. Speciality meats (45 lines).

TSC turnover by the end of the 1960s had climbed to around £300 000 on which it made around 30 per cent margin, and the company envisaged that the introduction of the new product lines would if properly carried out mean that sales of £750 000 could quickly be achieved.

The options

There were a number of options open to TSC each of which had advantages and disadvantages:

1. to set up a local sales operation in Bahrein with a direct salesforce to handle all TSC lines;
2. to concentrate the additional lines through their current agent Peninsular;
3. to find a new agent for the frozen and chilled goods while providing Peninsular with the remaining dry goods;
4. to achieve a broadly based agency system in Bahrein by offering differing lines to the various possible distributors.

Selling Overseas II: The Export Manager's Role 13

Once a company is involved in selling operations overseas it has to tackle the accompanying management issues regardless of the method of distribution that it has chosen. As is the case with most modern forms of organisation, once a decision is taken it is both difficult and costly to go back and the exporting firm must deal effectively with the realities arising from its decisions about overseas operations.

In chapter 12 we considered the question of overseas selling as being basically the expansion of the company's distribution network which was complicated by the fact of the company operating at some distance from its home base in different legal settings among people of diverse cultures. This approach is simple, giving clarity to exactly what exporting involves. Thus it is quite often the case that selling among foreigners is presented in such a way that the entrepreneur is mystified as to why, given the seemingly insurmountable obstacles, any company bothers with exporting. Yet the fact remains that these days few countries, certainly none of the large cities within them, are totally homogeneous and expanding companies – especially those based in federal states – will still have to confront customer profile and legal issues in expanding distribution networks at home.

There are, however, distinct practical, as opposed to theoretical, problems associated with selling abroad which must be resolved by overseas sales managers and it is with these that we shall be concerned in this chapter.

13.1 Controlling Overseas Markets – The Need for Export Managers

Generally speaking the greater the distance between the company and its markets the more severe the problem of exercising effective control over them. Although this plays an important role in determining the method of distribution chosen for the overseas markets, the influence of factors such as cost mean that many companies opt for agreements with overseas agents where their control over the market, as we have seen in the discussion in Chapter 12, is limited.

A survey of British exporters showed the following percentage using agents for distribution (though naturally not in all markets):[1]

Company size*	Use of agents (%)
1–100	68
101–500	79
501–1000	85
1001–10 000	85
10 000+	85

*By number of employees

These findings are reinforced by a survey of small American and Canadian firms which found that of those exporting 53 per cent used agents, while only 4 per cent sold direct.[2]

The recruitment of home-based export managers to spend time in the market alongside the distributor and his salesforce is the channel most frequently used by companies to secure a measure of control of their overseas markets.

Although many of the issues of salesforce management discussed elsewhere in this book also apply to situations arising in company markets abroad they will be complicated by factors which are outside the control of the company: cultural and linguistic differences, market idiosyncrasies, variations in legal systems, exchange control, currency and import/export regulations. In addition, we have seen that the company is likely to be using middlemen and is therefore further removed from the market. Thus there is a need for effective mechanisms to provide the company with direct experience of the market and to act as an effective channel of communication between the company and its overseas agents. There are various aspects to this which will now be considered.

Profits

A company may decide that ensuring that its overseas markets remain profitable requires the special attention of an export manager. This must therefore be seen as part of the overall sales strategy as well as being an investment. The company will have an interest in measuring the achievements of its exports managers against the profitability of the sales achieved in the markets for which they are responsible. Obviously these managers will be expensive to maintain with the necessary high level of travelling costs, and the necessity for them to have language skills. One survey showed that approximately 50 per cent of export sales management could speak a foreign language, rising to 66 per cent at director level.[3]

Setting priorities

No company can base its sales strategy solely on the experience of its overseas agents. The company itself must rely on the experience of its export management to take the decisions about the key markets based either on current sales achievement or likely sales potential. The analysis of present sales will clearly define the degree of likely importance of each market. It will be vital from such a base to define what expansion of sales could be achieved in various existing markets. For example, where the company might have a 40 per cent share of a £2 million market it would be unlikely that substantial additional market share could possibly be generated. Compare this with a similar sales value within a larger market: for example, a 5 per cent share of a £16 million market where it would appear that considerable gains in market share might be possible.

It would be logical for the company's export sales manager to allocate more time to the second market than the first unless there are other factors involved. Should the first market be facing increased competition which is creating serious problems for the agent, or one or other of the markets is limited on profitability or by government intervention, decisions will have to be made about the level of support that the company can realistically provide to each.

In many large countries it will also be important for the export manager to decide on behalf of the company, on the allocation of time and effort by region in relation to the overall company aims and objectives. In the USA especially, many companies concentrate initially on a limited region to ensure that effort is not too thinly spread. Where this is the case, the export manager will have to determine how much effort and time should be allocated to the various regions within the country.

The issue of potential business development within the country or region will be more difficult to evaluate. The time and effort allocated should ideally suit the overall potential for the firm, but this will be qualified by the difficulties inherent within the market. Such problems will include the amount of control that the company could exert via the agency agreements, the effect of government legislation on the nature and quantity of the goods that could be imported and the degree to which foreign exchange is controlled, and other political and economic factors.

Identifying opportunities

Experience also suggests that companies selling overseas will have sources of information about changing market conditions that are independent of those supplied by agents or distributors. It is only through the overseas sales manager or a similar mechanism that the company can link its own knowledge of its own markets to the selling skills of its agents to generate sales.

In all likelihood, every distributor will have a large product range of which the company's own goods is only a small percentage – rarely more than 20 per cent of total turnover with the exception of local sales operations that are exclusively directed to the company's products. The agent in consequence will view his total business operation in a different light to that of the supplier and will often miss new business potential as he is concentrating on the remaining 80 per cent or more of his turnover. For example, an agent involved in industrial cleaning might easily concentrate on the design and supply of equipment and product to a new industrial complex while ignoring less significant business for his overall product range which would be available in the local hospital. Should the supplier be more actively involved in the hospital field it would be obvious that concentration on this particular account would yield greater benefits than that of the industrial complex. This situation may be clear to the overseas sales manager but not necessarily so to the agent.

Agents may also not be aware of likely forthcoming requirements of specific customers for equipment or product that they currently do not order. The re-equipping of oil tankers with automatic tank-cleaning facilities would, for example, mean that ships' chandlers acting as agents for an industrial cleaning firm would experience a demand for the necessary sophisticated detergents that accompany the process. Again, the overseas sales manager would in such an instance inform the agent of the likely changes in customer demands because of this technical innovation.

Increasingly, international companies are co-ordinating their buying activity throughout the world. An export sales manager of a company supplying cooking oil to an international hotel chain may find that its agents are totally oblivious of opportunities in this area.

Technical assistance

To maximise the effectiveness of the overseas sales operation the firm will also have to ensure that overseas agents and customers can call upon its technical expertise as and when necessary. To do this, however, demands a level of active company involvement in the market. Companies frequently fail to realise this and therefore do not appreciate that they have a high level of skills in a number of areas which can make important contributions to the profitability of overseas operations. Yet it is a fact that it is impossible to learn from reports how well trained an agents' salesforce is; how well equipped they are to cope with a complex technical product; how well they are able to use literature; at what level they can negotiate; how much independence they can be given, and so on. There are various facets to the technical expertise that the company can supply to its agents overseas.

Company products

The more sophisticated a product the greater the agent's need for support in dealing with its technical features. With certain types of expensive equipment and with certain customers, the presence of the overseas sales manager may be essential if the agent is to achieve a sale. Goods requiring servicing may make it necessary for the company to maintain overseas offices in order to provide these services.

With highly technical goods the overseas sales manager will also provide on-site briefing to the company's technical staff about customers and their problems. He or she will also need to detail any specific installation requirements or technical modification that needs to be carried out during installation or servicing of equipment.

In the area of mass produced consumer goods, company expertise on storage facilities or warehousing of its products is another important, frequently overlooked problem, which can seriously affect efficiency. The difficulties are often relatively simple for the company expert to correct usually by introducing a training component – see training section below.

Company experience

Where a company is operating in similar markets in different countries it will be able to assist agents in sorting out various distribution bottlenecks.

It is generally the case that change in the market will herald the entry of companies with competing products. Agents may be concerned and will need reassuring about the entry of new products. If the agent has not faced competition before, he will need information about how competition has been dealt with in other countries – for example, he may need specialised support material. His supplier will probably also be familiar with the strategy that the competing company is likely to follow. Japanese companies when entering a market, for example, will more often than not use heavy discounts to become well established in the market. Counter-action by the agent in the form of special distributor price deals can substantially reduce the impact of such competitive arrivals.

Training

Close collaboration between the supplier and its overseas agents may often indicate that there are substantial benefits to be gained for a modest investment in ensuring that relatively simple tech-niques are understood. The potential importance of such activities will of course depend on the nature of the market in which the company is trading. In a more sophisticated market where the general level of education is high there may be less need for the company to be so concerned about warehousing. Yet even in these markets agents may still not understand the importance of stock or credit control.

The various aspects of the training issue are;

1. *Warehousing and storage.* Correct warehouse and storage pro-cedures can considerably reduce the amount of damage in-flicted on the company's products. Warehouse staff may need instruction on correct methods of stacking product on pallets, how many pallets can be stocked on top of each other, and ensuring that the product is the right way up.
2. *Stock control.* It is in the interest of any company using agents to ensure that standard stock and sales forms are understood and and are correctly and regularly filled out and returned to the supplier.
3. *Credit control.* There is also a need for set procedures to ensure that the agents' credit problems are minimised within the market and that all payments to the company are met on time. Such procedures identified an ice-cream agent in the Middle East running into financial problems and allowed the overseas sales manager to take corrective action before serious problems could arise.
4. *Distribution methods.* Different products will require different distribution styles. Introducing a range of chilled products may demand that the distributor sells such products from a refriger-ated van and the sales manager will advise the agent about the problems and opportunities that this approach will produce.

5. *Salesforces.* There are a number of areas in which training will provide substantial benefits for both supplier and agent:

Product knowledge. Agents' salesforces are quite commonly extremely limited in their knowledge of the product range that they are selling – its most important features, for example, and how the product stands in relation to the competition.

Support material. Analysis of the material that the salesmen use to illustrate the products in their range commonly shows that substantial improvement could be achieved with the use of suitable photographs and catalogue material.

Callage patterns. The amount of time that the agents' salesforce spends with each individual customer is rarely as efficient as it might be. Consideration of the time spent with each customer on an annual basis and the business derived therefrom can greatly increase salesforce effectiveness.

Customer knowledge. It is important that the salesforce should be aware that different features of a product may appeal to different customers. For example, a small warehouse would be more interested in the durability of a particular fork-lift truck whereas a larger warehouse would be more impressed by its cost-effectiveness.

Sales techniques. Improving the individual salesman's approach to the sale in such areas as preparation for the sale, gaining the attention and interest of the customer, creating demand, overcoming objections and closing the sale are all important in improving the ability of the salesforce to sell the supplier's products. These topics are covered elewhere in this book.

New products

The successful launch of a new product in an overseas market will require a special effort. New product launches accompanied by substantial promotional support are often a major investment by the supplier company. Careful monitoring is therefore essential to ensure that the company's resources are being used effectively.

The supplier has to make certain that agents and their salesforces are fully aware of all the features of a new product and that steps are taken to reduce any likely distribution problems. Should the product be launched to a group of customers at an exhibition or other special event it is desirable that the overseas sales manager should be present to provide answers to detailed questions about the availability of the product and any special customer requirements.

With the complex new product launch involving special demonstration equipment and display material, the overseas sales manager has to ensure that all facets are available, understood, and correctly used. For example, it will be necessary to check that the scheduling of commercials on the local radio or television coincide with the plans of the agent.

Promotions

The effective administration of sales promotions overseas involves fairly detailed planning. Liaison with the agent in the market concerned will always be important in ensuring the success of promotional activity: in understanding the nature of the customer and the opportunities in the market, particularly if there are any legal constraints. Furthermore many companies develop an overall promotional plan for their export markets which will involve the co-ordination of promotional print and visual material. There will almost certainly be some attempt by the supplier to evaluate the effectiveness of promotional activity. For example, a soft drinks manufacturer might run a bottle-top offer with various items as prizes. The supplier and its overseas managers would naturally be interested in ascertaining whether more of the product had been sold during the competition than was sold during a similar period outside the promotion. Ensuring that there was an effective mechanism to collect this data would be an important part of the contribution made by the overseas sales manager to the planning of the campaign.

Where the money is coming from to pay for promotional material is a good illustration of the co-ordinating efforts required in sales operations overseas and how they may vary between companies. Many companies spend all promotional appropriations through advertising agents locally based in overseas markets. This may be further complicated by the fact that the local agent may be contributing to the promotional budget and all material is provided from the combined budget. By contrast, other companies may have standard promotional campaigns resulting from industry and company pressures. A company such as Unilever producing a standard range of products world-wide gains immense economies of scale by producing standard promotional material in a single country. On the other hand for the Bata shoe group, which produces specific products for specific markets, localised production of promotional material is more logical. There are also companies operating under arrangements where both the company and agent provide a proportion of the budget. Some companies will not produce trade promotional material as a matter of policy; others may go to the opposite extreme with expensive leather gifts or other incentive items of high value.

In deciding between centralised or local production of promotional material a number of factors have to be considered. Local production will affect the type of material that can be used – multicoloured shopping baskets could not for example be made in the Middle East as the printing industry does not have the necessary equipment available. Complex plastic shelf material will be impossible in most of Africa, South America, and the Middle East. Printing leaflets is, however, a much easier task and local production of such material will almost always be feasible. The supplier may not, however, have a choice in the matter as many countries prohibit the import of printed material, even for advertising, to protect the local printing industry. For the sake of indigenous actors and actresses other countries ban foreign TV or radio advertisements.

The overseas sales manager may, however, wish to closely control material which will be crucial to sales performance such as descriptive panels for use at an exhibition. This will involve giving detailed attention to the accuracy of translation of the material since poor translation could turn the product into a local or trade joke.

There are times when an overseas sales manager has to supply promotional material quickly as when, for instance, an agent is faced with increased competition. The time involved in sending the artwork out to an overseas country, handling proofs and returning them would make local origination impracticable.

The overseas sales manager will need to define the quantity and type of promotional material required; the timing involved and the effects of not producing the material on time. Standard material for which there is no great urgency may be more cheaply produced at the periphery depending on the nature of the material and the quantity involved and will have a considerable effect on the unit price.

The opportunity cost implications, the failure to produce the material on time, should not be ignored. Suppliers frequently forget that it is often worth spending extra to ensure the arrival of the material in good time for the promotion.

13.2 Skills and the Overseas Sales Manager

So far our discussion has revealed that the job of the overseas sales manager is a potentially complex one.

As their effort will also be spread across a number of markets, they are unlikely to spend more than 25 per cent of their time in one particular market and it will still remain fairly simple for the distributor who after all is concentrating on it 100 per cent of the time, to continue to carry through a policy which is contrary to the interests of the principal.

An analysis of sales turnover at home and overseas shows this dilution of time highlighting how much more business turnover export sales personnel are responsible for when compared with those staff concerned with the home market:[4]

Company size	Home	Export
Small	220	727
Medium	400	719
Large	627	3 500

All figures in £'000s

Company policy on travel and time spent overseas will also have a bearing on the degree of control that it can realistically expect to exert on the markets concerned. For example, Berwick Batteries considered that their overseas sales managers should spend as much time as possible in the markets with the result that the normal length of time overseas was seven months.

As neither the agent nor the company manager will generally be devoting their time exclusively to promoting the company's products in a single market, success for both will depend upon the building of an effective working relationship. Securing this will to an extent depend upon the skills of the overseas managers as: (i) administrators; (ii) negotiators.

Administrative skills

As a company employee, the overseas sales manager will need a fair degree of administrative expertise. He or she will have to keep track of sales, often of more than one product, in a number of countries. He or she will also be involved in setting targets for products and markets; in planning and monitoring expenditure; organising market visits and stands at exhibitions; in evaluating promotions; in appointing and dealing with agents and distributors as well as being aware of the different nature of agreements with them, supply and credit terms and documentary requirements for each market. Countries differ as to the amount of documentation that is required to accompany an order. The Middle East for example insists on an accompanying Certificate of Origin; some countries demand laboratory analyses to accompany certain goods.

Incompetent administration is frequently at the root of poor relations between the principal and distributor. Oversights, small in themselves, feed on one another and can generate a high level of ill-feeling between the company and its distributors. A list of agents' most common complaints about the supplier company includes:

- failure to inform the agent of changes in packaging;
- minor damage in shipment;
- problems with quality control;
- shortages of promotional material;
- inappropriateness of promotional material to the local market;
- failure to inform the agent of problems of production leading to the agent running out of stock;
- failure to inform the agent about changes in the price of products or spare parts;
- failure to give the agent sufficient advance warning about a planned market visit.

Skills as a negotiator

A substantial part of the export manager's time will be given to negotiating the terms and conditions of agreements with distributors and customers. The skills required relate to a number of areas including agency agreements, terms of credit, pricing and supply terms.

Agency agreements and credit terms

The following are some of the questions that may be raised about agreements:

- What products are covered by the agreement – is it all of the company's goods or is it solely designated by brand? Such a question will be important when deciding whether the current agent should handle a new range of products.
- What requirements are laid down in the distribution agreement for the product range – must the agent maintain a certain level of stock cover over sales, or meet a certain time to service a given installation? This will be important in assessing the agent's performance.
- What are the credit levels offered by the company and how have they changed in the past?

A large sample of industrial exporters in the United Kingdom considered that the maintenance of an export salesforce was in the final analysis less important a method of influencing distributors than the use of financial constraints – changing the length of credit for example.[5] The overseas sales manager will need to be aware of the credit levels which the company will be prepared to offer in return for increased commitment or greater levels of sales achievement. Different payment methods may operate in different markets. They include:

(a) irrevocable letter of credit (LC) drawn on a London bank;
(b) standard letter of credit arrangements;
(c) sight draft arrangements;
(d) sight draft at 30, 60, 90 or 120 days.

Often these will be related to the level of business that the agent or customer is carrying out, the competitive position in the market and occasionally cash flow implications – 120 days credit in Australia will often mean financing stock including shipment time for 150 to 160 days.

Pricing and supply terms

Companies will have differing policies in relation to pricing and the
degree of flexibility in the various markets and also the level of
authority that the sales manager is given to negotiate pricing
levels. Some consumer goods companies will have a single price
list for all overseas markets: others will vary the pricing according
to market conditions. In both cases the negotiating power of the
overseas sales manager is likely to be limited once the prices have
been set – he will only be able to influence them at the annual
planning stage. With capital equipment or contracts the negotiating flexibility must be allowed in the market and the sales manager
is informed of the exact nature of the level of discount that is
acceptable in the overseas market.

There are various methods which the company may use to price
the goods that it offers to different markets. Essentially the two
issues involved are cost and control:

1. Ex-works. The product is costed to be available at the factory
   for collection by the customer. This reduces the cost of administration to the company to a minimum, but reduces control as
   the company cannot be sure where the goods will be going once
   they leave the warehouse. They also often introduce complications with VAT, in proving that the goods have in fact been
   exported.
2. FAS/FOB (Free Alongside, Free On Board). A far more common price offered to overseas clients. It has the advantage of
   ensuring that the goods do in fact leave the country resolving
   any taxation problems, and that the documentation requirements for the shipment will mainly be provided by the customer. It enables the customer to choose the shipping line he
   wishes to use, and to arrange his own insurance.

   It still reduces the level of control that the company can exert
   over the destination of the goods. A major whisky firm for
   example supplied a large order ostensibly for Eastern Europe
   FOB Rotterdam. Later investigation showed that instead of
   departing by road via Germany and Austria, the containers
   were immediately loaded onto a ship for the Middle East,
   arriving in one of the company's most profitable markets,
   damaging sales and profitability for six months and souring

relations with the agent. A similar lack of control has led to large quantities of toys supposedly for the Yugoslav market reappearing heavily discounted on British shelves just in time for Christmas!
3. C & F/CIF (Carriage and Freight; Carriage, Insurance, Freight). These pricing terms depend on the supplier undertaking all the shipping and administration issues. When the company establishes CIF terms it obviously will need to consider all the likely shipping lines that may be used during the year and in consequence will need to build this price on the highest tariff to ensure that the costs will always be covered. This is the 'conference' which is set in a similar fashion to airline fares should you wish to fly to Australia economy class it will cost the same whether you travel Singapore Airlines, QUANTAS, or British Airways. Like airlines, there are discount freight rates available from 'non-conference' shipping lines. A negotiating issue for the overseas sales manager is therefore frequently whether the agent can shift from CIF to FOB because of the potential savings on freight.

13.3   Conclusion

In order to achieve higher levels of control over the market the supplier is faced with the necessity of an increased level of investment, with the establishment of a direct salesforce solely concentrating on the company's product range eventually backed by either third party local manufacture or a full scale local production plant of a similar nature to that in existence in the home market, though the local conditions will obviously need to be considered. Recruitment procedure, payment terms and managerial control will all need to reflect the local environment. The payment of commission in Japan was, for example, frowned upon as being against group cohesion and it was only with difficulty that the US-based NCR managed to institute such a system for its Japanese operation.

The controls that then exist are very similar to those operating within the home market though there is the inevitable financial penalty – unless there is considerable volume already sold within the market the high overheads of creating and maintaining the salesforce will force the organisation to operate at a loss until this break-even or 'critical mass' position is achieved.

The complications of sales development in an international environment are therefore considerable with implications on company policy and speed of development following each choice of sales method and distribution path. Above all else, commitment to, and involvement in, export is essential to overall success as the problems will be considerable whichever distribution method is chosen. This is the most important factor identified across a wide range of British exporters:[6]

Factor	*Per cent identifying as major contribution to success*
Senior level involvement	67
Frequent contact	62
Good agents	56
Key market concentration	42
Own salesforce	39
Own local office	37
Good overseas service	34
Good literature	28
Foreign language ability	25
Allocation of manpower	15

The sample questioned was, however, senior management – different conclusions would probably be drawn from different levels within the organisation and certainly from the foreign customer.

Zeller Case Study

Background

France has for long been a major market for the consumption of certain British products but in many it still holds fast to well established traditions. The consumption of wine and spirits is no exception. Many aspects of the market are highly fragmented particularly the wine market which, except for the premium clarets and burgundies, is very regionalised; even the hypermarkets and supermarkets buying wine locally. There are, however, a number of alcoholic drinks which have strong national distribution, many of which are imported.

Product	Market size (FF million)	Growth (%)
Whisky	720	(5)
Cognac	200	(10)
Port	100	(2)
Rum	200	—
Cassis	300	10
Gin	50	25
Bourbon	40	20
Vodka	30	20
Liqueurs	200	(5)
Armagnac	120	—
Champagne	350	2
Beer	1100	3

There is also an extremely large vermouth and anise market dominated by Martini, Cinzano and Pernod.

Consumer tastes has been changing over the last ten years quite significantly. There is a continuing trend towards the consumption of lower strength alcoholic drinks – white wine instead of red, and beer instead of spirits. Kir, a mix of cassis and sparkling wine had shown continuing growth in popularity.

Over the last ten years there had been similar major structural changes within the retailing of alcoholic drinks. The growth of hypermarkets meant that more and more alcohol was purchased through these outlets – by the end of the

1970s market estimates put the percentage of most products bought through this sector at 70 per cent. In consequence there has been a rapid and spectacular decline of the specialist retailer. There has also been a considerable growth in own brands particularly in whisky and beer which pose the distributors of branded products considerable problems particularly when attempting to introduce new products into the hypermarkets. For very fast moving products such as beer and low-priced wine the turnover of the hypermarkets also often pose delivery problems for suppliers that were not locally based.

Due to the enormous size of the country distributors face serious problems. The distances between hypermarkets demand high manning levels in the field salesforce and consequentially higher numbers of sales managers. Additionally, travel expenses would remain high. Hypermarkets increasingly demand promotional packages across the distributor's product range to maintain presence or listing within the store, and are in the 1980s always looking to reduce the number of different brands within a given product sector. Only a few distributors maintain a national salesforce as the exercise tends not to be profitable. The major drinks producers finance distribution arms to maximise market share. Hennessy, Moet, Bardinet, Martell, Cointreau being examples of such distribution companies.

The problem

Zeller, a cognac firm, maintained a salesforce of 35 spread across France to ensure that the company maintained a presence in the French cognac market. In addition to cognac, it acted as agent for a number of other French and British firms in the French market. Their most important brand was Highland Fling, a whisky with an in-market sale of around 1 million bottles retailing at 68 FF (French Francs) but with a trade price (before tax) of 48. Port was in income terms the next most important product with a bottle retailing at 38 FF and sold to the trade at 26 FF, in volume around 0.8 million bottles. Cognac came next selling to the trade at 50 FF before tax, with a volume of 0.5 million. Cassis with a sale of 0.6 million bottles at 20 FF made up the list of the major brands, with minor gin brands and small speciality liqueurs.

The income statement (based on the gross margin made on each bottle) for the distribution company ran as follows:

Product	Income (FF million)	A&P	Net
Whisky	10	3.0	7
Port	9	3.0	6
Cognac	6	2.5	3.5
Cassis	5.5	—	5.5
Others	3	1.0	2.0

Expenditure:

Salesforce salary	5.6 million
Expenses	2.8 million
Head office costs	3.2 million
Distribution costs	4.0 million
Financing charges	3.0 million

Excess of income over expenditure: 5.4 million

In early 1984, Zeller lost both the cassis brand and the major liqueur brand which provided most of the 'others' income. In consequence the company was faced with a projected loss of around 2.0 million FF per annum. Furthermore, as the company lost brands it would become less important to the major hypermarket groups and would face the likely prospect of delisting. To offset this it would have to offer better promotional deals which again would adversely affect profitability. A further problem was that at this stage the recession was biting deep in France leading to the majority of drinks firms cutting prices to maintain volume.

Zeller to offset this commenced a policy of product diversification. It produced an own brand bourbon whisky called Prince Charlie, an own brand gin and vodka, followed by an own brand cassis. In order to minimise the drain on profitability, it held prices against the market trend and in consequence both its main suppliers of whisky and port suffered a 20 per cent volume drop, with no immediate sign of recovery.

The Zeller parent company as part of its investment plans bought distribution in the shape of a wine specialist chain through which it proposed to distribute a range of branded wines and speciality products such as overseas wines from California and China.

The suppliers of Zeller's whisky and port brands were both interested in developing volume in the highly competitive French markets. They had both invested heavily over the years to build up brand share and had been prepared to reduce margins to ensure that sales progressed satisfactorily. Both companies were part of multinational organisations with a strong emphasis on growth and market achievement. The decline in the French market would put senior management into a serious position.

The pricing structure for the two products at the end of 1983 was as follows:

	Port	Whisky
Ex-works (FF)	13	20
Freight/ins	1.2	1.0
Duties	1.5	8
Landed cost	15.7	29
Fixed costs	5	10
Variable costs/margin	4.3	9
Trade price (FF)	26	48
Wholesale margin	2	4
Retail margin	2	3
Sales tax	8	14
Consumer price	38	69
Volume (bottles)	800 000	1 000 000
Supplier margin (%) on ex-works price	40	50
Supplier advertising and promotion (FF)	3 m	6 m

The market showed a quite steep price elasticity with every 1 per cent increase in relative price leading to a 2 per cent decrease in total sales. Obviously the fixed cost of the distributor was dependent on volume achievement and this was one of the crucial factors leading to the decline.

Sommer Case Study

Sommer is a major Belgian distributor of imported alcoholic drinks based in the capital, Brussels. It handled a very large product range:

Whisky
  Banff Red
  Banff Black (12 Year)
  Antiquary
  Centurion
  Culloden
Brandy
  Ney VS, VSOP,
  Amphora
Rum
  Antigua
  Constantine
Vodka
  Kuopio
  Moskva
Port
  Douro Tawny
  Douro Ten-Year-Old
Gin
  Argyll
  Kerry
Aperitifs
  Peche Toi
  Ayan Bali
  Oriental
  Sol d'est
Acquavit
  Hague
Anises
  Anises

In addition it represented many of the leading French chateaux in Belgium; Rothschild, Talbot, Yquem were included amongst their list of around 200 wines all from France.

For many years Sommer had been heavily dependent on the sale of Banff for the bulk of their profitability. In recent years they had concentrated on building up the wine division and more importantly developing liqueur sales, especially of the banana flavoured Ayau Bali which had increased sales to around 800 000 bottles over two years. They had shown great innovation in the traditionally conservative Belgian market by advertising heavily on Luxembourg television, running campaigns on Culloden whisky, Ayau Bali, Douro Port, Antigua and Soleil d'Est. The company's main customers were four large retail chains which made up a large proportion of total Belgian trade.

Name	No. of stores	Trade (%)
GB	40	25
Delhaize	30	12
Colruyt	30	11
Makro	4	9

GB had come to prominence as the first developer of hypermarkets, and continued to follow a policy of building out of town sites and discounting heavily on certain key products. Delhaize had specialised in central store sites with an up-market quality image, in contrast to the other two groups Colruyt and Makro that concentrated on deep discounting. Colruyt attempted to follow the policy of building at a distance from the competition unless inexpensive central sites were available. With the economic climate in Belgium turning sour at the beginning of the 1980s the stores had become more and more aggressive on price to try and maintain market share. They had also become more demanding as to the level of service that they expected from their suppliers — one natural reaction to recession and increased competition being the reduction in the ranges that they stocked, and greater requirements to merchandise those restricted ranges. In consequence they largely concentrated on the main brands, ceasing to stock fringe products.

Profits of GB had declined from $20 million to $5 million over 18 months; the only other published figures, those of Delhaize, showed a static profit at $9 million. Independently owned specialist wine stores still made up about 30 per cent of the Sommer turnover, with restaurants and café's – a very important component of Belgian drinking patterns – the remainder.

When various sectors of the drinks market were analysed in greater detail, there were considerable differences in the way products were purchased by outlet types, and in growth patterns:

Product	Chains (%)	Specialist (%)	Café (%)	Growth (%)
Spirits	80	10	10	(5)
Anises	70	20	10	1
Aperitifs	50	30	20	6
Wines	30	40	30	8

Within this overall breakdown there were still certain variations: Delhaize for example held a far higher share of the wine sales than might be expected from their overall market share. There was an increasing emphasis on cocktails and 'lighter' drinks as the Belgians were becoming more aware of the problems of high alcohol consumption, many of which were supplied through the specialist stores.

At the end of 1983, all these customers were served by a Sommer salesforce of 12, geographically organised, each salesman dealing with all the potential outlets and the entire product range in the ascribed area.

The Problem

Banff, the leading Scotch whisky (with about 25 per cent market share or 1.85 million bottles) had become a major problem. Both the up-market twelve-year-old and blended version of the drink were extremely important products for both the profitability of Sommer and its customers as well. The problem began when one of the retail chains, GB, attempted to boost its share of the Banff market by selling the whisky at a loss. Because of the large volumes sold through GB the price at which they bought Banff, 385 BF compared favourably with the other chains (390) and the specialists/café's

(400). Even so, the chain proceeded to sell the brand at 380 -below cost price. This generated a great deal of ill-feeling among Sommer's other major customers – the specialist dealers and the three remaining retail chains.

The specialist dealers in various parts of the country proceeded to inform the salesforce that it was now cheaper for them to get their stocks directly from the GB retail outlets and that it simply did not make sense for them to buy the whisky directly from Sommer. The problem had been created by the distributor and should be resolved by it. The specialist store owners proved as good as their word – they began to refuse to stock the whisky at all, some contacted Sommer's competitor distributors. Others informed the salesforce that they were also looking at the wine alternatives being offered by the competitors. It also became impossible to persuade the specialist stores to stock Sommer's new liqueur acquisitions. Overall orders began to slump.

Belgium's traditions of high quality cuisine had created strong bonds between local restauranteurs and the specialist wine stores who often also acted as their suppliers. Many of the restaurant owners felt that they were being placed under similar constraints by the GB pricing policy on Banff. When Sommer launched a special PR drive designed to reassure the restaurant owners, its salesforce discovered that the discontent threatened a very important outlet for high-quality imported French wines.

Makro had also commenced a similar discounting policy with Antigua rum which had commenced its television campaign, undercutting the buying price by 15 BFr, down from 420 to 405.

The salesforce also soon became aware that the irritation had spread to other major customers. Another of the retail chains, their major wine customer Delhaize accused the company of varying its selling prices and favouring one customer at the expense of others, even going to the extent of threatening to take them to the European Court. The chain had looked at the costings involved in some detail before coming to this conclusion. It refused to believe that GB was selling Banff at a loss.

The impact of this situation was reflected in a serious decline in orders:

Spirits	−25%
Liqueurs	−35%
Wine	−15%

Since the salesforce salaries were partly based on commissions, their earnings were affected and they too became disgruntled. The owners of Sommer, a major drinks firm was also becoming more and more concerned about the loss of market share in the competitive whisky market.

The Future of Selling 14

The impact of social, economic and technological change in the past decade has created an environment where few people are without uncertainties about the future of their jobs. They may, for example, be worried about how new technology will affect their employment or about the scarcity of opportunities for promotion. It could be that this insecurity is no more than a reflection of a climate created by economic recession because there has always been change in employment and between 1945 and 1975 the nature of employment in the industrialised world had altered substantially without creating the mood of depression so prevalent in recent years.

Psychological and cultural factors therefore impinge on the issue of change and work, further complicating the issue. Thus in Britain nowadays the most likely door-to-door selling encounter will be between a Jehovah's Witness and a member of the public. The encyclopaedia and household appliance salesmen of the past were soon followed by those in insurance in quitting the front doorstep. Yet by contrast the door-to-door salesman is still an important force in Japan – the country with the Western world's most astonishing selling achievements. An explanation for this difference would almost certainly be couched in terms of culture and traditions, but pinning down the specific pattern for those interested in efficient sales management is almost certain to remain elusive. What is clear is that responses to change are not uniform.

Japanese managers do not have the same perceptions about similar patterns of change as their British counterparts and this will in turn influence the adjustments they make to keep their companies profitable. The same generalisation can still be made of two companies in the same market with similar salesforces, facing similar problems.

Predictions about the future of selling, about the adjustments that companies will make because of the impact of technology or changes in society seem doomed to failure. We can, however, examine trends that appear likely to continue to influence the way salesforces are shaped and used at least until the end of the century. These trends are based on the experience of companies, like the manufacturers of mass consumer goods under pressure from national retailing chains, that have in the past decade been compelled to fundamentally reappraise their markets and strategies because of change of one sort or another. Thus British manufacturing which was both extremely uncompetitive in 1979–81 and exposed to severe foreign competition was forced to improve its efficiency. Those companies that could not went to the wall, those that were more adaptable reflect some of the options for the future.

Trends include:

Industrial factors,
Cost factors,
Technology factors,
Personnel factors.

14.1   Industrial Factors

The concentration of purchasing power within fewer and fewer hands, a feature of the 1980s, and the increasing size and power of the transnational companies is likely to continue unless political action is taken to reduce the scope of their expansion. Whether it is feasible or desirable for governments to take such a step is a separate matter. By 1985 multinationals already employed 45 million people; state involvement in many countries throughout the world is also leading to the development of enormous buying units. Aware of this, some governments of countries burdened by debts and economic control measures demanded by the World

Bank and the International Monetary Fund have chosen to barter their raw materials for manufactured goods. Another illustration of the power of government in the market is Britain's National Health Service, now by far the largest single employer in Europe.

Companies with goods to sell, and those with buying power, must of necessity respond to these changes. As the size of the organisation increases the difficulty of achieving initial orders and the time that these will take to achieve will also lengthen.

Implications for the salesforce

The implications for those that are seeking customers is that commercial presentation skills will become more and more important within their salesforces as the size of the orders become larger and the number of buyers decreases. This is further emphasised by the steady decline in trading margins experienced by the majority of grocery manufacturers – similar trends are also occurring in other industrial sectors.[1]

These changes will expand the importance of the national accounts salesforce; they will demand an increasing level of negotiating skills to ensure that profitability is maintained and maximised. Customer account teams – which have already emerged among some major grocery suppliers as a result of the domination of the major retail chains – will grow in importance. The customer account team is usually a group of individuals each contributing towards the final commercial approach to a particular customer – marketing, finance and sales skills all blending to provide the best solution to a particular negotiation.

Such a change will inevitably mean that sales representatives will become more and more involved in the development and control of promotional activity, where and how merchandising should be carried out, and whether they need to be involved in the training of end-user staff.

Such structures which blur the distinction between 'sales' and 'marketing' will grow in importance as many companies attempt to ensure that new product introductions are successfully achieved; the influence of the 50–60 per cent of weighted distribution that will be provided by the top five or six outlets will be crucial in determining the overall performance and profitability of new products. As some of the case studies in earlier chapters make plain, the blurring of the lines between sales and marketing is already affecting the job of the sales representative in many companies and is the source of much conflict. If there is to be a fusion in the future, sales representatives' work will need to be re-oriented towards acceptance of selling as the long haul rather than the short sharp success; they will need to become more adept at presenting to committees rather than individuals, and they will need to increasingly tailor presentations to different interest groups.

Implications for buyers

Those who are buying are similarly concerned to increase the professionalism of buyers with major store groups reporting a steadily increasing length of time allocated to their training.[2] There will also be more and more demands for better and better information about how successful a product will be within the buyer's firm. Buyers will show a greater tendency to use more sophisticated appraisal techniques in defining their requirements such as vendor rating systems.[3]

14.2   Cost Factors

The cost of the salesforce has for the last 20 years outstripped the rate of inflation, in real terms the unit cost of the sales representative is a steadily increasing factor. This is largely due to the rising transportation costs which have grown at double the average rate of inflation over the past 15 years; they also partly reflect the competitive environment in many industries in recruiting and keeping able sales personnel, including the ever-spiralling costs of training.

Will such trends continue? In the view of the author selling skills will be more and more important in determining the future developmental path of the company, and in consequence the per capita cost increases are likely to continue. Companies will therefore be under greater pressure to reduce the numbers of sales representatives that they employ, or to change the nature and the remuneration of the total salesforce.

One option that has been explored by many companies is to separate the salesforce into two elements: one involved almost exclusively with merchandising, paid at a much lower rate than the salesforce average, and a reduced number of negotiating sales representatives. This trend is particularly marked in the grocery trade and with the continuing growth in market share of the large groups, will inevitably continue. For specific sales activities such as concentrated sales promotions, test markets, exhibitions, the trend towards using outside agencies to provide additional sales input will be seen as the logical way of retaining the sales representative's effectiveness allowing them to continue to concentrate on mainstream market sales and development. To a certain extent, however, the increased use of outside agencies for the specialised sales support activities will depend upon the company's perceptions about their effectiveness. They will not, for example, have the same back-up knowledge of, or interest in the company and its products as a trained member of the salesforce.

The increasing costs will put further pressure on the company to maximise the effectiveness of the sales representative by defining more closely the way in which he or she should spend the time available – by developing computer systems that evaluate the likely return on time employed; by developing routing systems which reduce the amount of wasted travel time; by defining more accurately the objectives of each sales call; by supporting the sales representative more effectively with sales material that will reduce the amount of explanation required and attempt to minimise the level of objections; by providing the sales representative with all the information necessary to make as effective a call as possible.

Effective recruitment and selection procedures become relatively more important as costs rise. Management will have to give more time to this than currently – the current industry average being 30 minutes – with greater emphasis on the selection board approach used by certain major companies which may extend over two working days. Some commentators suggest that this will lead to a further intensification of the use of aptitude tests and intelligence tests as a means of more effective recruitment; in the opinion of the author managers will probably become more adept at using role-playing to ascertain whether the practical sales skills are present, and longer standard interview sessions to evaluate the other elements in the selection process will emerge.

Similarly, the speed and intensity of training will have to change in line with the increasing salesforce costs to maximise the return on investment to the company. The analysis of salesforce strength and weaknesses will in consequence also require further development with the annual appraisal giving way to quarterly reviews of performance and problems. Management will need to give further attention to the appraisal systems in operation to ensure that the maximum possible benefit can be gained from the sales representatives employed by the company.

14.3 Technology

Already technological innovation is having a greater impact on many salesforces.

First, the way in which data is stored and retrieved will be increasingly dependent on the use of new technology with sophisticated data-base systems becoming more and more widely available for even the microcomputer. Other data applications will also be seen in the way in which the company tries to reach potential new customers in attempts to reduce the cost of gaining sales leads.

Secondly, the way in which orders can be received and transmitted will be increasingly determined by new technology with the slow introduction of personal computers into the salesforces of some major companies. Such systems also will allow the salesforce to analyse current customer records and receive updated information on specific developments. In addition, the use of the computer or other visual methods to improve presentations may grow in importance. The video or disc player present in more and more offices allows the sales representative to carry information in a form which can be entertaining and informative; techniques that apply to sales conferences with their use of comedians and presenters to put over a company message could easily expand to customer presentations. Similarly, the use of computer graphics which has proved very effective for many insurance sales representatives in showing how a particular individual's circumstances is reflected in likely benefits may find applications in many industrial contexts.

Thirdly, communication between the sales representative and the area or Head Office will improve with the introduction of radio-telephone links between Head Office and the sales representative, enabling the representative to be more fully integrated into the company's activities, hopefully reducing the time that will be spent in unproductive non-selling activities.

The impact of technology will hopefully lead to a greater integration of the sales representative in the firm's planning process and lead to an improved awareness of the firm's strategic requirements, reducing conflict and maximising effort in the most productive areas.

14.4 Personnel Factors

The increasing sophistication of the sales role will place greater and greater demands upon the sales representative. It is possible that the number of sales representatives who have passed through higher education will rise. In most companies there does not in the United Kingdom appear to be any substantial movement in this direction though it has always been a factor in the United States.

Throughout Western Europe the participation of women in sales and sales management has grown. One pharmaceutical company for example reporting that 80 per cent of its salesforce are women. There are increasing numbers employed in the grocery trade and a trend towards higher numbers in those most male preserves: office equipment and double glazing.

It is an interesting final speculation to consider whether the new more highly educated salesforce of the future with its high proportion of women will still suffer from the public view of sales representatives which has lasted since Chaucer's time to the most recent television poll which showed that while 85 per cent of the population trusted priests, and 80 per cent doctors, only 20 per cent trusted the sales representative who still came below journalists and politicians in public esteem.

References

1 Perceptions of Selling

1. See, for example, J. Fenton, *A–Z of Sales Management* (Heinemann, 1979).
2. G. Constedine, *Inside Media Research: Understanding the Industrial Buying Process* (Admap, 1971).
3. Constedine, *Inside Media Research*.
4. R. McTavish and A. Maitland, *Industrial Marketing* (Macmillan, 1980).
5. P. Kotler, *Marketing Management: Analysis, Planning, Control*, 5th edn (Prentice-Hall, 1985).
6. R. W. Hill and T. J. Hillier, *Organisational Buying Behaviour* (Macmillan, 1982).
7. K. J. Blois, 'The Effect of Subjective Factors on Customer Supplier Relations in Industrial Marketing', *British Journal of Marketing*, vol. 2 (1978).
8. See, for example, P. Hughes and T. Armstrong, 'The Micro Revolution', *Management Today*, no. 3 (1978).
9. F. E. Webster, 'The Industrial Salesman as a Source of Market Information', *Business Horizons*, vol. 2 (1965).
10. A. H. Maslow, original article in *Psychology Review* (1943) but see Kotler, *Marketing Management*, and G. Hughes, *Marketing Management* (Addison-Wesley, 1983).
11. See, for example, McTavish and Maitland, *Industrial Marketing*.
12. F. E. Webster, and Y. A. Wind 'General Model for Understanding Organisational Buying Behaviour, *Journal of Marketing*, vol. 36 (1972).
13. J. N. Sheth, 'A Model of Industrial Buying Behavior', *Journal of Marketing*, vol. 27 (1973).

14. See discussion in *Organisational Buying Behaviour.*
15. Fenton, *A–Z of Sale Management.*

2 Recruitment

1. A. Rodger, *N.I.I.P. The Seven Point Plan* (1952).
2. D. Mayer and H. M. Greenberg, 'What Makes a Good Salesman?', *Harvard Business Review*, no. 2 (1964).
3. R. Blake and J. S. Monton, *The Grid for Sales Excellence: Benchmarks for Effective Salesmanship* (McGraw-Hill, 1970).
4. See, for example, H. J. Eysenck, *Test your Own IQ* (Penguin, 1975).
5. See, for example, H. J. Eysenck and G. Wilson, *Know Your Personality* (Penguin, 1976).
6. See, for example, S. Broadbent and B. Jacobs, *Spending Advertising Money*, 4th edn (Business Books, 1984).
7. N. C. Parkinson, *Parkinson's Law* (Penguin, 1965).

4 Achieving the Sale and Keeping the Customer

1. G. A. Luffman, 'The Processing of Information by Industrial Buyers', *Industrial Marketing Management*, vol. 3 (1974).
2. See *Organisational Buying Behaviour.*
3. See, for example, W. J. Stanton and R. H. Buskirk, *Management of the Sales Force*, 6th edn (Richard D. Irwin, 1983).
4. M. J. Baker, *Marketing New Industrial Products* (Macmillan, 1975).
5. B. Klass, 'What Factors affect Industrial Buying Decisions?', *Industrial Marketing*, vol. 3 (1981).
6. See, for example, Ehrenber (ed.), *Consumer Behaviour* (Penguin, 1965).

5 Training and Support Systems

1. D. McFarland (ed.), *The Oxford Companion to Animal Behaviour* (Oxford University Press, 1981).
2. *Financial Times* (11 Feb 1985).
3. P. Peters and R. H. Waterman, *In Search of Excellence* (Harper & Row, 1982).
4. *The Economist* (12 July 1985).
5. *Financial Times* (15 Aug 1985).
6. M. J. Naples, *Effective Frequency: The Relationship between Frequency and Advertising Effectiveness* (ANA, 1979).
7. H. A. Zielske, 'The Remembering and Forgetting of Advertising, *Journal of Marketing*, vol. 1 (1954).

6   Motivation and Compensation

1. B. O. Pettman (ed.), *Labour Turnover and Retention* (Gower, 1975).
2. F. Herzberg, W. Paul and K. Robertson, 'Job Enrichment Pays Off', *Harvard Business Review*, vol. 2 (1969) and references cited.
3. See, for example, H. J. Eysenck, *You and Neurosis* (Scientific Book Club, 1977).
4. *The Economist* (11 October 1985).
5. Mayer and Greenberg, 'What Makes a Good Salesman?'.
6. PA Fringe benefits report 1985.
7. F. Hertzberg, *Work and the Nature of Man* (Collins, 1966).
8. J. E. Muckley, 'Dear Fellow Shareholders', *Harvard Business Review*, vol. 2 (1984).
9. R. Lidstone, *Motivating your Sales Force* (Gower, 1978).
10. Pettman, *Labour Turnover and Retention*.
11. Tack Research Ltd, *Salesmen's Pay and Expenses* (1985).
12. BIM, *Remunerating Sales and Marketing Staff* (1976).
13. See, for example, Stanton and Buskirk. *Management of the Sales Force*.
14. R. Korlin, *Profit Centre* (Sales Management Business Books, 1976).
15. T. R. Wotruba, *Sales Management, Planning, Accomplishment and Evaluation* (Holt, 1971).

8   Appraisal and Discipline

1. R. Lickert, 'A new Twist to People Accounting', *Business Week*, no. 21 (1972).

9   Defining Sales Structures

1. P. T. Fitzroy, *Analytical Methods for Marketing Management* (McGraw-Hill, 1976).
2. J. Semlow, 'How Many Salesmen do you Need?', *Harvard Business Review*, vol. 23 (1959).
3. C. D. Fogg, and J. W. Rokus, 'A Quantitative Method for Structuring a Profitable Sales Force', *Journal of Marketing*, vol. 37 (1973).
4. W. J. Talley, 'How to Design Sales Territories', *Journal of Marketing*, vol. 35 (1971).
5. A. A. Brown, F. T. Hulswitt and J. D. Kettelle, 'A Study of Sales Operations', *Operations Research*, vol. 9, (1956).
6. L. M. Lodish, 'Callplan: An Interactive Salesman's Call Planning System', *Management Science*, 18 vol. 4 (December 1971).
7. R. F. Vizza, 'ROTI Profitable Selling New Maths', *Time and Territory Management* (1976).

10 Sales Budgets and Forecasting

1. E. C. Bursk and J. F. Chapman (eds) *New Decision-Making Tools for Managers* (Mentor, 1963).
2. C. Pearce, *Prediction Techniques for Marketing Planners* (Associated Business Programmes, 1971).
3. C. Chatfield, *The Analysis of Time Series: An Introduction*, 2nd edn (Chapman & Hall, 1980).
4. C. W. J. Granger and P. Newbold, *Forecasting Economic Time Series* (Academic Press, 1977).

11 Sales Strategy and the Marketing Mix

1. See Kotler *Marketing Management: Analysis, Planning, Control*; and Hughes *Marketing Management*.
2. D. Cowell, *The Marketing of Services*. (Heinemann, 1985).
3. See J. Winkler, *Pricing* (Heinemann, 1982).
4. Peters and Waterman, *In Search of Excellence*.
5. See, for example, B. Heirs and G. Pehrson, *The Mind of the Organisation* (Harper & Row, 1982).
6. D. L. Kurtz and C. W. Hubbard, *Sales Function and its Management* (General Learning Press, 1971).
7. N. K. Dhalla, 'Assessing the Long Term Value of Advertising', *Harvard Business Review*, vol. 1 (1978).

12 The Problem of Distribution

1. T. Cannon and M. Willis 'The Smaller Firm in Overseas Trade', *European Small Business Journal*, vol. 3 (1983).
2. E. Kaynack, 'Export Behaviour of Small Manufacturers: A Comparative Study of American and Canadian Firms', *European Management Journal*, vol. 2 (1984).
3. BOTB Report 1982.

13 The Export Manager's Role

1. D. Shipley, 'Selection and Motivation of Distribution Intermediaries', *Industrial Marketing Management*, vol. 13 (1984).
2. Kaynack, 'Export Behaviour of Small Manufacturer'.
3. PE Consultancy Group report, *Languages and Export Performance* (1974).

4. BOTB Report 1979.
5. See, for example, W. Keegan, *International Marketing* (Prentice-Hall, 1983).
6. BOTB Report 1979.

14 The Future of Selling

1. R. W. Ballance and S. W. Sinclair *Collapse and Survival: Industrial Strategies in a Changing World* (Allen & Unwin, 1983).
2. G. Wingate, *Retail Buying* (McGraw-Hill, 1978).
3. Hill and Hillier, *Organisational Buying Behaviour*.

Index